WHITE HOUSE CHEF

ELEVEN YEARS, TWO PRESIDENTS, ONE KITCHEN

Walter Scheib and Andrew Friedman

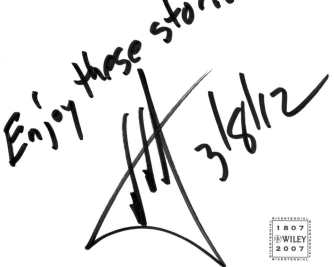

Enjoy these stories

3/8/12

BICENTENNIAL
1807
WILEY
2007
BICENTENNIAL

JOHN WILEY & SONS, INC.

Copyright © 2007 by Walter Scheib

Published by John Wiley & Sons, Inc., Hoboken, New Jersey
Published simultaneously in Canada

Design by Elizabeth Van Itallie

Library of Congress Cataloging-in-Publication Data:

Scheib, Walter.
White House chef : eleven years, two presidents, one kitchen / Walter Scheib and Andrew Friedman.
    p. cm.
  Includes index.
  ISBN-13: 978-0-471-79842-2 (cloth)
  1. Entertaining. 2. Cookery. 3. Clinton, Bill, 1946- 4. Bush,
George W. (George Walker), 1946- I. Friedman, Andrew, 1967- II. Title.
  TX731.S292 2007
  642'.4—dc22
                         2006022832

Printed in the United States of America

10 9 8 7 6

For the "Three Women"
My mother, for her early inspiration and encouragement,
My wife, Jean Scheib, for pushing me to take the shot, and
Hillary Rodham Clinton, for the opportunity of a lifetime and for taking a chance
on an unknown commodity.

CHIEF OF STAFF TO THE PRESIDENT
THE WHITE HOUSE

December 21, 2001

Mr. Walter Scheib
Executive Residence
The White House
Washington, D.C.

Dear Chef,

This letter is just to thank you for all that you do here at The White House. Just over one year ago, President George W. Bush asked me to be his Chief of Staff. The last eleven months have been filled with remarkable challenges and achievements, and for all of us serving on his team, it is an incredible honor.

As 2001 comes to an end, I hope you will take time to reflect on your contribution to the Administration and the country. In the wake of the tragic events of September 11th, you and your colleagues continue to show courage and resolve, dedication and compassion, grace under pressure, and above all, love of this great country and all that it represents.

On his second day in office, President Bush gave all of us a charge: "Let us begin the work we were hired to do and leave this a better place than we found it." You should be very proud of your service at The White House. America and the world are better for it.

President Bush and Vice President Cheney are grateful for your efforts; and, they know that the success of this Administration depends on the hard work of a competent and devoted team. Whether you came to The White House with this Administration or have been here through many, you are a valuable part of that team.

Kathi and I look forward to the year ahead, and we wish you and your family a wonderful holiday season. May God continue to bless America.

Sincerely,

Andrew H. Card, Jr.

The President and Mrs. Clinton
welcome you to
The White House
on the occasion of the

White House
Millennium Dinner

Saluting American Achievement

Friday, December 31, 1999

Hillary Rodham Clinton

Thanks to everyone for a wonderful state dinner! Magnifique!
HRC

TEE BALL
ON THE
SOUTH LAWN

Contents

Author's Note

This book tells the story of my eleven years as White House Executive Chef, from the time I interviewed for the job in 1994 to my departure in 2005.

I was hired by First Lady Hillary Rodham Clinton, and following her mandate, I helped the Clintons redefine how food was thought about and served at the White House. Then, starting in 2001, I again revamped the White House food program to meet the very different criteria of President George W. Bush and First Lady Laura Bush.

In its role as the "people's house," the White House hosts tens of thousands of visitors every year. Accordingly, my team and I served thousands of meals to the First Family, and prepared food for thousands of events ranging from intimate garden parties to state dinners for hundreds.

To fit this story into the space allotted here, I've made some decisions. For the most part, I've chosen not to focus on the minutiae of what we did, but rather to paint in broad strokes a picture of how we did it, sharing some colorful exchanges, humorous incidents, and taxing challenges along the way.

I've also made what for me was an easy decision: There's no so-called "dirt" to be found about the First Families here, and no commentary on the personal or political challenges faced by either of the administrations I served. There are three reasons for this. First, there's a bond of honor between the White House staff and the First Family, and I won't violate that confidence and trust. Second, as a chef, even at the White House, I'm no expert in such matters. And third, they were none of my business.

I should add that where my personal relationships with other government personnel are concerned, I feel no such compunction, and so am very candid in my descriptions of certain discussions and interactions with those employees.

A few additional notes about how this book was written are in order: Menus and dishes have been recreated primarily from my extensive records, which occupy four lateral filing cabinets in the basement of my home.

Conversations have been recreated from memory. While they are, of course, not necessarily verbatim, they are accurate in their content and tone.

I'm very indebted to three social secretaries with whom I worked—Ann Stock, Capricia Marshall, and Catherine Fenton—for agreeing to be interviewed for this book. They helped verify and complete my recollection of certain events and decisions, some of which dated back more than a decade.

In the interest of full disclosure, I should add that some details of state dinners, summits, tee ball games, and other functions have been recreated or expanded upon with the help of news accounts, interviews with the social secretaries, and materials from the White House and Parks Service communications offices. As the chef, I was often in the kitchen while the events were taking place; consulting these sources enabled me to provide a full sense of the players, the action, and the atmosphere.

Walter Scheib
Great Falls, Virginia

Introduction

For eleven years, from 1994 to 2005, I had the honor of serving as White House Executive Chef, a position in which I was responsible for all of the food prepared for the First Family, as well as the staff of the residence and guests at functions ranging from intimate holiday gatherings to congressional picnics to gala state dinners for visiting foreign dignitaries. I was personally hired by First Lady Hillary Rodham Clinton one year into President William Jefferson Clinton's first term, and stayed at the White House through the next seven years of his presidency and the entire first term of President George W. Bush.

Thanks to Mrs. Clinton, my tenure as White House Executive Chef was unlike that of any of my predecessors. Mrs. Clinton set a very ambitious mission for me and my team: remake the White House food program—traditionally very conservative and skewed toward classic French gastronomy—to reflect contemporary American cuisine. "I have a lot of ideas about what I want the food at the White House to be," she told me in an early meeting. "They all have to do with highlighting what's best and most unique about *American* food and wine, and entertaining at the White House."

It was a challenge and an honor to have so much asked of me. It was also an adventure unlike any other, because working in the White House—even as the chef—means being eyewitness to history from a unique vantage point. I was there for the happiest of occasions, such as the Millennial New Year's Eve, when the party went so late that butlers could be seen napping in the corridors, and I was there for the saddest of days—the darkest, of course, being September 11, 2001.

Working in tandem with Mrs. Clinton and her staff, I modernized and Americanized the White House food program, making it more healthful, upgrading the quality of staff meals, creating a vegetable garden right on the roof the White House, and serving contemporary American food—by which I mean a thoughtful but creative mix of regional American dishes, with myriad international flourishes—to visiting heads of state.

In this book, I share the behind-the-scenes story of my tenure as White House Executive Chef, tracking each step of how we reinvented the food served at the "people's house." I explain how we elevated the House's "market basket" by seeking out fruits and vegetables from the best farmers, and bringing then-obscure fish, meats, and other foods to the table for family meals and state dinners alike. We tried everything we could get our hands on, and experimented with new recipe ideas as much as possible, often serving them to the First Family to secure their approval before putting them on the menu for large-scale public events. We even remodeled the kitchen.

Additonally, this book describes the unique aspects of being White House Executive Chef, such as having each and every decision and menu scrutinized by the national and international media. I also share personal observations and anecdotes, from how I got the job, to my very fond memories of Christmastime under the Clintons, to the "Chelsea Clinton Cooking School," a series of one-hour private lessons I gave Chelsea Clinton over a six-week period before she departed for Stanford University, enabling her to cook for herself when she got there.

From my service to President Bush and his family, there are the kitchen's semi-daily guessing game about what the President would order for lunch, and the miniature baseball stadium that was created right on the South Grounds for a children's event, authentic down to how the hot dogs were cooked; an avid baseball fan and onetime owner of the Texas Rangers, President Bush saw us grilling hot dogs and sent word to us that "ball park dogs are *steamed*, not grilled."

The two administrations I served had dramatically different culinary and entertaining sensibilities, styles, and needs. Accordingly, I have divided the book into two parts, the first covering the Clinton years from the time I came on board in 1994, and the second covering the Bush years, up to my departure in 2005.

The Clintons, for example, had me travel to many destinations for state functions of various sizes; the Bushes preferred to escape to Crawford, Texas, as much as possible, and to take minimal staff with them. Moreover, history played a big role in the tenor of the first Bush administration; there were very few festive events for a long time after September 11, 2001, when the focus was more on working lunches with visiting world leaders. Scattered among the anecdotes in each chapter are recipes that invite you to cook and serve some of the same dishes enjoyed by our most recent First Families. Since I left my role as White House chef, I have given dozens of talks and cooking demonstrations at which people ask me about the First Families' favorite personal dishes, how we decided what to serve at state dinners, and other subjects unique to my former job. You'll find the answers to those questions here, along with illustrative recipes. Generally speaking, I've selected simpler dishes from all that we made, knowing that you will not have the same time and resources as I did at the White House. Where the recipes are a little more challenging, I've broken down the recipes into components so if you do not want to make all of them, you can make the parts you like. At the back of the book, you'll find two appendices that complement the recipes—a Recipe List to help you find a particular kind of dish, and Sources, which offers a list of Internet and mail-order purveyors who will ship just about any meat, fish, spice, or piece of equipment to your door.

The People In My Story

This is not a complete list of White House staff or other groups that I discuss. Rather, it is a who's who of people who appear regularly or repeatedly in the book and the job they held, or role they served, during the years covered in the story.

CLINTON YEARS (1994 TO 2001)

FIRST FAMILY

President William Jefferson Clinton, 42nd President of the United States

First Lady Hillary Rodham Clinton

Chelsea Clinton, President and Mrs. Clinton's daughter

EXTENDED FAMILY

Mrs. Virginia Clinton Kelley, President Clinton's mother

Mr. Richard Kelley, President Clinton's stepfather

Mrs. Dorothy Rodham, Mrs. Clinton's mother

Hugh Rodham, Mrs. Clinton's brother

Tony Rodham, Mrs. Clinton's brother

FIRST LADY'S STAFF

Neel Lattimore, Deputy Press Secretary and spokesperson (through 1997)

Capricia Marshall (Special Assistant to the First Lady, 1993 to 1997; Social Secretary 1997 to 2001)

Ann Stock, Social Secretary (through 1997)

Maggie Williams, Chief of Staff (through 1997)

KITCHEN STAFF

Adam Collick, Steward

Cristeta Comerford (Service by Agreement Cook, 1995; hired as Assistant Chef, 1995)

Keith Luce, Assistant Chef (through 1995)

Roland Mesnier, Executive Pastry Chef

John Moeller, Assistant Chef

SERVICE BY AGREEMENT COOKS

Leland Atkinson

Gordon Marr

Patrice Olivon

MILITARY COOKS

Sergeant Denzil Benjamin

Sergeant Brian Williams

BUTLERS

Buddy Carter

George Haney

James Ramsey

GROUNDS STAFF

Dale Haney, Horticulturist

USHERS

Dennis Freemyer, Assistant Head Usher charged with among other things, coordinating White House construction and engineering projects

Daniel Shanks, Assistant Usher specializing in wine and service (hired in 1995)

Gary Walters, Chief Usher

OTHER STAFF

Nancy Clarke, Chief Florist

Chris Limerick, White House Director of Housekeeping

BUSH YEARS (2001 TO 2005)

FIRST FAMILY

President George W. Bush, 43rd President of the United States

First Lady Laura Bush

Barbara and Jenna Bush, President and Mrs. Bush's twin daughters

EXTENDED FAMILY

Mrs. Barbara Bush, President Bush's mother

President George H.W. Bush, President Bush's father

Governor Jeb Bush, President Bush's brother

FIRST LADY'S STAFF

Andrea Ball, Chief of Staff (through 2005)

Lea Berman, Social Secretary (hired in 2004)

Catherine Fenton, Social Secretary (2001 to 2005)

KITCHEN STAFF

Adam Collick, Steward

Cristeta Comerford, Assistant Chef

Thaddeus DuBois, Executive Pastry Chef (hired in 2004)

Roland Mesnier, Executive Pastry Chef (through 2004)

John Moeller, Assistant Chef

BUTLERS

Buddy Carter

George Haney

James Ramsey

USHERS

Dennis Freemyer, Assistant Head Usher

Daniel Shanks, Assistant Usher

Gary Walters, Chief Usher

OTHER STAFF

Kenneth Blasingame, design consultant to the Bushes

Nancy Clarke, Chief Florist

Chris Limerick, Director of Housekeeping

Rick Paulus, Chief Calligrapher

MY CLINTON YEARS

America On The Menu
Getting the Job, Start Up, and Development

In 1994, I applied for the position of White House Executive Chef and, to my everlasting amazement, was hired.

The interview process for a job like this is, by design, quite taxing—created as much to evaluate the cuisine the candidates will cook as to uncover any temperamental or organizational tics that might prevent them from succeeding in a pressure-cooker environment.

This was a life-altering assignment, even before I began. Surprisingly, the food itself would prove the least challenging aspect; creating an environment in which to provide it was the much bigger task. That, and learning how to function under the intense internal and external scrutiny that greets any new White House team member.

JOB OPENING

"The chef of the White House just resigned," said my wife Jean, reading from a copy of that morning's *New York Times,* an article announcing that Pierre Chambrin was leaving after two years in the position, reportedly because he couldn't—or rather wouldn't—break away from rich, traditional

French cuisine to cook in the healthful, American style the Clintons desired. The situation was succinctly encapsulated by the article's headline, "High Calories (and Chef!) Out at White House."

She looked up at me. "You should apply for that job."

Under normal circumstances, I might have come to that realization myself. But these weren't normal circumstances. It was the first week of March 1994 and we were boarding a flight from San Diego back to our home of West Virginia, where I had been executive chef of the Greenbrier—an opulent, colonial-style hotel and spa with a number of upscale dining rooms and cafés—for two and a half years. Jean and I lived in a nice house in nearby Lewisburg, where we were raising our two sons, Walter and Jim, then ages five and two, respectively.

Life was good, and I saw no reason to rock the boat.

"Jean," I snapped, "I'm not interested in any job. I just want to get home."

I don't normally speak to my wife in that tone, but this was one of the worst weeks of my life. My mother had just died following a long bout with cancer, and we had flown west for the funeral. All I wanted to do was get home, lick my emotional wounds, and lose myself in my work.

My mother, coincidentally also named Jean, was the person who first introduced me to food and cooking. In the roast-chicken-and-meatloaf days in which I grew up, she was a gourmet who'd clip recipes from magazines, experiment with ingredients most Americans probably couldn't pronounce, and encourage me to try new things such as pot au feu, paella valenciana, and smoked beef tongue. When my father dismissed the idea of cooking school, it was my mother who paid my tuition at the Culinary Institute of America from her personal savings.

In short, I owed her everything. She was my hero and my inspiration, and I was going to miss her more than I'd ever missed anyone or anything.

APPLY YOURSELF

Jean and I got back to the East Coast, the frosty indifference of winter the perfect reflection of my deep, deep sorrow. Sticking to my plan, I dove right into work.

After trudging through two days, I was home one morning, working at my desk, when Jean said to me, a mischievous glimmer in her eye, "I sent your resumé in."

It seemed like a total non sequitur. "What do you mean, you sent my resumé? Sent it to who?"

"To the White House."

I was incredulous. "You sent my resumé to the White House?"

She couldn't have been more matter of fact. "Yep. You should probably give them a call."

We dropped what we were doing and proceeded to discuss the pros and cons of my going to work for the White House. It quickly became apparent that of the two of us, she was the clear-thinking one at that moment, because there were no cons. We had wanted to move back to D.C., and this would be a plum job, unlike any other in the country, maybe the world.

I walked over to the phone, called D.C. directory assistance, and was connected to the White House. The operator transferred me to the Usher's Office, home base for the staff that runs the First Family's domestic affairs.

An administrative usher answered.

"Hi. My name is Walter Scheib and I sent my resumé in for the chef's position."

I was greeted with an undisguised chortle. "Yeah," she said. "You and about four thousand other people."

She went on to explain that so many resumés had arrived that they had been boxed up in crates and set aside temporarily. The picture she painted made me think of that huge warehouse at the end of *Raiders of the Lost Ark*, a hopelessly mammoth hangar from which artifacts are never retrieved.

I politely explained that I was the executive chef of the Greenbrier, and suggested that she or one of her associates dig out my resumé and pass it along to the proper authorities.

"I don't for a minute think I'm the only qualified candidate for the job," I told her. "But I know I'm one of the few qualified candidates in those boxes you're talking about."

That might seem a rather boastful claim, but I was immensely proud of my hotel background. Restaurant chefs may get more of the glory in the glossy magazines and television shows, but the multiple kitchens I ran at the Greenbrier and the thousands of meals we served every day gave me great confidence that I had the chops for this assignment. In fact, I was convinced that a hotel chef was the only way to go in their search for a new White House chef.

"O.K. I'll make sure someone looks at it."

I thanked her and hung up, not knowing what to expect.

About four hours later, I got a phone call from a man who identified himself as Gary Walters, the chief usher of the White House. With the efficiency of an attorney, he dispensed with the small talk and got right to the point. "Can you come into town and see us the day after tomorrow?"

Washington, D.C., was about 250 miles from us. I had just returned from some very sad family business that had taken me away from my job. And it didn't make things any easier that I couldn't tell my higher-ups at the Greenbrier why I'd be absent on the day of the interview.

But this was the White House. So I said what any proud American chef would say when the office, or at least the home, of the president called on him: "No problem."

FIRST IMPRESSIONS

Two days later, I drove to the White House. A Maryland native, I had walked or driven by the "people's house" my whole life, but had always admired it from afar, like any other D.C. resident or tourist.

This time, I drove up to a gate at the perimeter of the White House grounds, and was cleared through the first of two checkpoints—little white guard houses manned by the Uniformed Division of the Secret Service, recognizable by their standard-issue uniform of black pants, white Oxford shirt with a crest on the left breast pocket, and police officer's hat. On their belts were a holstered gun, handcuffs, a canister of Mace, and a walkie-talkie.

As I got closer and closer to the White House itself, its columns came into high relief. Seen from the street, it's not much different from looking at a photograph, but up close, you begin to sense its innate grandeur.

Once inside, this effect increases exponentially. As a member of the Uniformed Division escorted me in through a side entrance, our shoes clacking along the floor, I felt American history coming alive all around me. The chandeliers hanging overhead in certain rooms, the framed portraits on the walls, and the marble flooring underfoot were so immaculately maintained that in many ways, this place felt more like a museum than a house—and in many ways, it is.

I kept a poker face, but there was no denying it: I was getting excited. I was in the White House to discuss the possibility of coming to work there. I had to fight to keep from grinning like a little kid.

Arriving in a corridor of administrative offices, I was greeted by chief usher Gary Walters and Mrs. Clinton's social secretary, Ann Stock. They led me into a room where we sat down and began talking.

Ann Stock, with her short coiffed blond hair and smart skirt suit, looked very buttoned down, but was surprisingly informal in tone and demeanor. Though clearly an organized and strategic thinker—she kept me focused on a series of topics such as family meals and cooking for large groups—she engaged me in a fun and energizing discussion of my culinary ideas for the White House, my cooking style, and so on. She asked me what I thought made a reception good, and how I'd attack a state dinner. She asked me to describe my style. "I'm classically trained, but I don't execute classically," was my answer, and I went on to explain how I had kept up with contemporary American food, weaving international elements, especially Asian and Mediterranean, into my cooking. She even challenged me a bit by downplaying my Greenbrier experience, indicating that perhaps it was too conservative for what Mrs. Clinton had in mind. The implied question was: "Okay, Mr. Scheib, you're a world-class hotel chef, but can you let your hair down and make food innovative and exciting. Are you ready to go out on a limb?"

Clearly Ann Stock and Mrs. Clinton had spent a lot of time talking about what they wanted from the White House chef. She described to me that one of the Clintons' overarching goals was to have the White House "look like America," reflecting essential aspects of our nation, especially its diversity. Special events and the food served at them, she explained, were one way to accomplish this, with menus influenced by the cultures of the world. She also explained that the Clintons had huge ambitions, and wanted to host state dinners and other functions bigger and more audaciously ambitious than anything that had been attempted there.

Gary Walters took a different approach. A fit, trim, all-business professional in his late forties or early fifties, with gray hair and a dark suit, Gary might easily be mistaken for an FBI agent; in fact, I would later learn that he had been a member of the Secret Service Uniformed Division at one time. He talked to me about the business side of the job, the protocols and logistics within which the chef of the White House is expected to operate.

You might say that Gary Walters and Ann Stock represented, respectively, the left (logical) brain and right (creative) brain of the administration. I remember thinking that my background and demeanor were oddly suited to both sides. My hotel experience, while perhaps not as overtly "sexy" as that of a hot, new restaurant chef, was a perfect fit with the wish to do the bigger and grander events described by Ann Stock; and my strict upbringing—my father raised me to address everyone, even peers, as Mr. or Ms., prompting people to frequently mistake me for a military man—made it possible for me to relate to the conformity clearly sought by Gary Walters.

Gary Walters also said something that I've never forgotten: "The money might not be as good as you're used to, but if you get this job, you'll be part of living history."

After about two hours, we all shook hands, and I made the long drive back home.

Was I going to make the first cut? I had absolutely no idea.

HERE WE ARE NOW, ENTERTAIN US

That Friday, Gary Walters called me again.

"We'd like you to come cook for the First Lady and her staff on Tuesday," he said. This is not at all unusual for a chef candidate: to prepare an "audition" menu for his prospective employers.

"What do you want me to make?"

"Whatever you want."

That was a curveball. Whatever I wanted? For the First Lady and her staff? Daunting, to say the least.

"Well, how many people will be there?"

"About ten."

"How many courses?"

"As many as you want."

So they weren't even going to tell me how much food?

I had to laugh. "So you're not going to tell me anything. You're just going to throw me to the wolves?"

"Yeah, basically," he said, then softened. "Look, we don't want to give you any preconceived notions. We want to see what you do."

Fine, I thought. I can do that. I'll cook the stuff I know I do best. "Very good, Mr. Walters. I'll look forward to seeing you on Tuesday."

In the days since my interview, I had looked up some articles about Mrs. Clinton and her quest for a new chef. "We're not going to entertain until we have the chef I want," was her oft-repeated reason for why they hadn't thrown any state dinners in the fifteen months they'd been in the White House. In those same articles, I had identified the kernel of what would become my approach to the audition. Mrs. Clinton wanted to modernize the White House menu, moving away from its traditional French style and toward contemporary American cuisine and service, thereby making the White House a showcase for what our farmers and other culinary purveyors were creating, and also for the style being forged by modern American chefs who wove indigenous American ingredients and international elements and styles together into an exciting, ever-changing cuisine that defied easy description—and was garnering a great deal of attention from coast to coast and around the world.

I spent the weekend holed up in the kitchen at the Greenbrier with some of my best cooks, working on a few "new menus"—the reason for which, of course, I couldn't fully explain to them. I built the menus around the best seasonal foods of the moment such as morel mushrooms, which were just becoming available, young spring lettuces, and ramps (wild leeks), which were growing everywhere in West Virginia. Because the waters were still ice cold, we were still in peak lobster season, so those went on as well. And I made room for elements that, in my research, I had discovered Mrs. Clinton enjoyed. For example, having read that she liked spicy food, I added a mousseline of curried sweet potatoes. To meet the expectation of modernity, I also included some international flourishes such as the sauce for the lobster, which featured ginger, scallions, and cilantro.

In all, we prepped three menus of three courses each. My thought was this: If there were ten people at the table, I'd serve alternating menus to each person, so no matter where you were seated, you'd have one dish before you and be able to see the other two dishes simply by glancing to your immediate left and right, and maybe taste them if someone was willing to share.

Moreover, the three menus I had designed each comprised dishes that could be produced on a large scale for special functions, such as the much-anticipated state dinners. I didn't know if I'd have a chance to address the First Lady directly during my audition, but if I did my mission was clear: convey to her that this wasn't just a lunch; it was a preview of what she could look forward to serving visiting heads of state, foreign dignitaries, and others guests of honor.

On Monday, the guys helped me pack the sauces, vinaigrettes, and prepared vegetables into half-quart and one-quart containers. They must have known by this time that the food wasn't meant for the hotel, but they were kind enough not to ask me any awkward questions. Thanks to them, the only actual cooking I'd have to do at the White House would be the preparation of more delicate items such as leafy greens, and of course the poaching, searing, and roasting of any fish and meat.

That night, sitting in bed on the eve of my Big Day, Jean reminded me of something I had long forgotten. Years earlier, she had asked me what my professional dreams were. I had replied that one was to become an executive chef within five years; another was to apprentice at the Greenbrier; and the third was to be the chef of the White House.

I had to laugh. The third ambition had been such a pipe dream—the outlandish utterance of a young cook, shared as mere fantasy at the time—that I had long forgotten even saying it. But now here I was, with that once-ridiculous goal in my sights, and Jean's message was clear: having combined and attained the first two goals, why not expect that the loftiest of the three was truly possible?

I must say, the whole thing was beginning to have an air of destiny about it—in many ways, I felt my mother's presence, convinced she was looking down on me. It was, after all, on the trip home from her funeral that this had all begun.

And there was something else, something that had only deepened as I reflected on my first interview. The White House was simply a place like no other. It would be more than a job to work there. As they said in the Navy recuitment ads of the time, it would be an adventure.

My heart pounding, I was so filled with adrenaline that I could've cooked my audition meal right then. But I had a long drive to make, and I'd have to begin it at about two o'clock in the morning. So I took a deep breath, turned off the light, and made myself go to sleep.

★ ★ ★

At seven thirty the next morning, I was cleared into the White House and shown the kitchen. I was rather dismayed at what I found. I had seen it briefly during my initial visit, but now that I had a chance to study it—indeed, cook in it—the evident wear and tear was disconcerting. It seemed to me that most of the equipment hadn't been replaced since the 1970s, so not only did it look a generation behind but it was also incapable of generating the kind of power required to produce the volume of food that was prepared there.

Along the south wall was a bank of ranges, and along the opposite wall there were a pot sink, a produce sink, a broiler in the corner, a deep fryer, a flat top (griddle), and a battery of burners. There was a pastry bench along one of the adjacent walls, and two work tables in the center of the room. Glancing down, I noticed that the floor was a peculiar blue color with yellow streaks down the center.

Everything was there that should have been there, but it was all hopelessly out of date, and it occurred to me that the kitchen was an obvious symbol for what Mrs. Clinton was hoping to reverse—a backward-looking spectacle that recalled the American attitude toward food as fuel, and little more.

Nonetheless, this was the kitchen I was presented with, so I got to work, unpacking the coolers of food I had brought from home, preheating ovens, and so on.

Before too long, Gary Walters entered accompanied by the maitre d' (highest ranking butler), who asked me what I'd need in the way of service ware and cutlery. I handed him a prepared list and he left the room. Gary informed me that the First Lady wanted to have lunch around one o'clock. "No problem," I said, and he left, too.

Forty-five minutes later, Gary returned and told me it'd be more like noon. Again, I replied that this would be no problem.

A short while after that, he retuned yet again and let me know that twelve thirty was the more likely time.

At this point, I began to realize that I was being tested, pressed to see how well I could manage a moving target. Sorry, guys, I thought, You're not going to psych me out that easily.

"No problem," I said barely looking up from the freshly poached lobster I was removing from its shell. Just to make clear how absolutely flexible I was, I added, "We'll do it now if you like."

At about ten o'clock I realized that my service ware and such hadn't arrived. I asked a nearby butler where the maitre d' I'd met earlier had gone.

"He went home," was the unsettling answer.

"Did he give you the dishes?"

"No."

"Okay," I said as another obstacle was dropped in my path.

To the butler's surprise, I produced a second copy of the list from my notebook. Having worked in a number of enormous kitchens, I was used to having a back-up duplicate of everything.

"Here's the list," I said to him. "You might as well take care of it."

"I don't know," he said, dramatically looking at his watch. "I hope I have time to get it."

"I hope so, too, because it's gonna look awfully bad when I serve the First Lady on paper plates because I didn't receive what I asked for."

I have to admit, I was getting a little hot under the collar by this point. I was beginning to wonder how many of these challenges were real and how many were manufactured. It didn't really matter. This was the biggest day of my professional life, and I wasn't about to be undone by the china.

Turns out that fluctuations of the schedule and a disappearing butler were the least of the obstacles in my path. In the White House, I was told, you prepare most of the food in the ground-floor kitchen in which I was working. But it's finished and delivered to the First Family from a smaller kitchen on the second floor, adjacent to the formal President's Dining Room. Accordingly, at eleven o'clock, I was to get into the tiny little elevator that shuttles staff members up and down to move the food upstairs. What nobody told me was that the staff began taking their lunch at eleven, at which time the elevator is occupied more or less nonstop for much of the hour as they make their way to and from the cafeteria on the basement level.

So there I stood, at the threshold of the most important moment in my career, with all of my meticulously thought-out food on a cart, ready to be transported to the private kitchen of the First Family, and I couldn't move. I stood there, paralyzed, as the doors opened again and again only to reveal that the car was packed to capacity. Finally, after about thirty minutes (at least it seemed that long), the elevator freed up and I got to the second floor.

After navigating a short series of corridors that lead from the elevator, I stepped into the second-floor kitchen and blinked a few times, surprised by what I found there. Rather than a commercial prep and finishing area, the room had the exact look and feel of an all-American eat-in kitchen. There were charming cupboard cabinets, a casual wooden dining table and chairs, and even a television set. It was as though I had left the White House and entered a suburban family kitchen not unlike the one in my own house. (Before my day was done, an usher would inform me that the First Lady, put off by the idea of dining in the ornate and formal President's Dining

Room on a regular basis, had ordered this room redesigned almost as soon as the Clintons had moved in, and it was here that they usually enjoyed meals together when they didn't have guests.)

After a cursory look around to take all of this in, and to check that the plates I had requested had been delivered (thankfully, they had, and were piled neatly on the counter), I began unpacking my food.

Gary Walters came into the room.

"Lunch isn't going to be served at twelve-thirty. It's going to be served at eleven fifty," he said.

I looked at my watch. It was already eleven forty!

I took a deep breath. Okay, I said to myself. Let's see what we can do.

As I began putting together the first courses, making small alterations in garnishes and presentation to account for the sudden lack of time, I could hear Mrs. Clinton and her staff filing into the dining room next door. It was thrilling to hear her famous voice just one room away, but it was also nerve-wracking.

As the plates were completed, they were whisked away by a small team of tuxedoed butlers and taken out into the dining room.

The whole meal, all three courses, happened so quickly that I didn't know if I had sent out something great, or the worst meal of all time. I had been running on pure instinct and adrenaline, not focusing on anything but the food and not even trying to determine how it was being received. Now that the work was done, I began to notice audible oohs and ahhs drifting in from the dining room, the unmistakable sounds of happy diners, who were telling each other, "You have to try this," "This is delicious," and so on.

An usher led me into the dining room, and I found myself in uncharted territory: Hillaryland.

Hillaryland was the name given to the inner circle of folks, women mostly, who worked for the First Lady, including Ann Stock, who had interviewed me on my last visit; Mrs. Clinton's chief of staff, Maggie Williams; her deputy chief of staff, Melanne Verveer; Capricia Marshall, her special assistant; press secretary Lisa Caputo; spokesperson Neel Lattimore; deputy assistant to the President, Patti Solis, and so on—her most trusted advisors and staff, an intimate group who fluttered around her at all times.

It was such an energetic scene that it actually took me a moment before I focused on Hillary Clinton, sitting right there at the head of the table. She exuded that effortless star power for which the Clintons were already famous at the time, but she also seemed more laid back than the First Lady I had seen on television. Though clearly the leader of this group, she seemed to be enjoying a fun afternoon with friends as much as she seemed to be working.

A surreptitious glance down revealed that she had cleaned her plate—always a good sign to a chef.

The members of Hillaryland all had big smiles on their faces, and as they detected my presence, they turned to the First Lady, deferring to her.

After a moment, she spoke. "That's the best lamb I ever had."

"Thank you, ma'am," I said.

There was an infinitesimal pause, a moment in which nobody was saying a word. I realized that this was my opportunity, the opening for me to launch into my rehearsed pitch.

"Now, Mrs. Clinton," I said, surprising the members of Hillaryland. "What I want you to know is that this menu wasn't designed to be a precious restaurant menu. All nine of the dishes you've seen today—the three you tried and the ones to your left and right—can be reproduced for 150 people in a state dinner setting and in a timely fashion."

I could swear I saw a small spark go off in her eyes as she considered this.

"That's very interesting," she said, leaning slightly forward. "Tell me more about that."

"Well, there are probably one thousand chefs in the country who could make you a restaurant meal that would impress you and your family. But from what I've read in the papers, that's not what you're looking for. You've said you're not going to entertain until you find the chef you want. And that you're looking for a chef who can do large parties, not just show off his culinary skills for ten people."

"You know, you're the first one to say that," she said.

I later learned that chefs had come in and treated the First Lady to the biggest, wildest, most opulent dishes imaginable, with architectural presentations and luxury ingredients. My food was contemporary, to be sure, but also practical.

My brief presentation complete, I left the dining room and retreated to the kitchen. The assistant pastry chef—a woman in her thirties—was there and I noticed that she had a camera at her station. I asked her if she could do me a favor.

"Would you mind taking a picture of me here?" I said. "I want to be able to show my kids that at least their old man got a chance to audition for this job."

"Sure," she said.

I stood in front of the window, smiled through my exhaustion, and off went the flash.

Pecan-Crusted Lamb with Morel Sauce and Red-Curried Sweet Potatoes

SERVES 4

This was a karmic dish selection for my White House audition lunch because it turned out that Mrs. Clinton's favorite meat is lamb. Her taste for spicy food made the curried sweet potatoes a big hit as well. The dish sparked my brief but all-important dialogue with the First Lady following the lunch.

It was meant to show what kind of food I thought we could pull off for a state dinner, and it obviously did the trick in helping me get the job. (The original also featured a mix of spring vegetables, which I've omitted here for simplicity's sake.) For less formal occasions, you can serve these components family-style rather than plating each dish. You can also simply spoon the potato puree onto the plates rather than piping it out of a pastry bag.

FOR THE PECAN CRUST
⅔ cup pecan halves (about 2½ ounces)
⅓ cup fresh white bread crumbs
Pinch of ground cumin
Pinch of cayenne
Pinch of ground coriander
Pinch of freshly ground black pepper

FOR THE LAMB
One 8-rib lamb rack (about 1½ pounds), trimmed of excess fat
Salt and freshly ground black pepper
1 tablespoon canola oil
1½ tablespoons Dijon mustard
½ tablespoon honey
¾ teaspoon roasted garlic puree (see box, page 23)

TO ASSEMBLE AND SERVE
Red-Curried Sweet Potatoes (page 24)
Morel Sauce (page 24)

1. Make the breading: Lightly toast the pecan halves in a small, heavy-bottomed sauté pan over medium heat until fragrant, 3 to 4 minutes. Let cool, then transfer to the bowl of a food processor fitted with the steel blade and pulse to a medium-fine grind. Transfer to a medium bowl. Add the bread crumbs, cumin, cayenne, coriander, and pepper and stir to combine. Set aside. (At this stage, the breading can be refrigerated in an airtight container for up to 24 hours. Let it come to room temperature before proceeding.)

2. Precook the lamb: Preheat the oven to 325°F. Season the lamb on both sides with salt and pepper. Heat the canola oil in a large, heavy-bottomed sauté pan set over high heat. Add the lamb and sear well on both sides, 2 to 3 minutes per side. Transfer to a plate and let cool.

3. In a small bowl, stir together the mustard, honey, and roasted garlic to make a glaze. Using a pastry brush, paint the glaze onto the meat portion of the lamb. Coat the lamb with the pecan breading by rolling the meat in the breading and lightly pressing it on by hand. (Be careful to not get any glaze or breading on the bones or it will scorch and blacken them.)

4. Put the lamb in a roasting pan and roast until an instant-read thermometer inserted into the thickest part reads 135°F to 140°F, about 20 minutes. Remove from the oven and let rest for 8 to 10 minutes.

5. To serve: Put the sweet potato puree in a pastry bag fitted with a medium tip, if using. Reheat the sauce, if necessary. Slice the lamb between the bones to make 8 chops. Pipe or spoon about 3 tablespoons of sweet potato puree in the center of each of four dinner plates. Place two lamb chops on each plate, spoon some sauce and mushrooms around the lamb, and serve.

TO MAKE ROASTED GARLIC PUREE: Preheat the oven to 350°F. Put a head of garlic in a small ceramic baking dish or ramekin. Drizzle with 1 tablespoon olive oil and 1 tablespoon water and season with salt and pepper. Cover with a lid or aluminum foil and bake until the cloves are soft, about 40 minutes (a small, thin-bladed knife will easily pierce right through). Remove the dish from the oven. When the garlic is cool enough to handle, separate the cloves and squeeze the garlic out of the papery skin. Mash smooth with a fork. One medium head of garlic will yield 3 to 4 tablespoons of puree. The puree can be refrigerated in an airtight container for up to 3 days. Stir leftover puree into soups and sauces, or into softened butter for an extra-flavorful spread.

Red-Curried Sweet Potatoes

2 medium sweet potatoes (about 6
  ounces each)
1½ cups orange juice, preferably
  freshly squeezed
2 teaspoons packed light brown
  sugar
About ¾ teaspoon red curry paste,
  depending on desired heat level
3 tablespoons coconut milk solids
  (skimmed from the top of a can of
  unsweetened coconut milk)

1. Preheat the oven to 325°F. Arrange the sweet potatoes in a single layer on a baking sheet or baking dish. Roast until tender to a knife tip, about 1 hour. Remove from the oven and let cool. Peel the potatoes and transfer them to the bowl of a food processor fitted with the steel blade. Puree until smooth, then push them through a fine-mesh strainer set over a large bowl, pressing down with a rubber spatula or the bottom of a ladle to extract as much puree as possible.

2. Put the orange juice and brown sugar in a small, heavy-bottomed saucepan. Bring to a simmer over medium-high heat and cook until reduced to a syrup, about 10 minutes. Stir in the curry, then fold the mixture into the sweet potato puree.

3. Transfer the puree to a large saucepan over medium heat. Thoroughly fold in the coconut solids. Cook, stirring occasionally, until the mixture dries to piping consistency, 3 to 4 minutes. (At this stage, the puree can be kept warm in a double boiler set over simmering water for up to 2 hours.)

4. Serve with a spoon, or transfer to a pastry bag fitted with the medium star tip.

Morel Sauce

3 ounces lamb stew meat, cut into
  ½-inch cubes
1 tablespoon chopped shallot
¼ cup cabernet sauvignon or other
  full-bodied red wine
Freshly ground black pepper
2 sprigs fresh thyme
1 cup veal demi-glace (available
  from specialty grocers or online;
  see Sources, page 302)
1 teaspoon roasted garlic puree
  (see page 23)
Salt
1 teaspoon canola oil
1 ounce morel mushrooms, trimmed
  and cleaned

1. Heat a medium, heavy-bottomed saucepan over medium-high heat. Add the lamb stew meat and cook, stirring often, until well browned, about 5 minutes. Add the shallot and cook until softened but not browned, about 3 minutes.

2. Add the wine and stir, scraping up any flavorful bits stuck to the bottom of the pot. Add a pinch of pepper and the thyme. Simmer until the wine is reduced by three quarters. Add the demi-glace and the garlic puree and simmer until reduced by one fourth.

3. Strain through a fine-mesh strainer set over a bowl and season to taste with salt and pepper. Keep covered and warm. Discard solids.

4. In a sauté pan, heat the oil over medium heat. Sauté mushrooms 3 to 4 minutes until tender. Add to sauce. Serve. Add the sautéed morels before serving. (Sauce can be cooled and refrigerated in an airtight container for up to 24 hours. Reheat gently before proceeding.)

THREE WOMEN

Over the next few days, the entire audition began to fade into a dreamlike memory. I didn't hear from anyone, and a news account in the paper mentioning candidates for the job of White House Chef didn't even include my name. I felt the air going out of my candidacy, so much so that when Jean said that getting the job would be "the greatest thing that ever happened," I simply replied that I wasn't going to get it.

But I still wanted the gig. I remember talking with my direct boss, Greenbrier's vice president of food and beverage, Rod Stoner, one day. He had seen an article about the search for a White House chef, and commented to me, shaking his head in confusion and distaste, "Who would want to go cook for just three people?"

With dreams of preparing state dinners for hundreds swirling around in my head, despite the lack of communication from the White House, I couldn't help but reply, "Well, I think it might be a bit more complicated than that."

A week later, on a Wednesday night at about ten o'clock, Gary Walters called our home, asking me to be at the White House at seven o'clock the next morning. I immediately showered, shaved, got into my car, and drove the five hours to D.C. I hit the city at about five thirty in the morning, and promptly pulled over and took a nap in the car.

When I got to the White House, an usher took me to the medical office where they performed a number of tests. I didn't know what to make of it. Maybe they were doing this to all candidates who had made it this far?

At about 10:00 a.m., I was led to the Yellow Oval Room, a parlor-like sitting room on the second floor of the residence. There again were the First Lady, chief of staff Maggie Williams, Ann Stock, and the rest of Hillaryland. Someone motioned for me to have a seat on the settee in the center of the room.

No sooner did I sit than Bill Clinton, the President of the United States, appeared in the doorway, pink-cheeked and brimming with energy. Following the lead of the rest of the room, I quickly stood back up.

There is no way to adequately explain the charisma—the sheer, attention-grabbing, rock star–level wattage—emanating from President Clinton. I had heard about it, but it was exponentially greater than what I might have expected. I mean, he was just standing there, just standing in the doorway, and I could not take my eyes off of him.

He noticed me as well, though for very different reasons.

"Hey, is this the new guy who's gonna cook me all those Big Macs from here on in?" he said in his big, hearty drawl, then cracked up at his own joke. "Aw, don't worry about that. I don't really eat much of that stuff. That's just the press."

And—whoosh—as fast as he had appeared, he was gone.

But what he said wasn't lost on me. He was talking as though I had the job. But I hadn't been offered the job. What to do?

The most prudent thing seemed to be to just sit there and see what happened next.

"OK, everybody, let me and Walter have the room, please," said Mrs. Clinton. The denizens of Hillaryland fell into a neat little formation and filed out of the room.

Mrs. Clinton sat down on the settee beside me.

"Walter," she said. "I have a lot of ideas about what I want the food at the White House to be. They all have to do with highlighting what's best and most unique about American food and wine, and entertaining at the White House."

As she proceeded to outline her goals for the White House chef—which she ran through without the aid of any notes—I pulled out my yellow legal pad and started writing. These were the goals she laid out for me:

1. Showcase American regional cuisine and products, which she described as the "Number One" priority.
2. Make the food as good as anyone's (which I took to mean as good as any restaurant's food) and serve restaurant-caliber food for both state dinners and other functions.
3. Develop a more nutritional and low-fat style for all White House food, including staff meals, and keep amounts of red meats on menus to a minimum.
4. Provide family meals for a real family; learn likes and dislikes of all members. Make them nutritious, but informal. Keep meals with friends interesting, but also informal.
5. Make receptions at the White House more eclectic and interesting.
6. Start a rooftop garden for vegetables and herbs for use in preparations.
7. Upgrade the quality of food purchasing.
8. Think about what role the chef has in the history of the White House.
9. Develop a guest chef series.

After about forty minutes, the key members of Hillaryland—Ann Stock and Maggie Williams—returned along with Gary Walters, and began talking to me about a variety of upcoming functions, and the menus they would require. It's fair to say that my head was spinning.

In the midst of all this, Mrs. Clinton turned to me. "What do you think?" she said.

"It all sounds very interesting, Mrs. Clinton. But, you know, I haven't been offered the job."

She thought about this for a moment, then tossed her head back, and let out what I would soon learn was a trademark, joy-filled burst of laughter—in strong contrast to the somewhat studied, reserved persona she displayed in public.

"Oh, Walter," she said, laughter still reverberating in her voice, "Of course, you can have the job."

She looked me right in the eye, knowing what a big moment this was for me.

"Do you want the job, Walter?"

"Yes, ma'am."

And just like that, I became White House Executive Chef.

We spoke for a few minutes longer, then I said my goodbyes and was escorted out of the residence.

I got in my car and started the long drive home. In Strasburg, Virginia, where 66 West becomes 81 South, I pulled into the parking lot of the Strasburg Hotel, a big Victorian relic. I walked into the lobby and dialed my home on a payphone.

Jean answered.

"Jean, I—"

"You got it! You got it! You got it!" she exclaimed. Somehow the news had leaked and she had already received a number of inquisitive calls from the media, though—not having spoken to me yet—all she could do was tell them the truth: that she hadn't heard a thing.

We talked for a minute, then hung up, and I headed back out into the parking lot.

There was another call I wanted to make, but that opportunity had passed. I wished I could have shared the news with my mother, whose moment this was as much as it was mine. That she had missed it by mere weeks made her absence all the more painful.

Rather than dwell on the sadness, I resolved to make her proud, wherever she was, to do a job that would honor her, as well as my wife, who had pushed me into this new life, and the First Lady, who was taking a big chance on someone she barely knew, on the biggest stage in the world.

The adventure had begun.

MY CRASH COURSE IN MEDIA RELATIONS

Imagine landing the dream job of your life and not being able to tell the world about it. That was the situation in which I found myself after Hillary Clinton offered me the position of White House Executive Chef.

Though Mrs. Clinton hired me, my official supervisor was chief usher Gary Walters, who had instructed me, conveying the wishes of the First Lady's spokesperson Neel Lattimore, not to discuss my new job with the media. I was even given a script to follow. If asked by a reporter, my response was to be, "No position has been offered; no position has been accepted."

I was allowed to tell my family, of course, as well as my then-current employers, and it was interesting to see how each responded. Everybody, it seems, has a different reaction to this kind of news.

Our kids, just shy of three and six, didn't really understand the concept of moving, though they were excited that their dad was going to work at the White House, a place they saw on television all the time. In fact, they had the idea we were going to live there ourselves, until I told them otherwise.

The most amusing reaction came from Rod Stoner, the guy who had made that crack about how boring it must be to be chef at the White House. When I told him the news, it did little to change his oft-repeated slogan: "Nobody ever leaves the Greenbrier for someplace better."

More supportive was Ted Kleisner, the hotel's managing director, for whom I had also worked in Boca Raton, Florida.

My departure wasn't going to make Ted's life any easier, as locating a new Greenbrier chef would be almost as hard as finding the right White House chef. Nonetheless, when he heard the news, Ted—realizing the public relations bonanza this meant for the hotel—brightened like a Christmas tree, and exclaimed, "This is one of the best things that's ever happened to the Greenbrier! Congratulations."

The Greenbrier was a complex operation. Accordingly, I gave Rod and Ted ample notice, so they'd have time to find a replacement, or at least set up a workable contingency plan for any lapse between my departure and the selection and arrival of a new chef.

What none of us could plan for was the fact that journalists would begin coming out of the woodwork, calling me, Rod, Ted, and other executives and department heads for comment.

I kept in mind my orders from the White House and rehearsed my answer, trying to make it convincing through intonation and facial expression: "No position has been offered; no position has been accepted." "No position has been offered; no position has been accepted." Finally, I settled on a tone and delivery style, an affable but stern declaration, punctuated at the end by a bemused chuckle.

I had my routine down. I was ready to face any journalist and answer any questions.

There was just one catch. Every reporter who showed up seemed to have it on good authority that I had been hired. They weren't fishing around for clues; they clearly knew that I was the new White House chef. I called Gary Walters for counsel, and he urged me to stick to my instructions from the press office. Each new day was an adventure in navigating a sea of sleuths in our midst. Not only did they call; a few intrepid souls even staked out the Greenbrier lobby, in hopes of spotting me, then pulling me aside for a spontaneous heart to heart.

For example, Phyllis C. Richman, the *Washington Post*'s restaurant critic, showed up one day and introduced herself to me, saying, "I understand you're the new White House chef."

"No position has been offered; no position has been accepted," I said in my by-now rote delivery style.

She cocked an unconvinced eyebrow in my direction.

"Okay, look," she said, "why don't we have a generic discussion. I'll ask you hypothetical questions, but you don't have to acknowledge that you have the job."

That seemed harmless enough, so I agreed. We took a seat at one of the Greenbrier's indoor cafés and she proceeded to ask me questions that were about the White House but without naming it, such as "How do you think what you do here would apply to an informal dinner . . . for the First Family?"

It was a friendly if ridiculous exercise. I was reminded of Jackie Gleason's old Ralph Kramden routine on *The Honeymooners*: "I know that you know that I know that you know . . ."

In time, I realized that there was no point in denying the obvious. Television news broadcasts were announcing my appointment as undisputed fact, as did brief articles in the *New York Times* and *Washington Post*, which even detailed my audition lunch and subsequent meeting with Mrs. Clinton, although Neel Lattimore was cited in the pieces as saying that no one had officially been hired. And the fact that wire-service stories began to be picked up in smaller papers from coast to coast only increased the sense that everybody was well aware that I had been hired.

I called Gary again and pleaded my case for just telling everybody the truth, going so far as to tell him that I thought it was "silly" to bother denying it anymore. "Do what you will," he said. "But I'm telling you, the media isn't going to help you, and you've got nothing to gain from talking to them."

With that permission, I made a judgment call not to participate in any more denials, and began talking openly about the job.

The next decision I made was to whom I would give interviews. I was being approached by everybody, from the smallest of the small papers such as my hometown paper, *The Montgomery Journal*, and the local West Virginia paper, the *Roanoke Times*, to the biggest of the big newspapers such as *USA Today* (which I turned down, and which proceeded to get my name wrong in the blurb they

Berry's World

"GREAT burger! My compliments to the new chef."

Although becoming the White House chef was of great importance to me, I didn't realize that the news media and even a few political cartoonists would find it so significant.

published) and *People* magazine, and not just from the United States; journalists from all over the world were looking for me.

I decided to give a limited number of in-depth interviews. I talked to those papers in Roanoke and Montgomery, and via telephone to Marian Burros of the *New York Times*.

I also made some time to speak with cookbook author and *Washington Times* reporter Judith Olney, who found her way back to the Greenbrier kitchen one day and caught me in a talkative mood. Judith instantly struck me as an unlikely representative of the right-leaning paper for which she worked: a '60s-folk-type who had also written books on gardening, she had a pleasant, neo-hippy aura about her, a voice that practically sang "I'm okay, you're okay," and a bright, sincere smile.

Though she had come to get what she could from me, I ended up getting more from her. "I want to give you some

tips about working with the press," she said to me. As a newcomer to the spotlight, I was only too happy to listen.

"First of all, reporters are never, never your friends. They are out to write a story. If you can help them, that's great. If not, then don't. And don't offer them stuff off the record. There's no such thing as 'off the record.'"

She went on to explain to me the pitfalls of, well, of just being straight with people who might take your words out of context, using them to wrest a story from their time with you.

After this nearly forty-minute tutorial, we returned to the subject of our interview: me.

"Are you happy to be leaving West Virginia?" she asked.

"Yeah, I am. Mostly for the boys," I said, referring to my two sons. "You know the schools in West Virginia aren't the best. It's practically as bad as Tennessee or Arkansas."

She stopped writing and looked at me with a disapproving frown.

"Walter, let me repeat what you just said. You just mentioned Arkansas and Tennessee. Do you happen to know where the Clintons and Gores are from?"

Damn, I thought, instantly recalling that the President had previously been Governor of Arkansas. And Vice-President Al Gore had most recently been a senator from Tennessee.

"Do you know what my editors would give me for that quote?" she said, politely scolding me.

I gulped, imagining my sentence plastered across newspapers from coast to coast. Would it be grounds for withdrawing the job offer or, if not, would I be persona non grata on Day One of my tenure in the White House kitchen?

"I'm going to give you a pass on that one," she said, and my entire being relaxed. "But you really need to keep your foot out of your mouth in this job."

And I thought all I had to worry about was what to make for breakfast, lunch, and dinner.

It wasn't the last time I'd say something ill-considered to a journalist, or an official, but I'll always be grateful to Judith Olney. If it weren't for her, I'd probably have said even worse things, and with greater frequency.

EYE OF THE STORM

Before too long, the volume of calls to the Greenbrier was overwhelming. I was getting five or six an hour, minimum. I couldn't get out of the office, and neither the kitchen manager nor I could get anything done.

And the calls weren't just affecting me. They were such a switchboard-smothering distraction that the powers that be politely released me from my post. "We'll pay you for a month," Ted Kleisner told me, unable to find a better solution. "Just go home and let us do some business."

The calls to our home were equally unyielding. Jean and I changed our phone number to an unlisted one, but that mattered not at all. Within a few hours of when the new number took effect, they resumed.

The distractions were so constant, so unending, that we could barely get anything done. I couldn't even find the time to enlist a broker to sell our home. When this fact hit Jean and me, I made a joke out of the situation: I grabbed a mop, sawed off the sponge end, handwrote the words "For Sale" on a piece of cardboard, taped it to the sign, and stuck it in the front yard.

The very next day, a car screeched to a halt in front of the sign, kicking up dust. The driver got out and asked for a look around. Within a month, he had bought the place from us.

Jean and I first met in Washington, D.C., and we had kept the house we built in Great Falls, Virginia, about twenty-two miles out of town, renting it during our time in Florida and West Virginia. We gave our tenants notice and returned to the area, staying in a friend's townhouse in Reston, Virginia, for a few weeks.

I was surprised that there was virtually no contact from the White House at this time, and I never received any paperwork, outside of the standard tax forms and such one has to fill out for any job. There was no employee manual, no map of the house, not even a list of do's and don'ts.

A workaholic chef not used to having time on his hands, I found myself consumed with nervous excitement. I was thrilled to have the opportunity awaiting me, but it was so beyond anything I had ever attempted that I teetered precariously on the brink of panic.

I channeled the energy into my preparation, leafing through many of my cookbooks (my collection housed more than one thousand at the time) for ideas to satisfy the First Lady's mandate for healthful food, vegetarian dishes, and international influences. I immersed myself in the books for hours and hours, trying to just think about food.

Finally, I heard from the Usher's Office, who phoned with the only instruction I received during this time: to report to the White House on Monday, April 4, for a photo op and to return the following morning to start work.

MEET THE FAMILY

Every year, the White House stages an Easter Egg Roll, in which young children push eggs down a runway with slotted spoons, on the Monday after Easter. In 1994, this festive event took place on April 4.

The adventure begins: A photo op with my family and the Clintons, the day before I started work. *(Courtesy William J. Clinton Presidential Library)*

As thousands of children—a group that in later years would include our own sons—participated in the ritual, Jean, Walt, Jim, and I arrived on the White House grounds. It was Monday, but we were in our Sunday best—Jean in a springy yellow dress, me in a suit and tie, and Walter and Jim in blue blazers.

"Now, remember, boys, these are very important people we're meeting today," I told them before heading to the White House. I was very anxious about meeting President and Mrs. Clinton in my official capacity, but more than anything, I was terrified that my young children might, as young children will, say something inappropriate.

On our way into the White House, we passed by one of the many news crews who were covering the event.

"What are you doing here, young man?" asked a woman reporter, as her cameraman trained his lens on our younger son, Jim.

Jerking his head in my direction, he said, "Well, my father came here to get a job."

I quickly took him by the hand, and we all proceeded into the White House, where an usher took us to the Blue Room.

We met President and Mrs. Clinton there. It was quite a thrill to introduce my wife and children to the First Family.

As we all shook hands, the President looked down at Jim.

"What's your name?" he asked.

After a thoughtful pause, my boy responded, "Well, I have three names."

My stomach sank as he continued to make wisecracks, listing his various monikers to the leader of the free world: "Jim, Jimmy, and James." He considered for a moment, then added, "I like you. You can call me Jimmy. All my friends do."

"That's quite a little firecracker you have there," the President said, laughing.

"Yes, sir," I said, amused at Jim's spirit.

ARE YOU NOW, OR HAVE YOU EVER BEEN . . .

Later that afternoon, I was enjoying my last evening before starting the job. To clear my head and let off some pent-up steam, I was in the backyard, mowing our lawn, sweaty in my gym shorts and T-shirt, and feeling great.

In the distance, I noticed a trench coat-clad figure with a little mop of gray hair on top of his head, making his way from house to house. As he approached my front yard, I turned off the lawnmower and went up to meet him.

We got closer to each other, and I realized that he was a real-life incarnation of Lieutenant Columbo, a diminutive guy in a brown suit who shuffled in my direction not unlike Peter Falk.

"Can I help you?" I said.

With a gravelly, Columbo-like voice, he introduced himself, telling me that he was an agent from the FBI. "I'm completing a background check prior to your beginning work at the White House."

I was bemused, both by his persona and his timing. "Aren't you a little late? I start work tomorrow."

He ignored my comment and, in an inscrutable staccato, asked, "Is there some place we can talk, Mr. Scheib?"

I invited him in and he, Jean, and I pulled up chairs around the kitchen table. He declined our offer of a drink, even water.

Removing a steno pad from his coat pocket, he began asking us questions in an utterly detached monotone.

"Do you have any reason to believe that you might have any psychological illness or damage?"

"No," I said, then made, I thought, a harmless domestic joke. "But my wife thinks I do."

He considered this for a moment, then began scrawling in his pad, muttering to himself, " . . . wife thinks he does . . . "

"No, no that's a joke," I said.

He stared at me uncomprehendingly for a few moments—who would make a joke to a G-man during a background check?—then flipped back through his notebook and continued with the questioning. Where had I lived? Did I have a criminal record? And on and on and on.

Once he got past the pro forma stuff, he proceeded to questions inspired by his canvassing of the neighborhood.

"Now, Mr. Scheib, one of your neighbors said that he said hello to you one time and you didn't say hello back. He wonders about your temperament."

"I don't remember that. Maybe I don't like the guy you're talking about."

He nodded again, giving away nothing, then scribbled something in his notebook.

And so it went, for an hour and a half. Finally, he arrived at his last question: "Are you now, or have you ever been a member of a group that advocates the overthrow of the government of the United States?"

He paused, then added, "If yes, please explain."

A number of jokes occurred to me—I mean, if I did belong to such a group, would I cop to it that easily?—but I decided to keep them to myself.

"No," I said.

I was learning, slowly but surely, that there are many times in public life when saying as little as possible is the best way to go.

WELCOME TO THE WORKING WEEK

The next morning, Tuesday, April 5, I woke up at 4:30 a.m., got dressed, hopped into my car, and drove to work at the White House.

It was dark out, and there wasn't much traffic, though when I arrived at the White House, there were a number of people already well into their workday.

As I did for my interviews, I passed through the two checkpoints. In time, I would be on a first-name basis with the Uniformed Division, but on my first day I was thoroughly checked out. They were most interested in my knife kit. Knives are a very personal choice for a chef, so most chefs bring their own knives to any job. Mine were a hodgepodge of knifes, about twenty-five in all, which I had been amassing since my cooking school days. Though made by several different companies, they all had my name emblazoned on the blades in black.

A member of the Usher's Office led me to my office, located on the third floor, which I was to share with Roland Mesnier, the executive pastry chef who had been at the White House for about 15 years at that point, and had enjoyed quite a bit of fame.

In the office there were two single beds and Roland's desk. To this day, I'm not sure why there were two beds there, but I knew I'd be getting rid of one of them before too long.

During my first day, I could see that I'd have a lot of work to do just to feel grounded in the office. I've always believed that the kitchen is only half of a chef's domain; each of us also needs a place—usually an office—to put down his or her anchor. If you don't have a sanctuary to keep order, your universe—and your mind—can get very messy very fast.

Then it was off to the kitchen, the thirty-by twenty-six-foot room where I was to transform menu planning for the First Family and their guests. Any thoughts I had of setting up my office were immediately postponed because Job Number One would clearly be to get the kitchen cleaned up and ready to operate.

A few challenges of this space were immediately apparent. One was that the kitchen had an open wall on one side, and that the kitchen doors were always open. As a result, there were flies everywhere, which amazed me.

During my audition, I learned that the equipment was outdated, but I had no idea how deeply this problem extended. For instance, there was a big deck oven, like a pizza oven, with one shelf—a huge devotion of space to something with limited utility and output. Also, owing to the meager refrigeration space, fresh fish was kept in ice-filled drawers, which, in addition to being a far-from-failsafe means of preservation, also threatened to damage the delicate flesh of most fish.

To put it as succinctly as possible, the kitchen was ugly, inefficient, and most pressing, dirty, so one of my first orders as chef was the distinctly unglamorous one of having the place scrubbed from floor to ceiling.

During the first week or two, I was constantly and unpleasantly surprised by new issues. For example, on my second or third day, one of the cooks came into the kitchen with a plate of hamburgers. He put them on the grill to mark them for staff lunch. As soon as they hit the grates, the tiny room began to fill with smoke.

"Turn up the fan," I said, referring to the rotating blade under the ventilation hood.

"That's full speed," he replied. At this point, I could barely see him through the haze of smoke. "That's as good as it gets."

There was a lot of work to be done.

Ann Stock
White House Social Secretary, 1994 to 1997

White House social secretary is a big job for anybody. After the First Lady, the social secretary is the hostess of the House.

Under the Clintons, the job of White House social secretary was growing. To meet their grand ambitions, they searched for someone with the experience and sophistication to plan and execute enormous parties with style.

The person they found was Ann Stock, a native of Lafayette, Indiana, who left her job as vice president of public relations for Bloomingdale's in New York to work for the Clintons. But Ann was no stranger to politics, having served as deputy press secretary to Walter Mondale while he was Vice President. She was also no stranger to Washington, D.C.—she had been commuting to her Bloomingdale's job from her home in the area, and was active in D.C. organizations, having founded the Washington Woman Roundtable and Washington's Race for the Cure against breast cancer.

In other words, Ann's background touched on all the areas that intersected at her desk: politics, special events, large scales, and style. She also had a nose for what would play well in the media, and what wouldn't. On occasion, especially before state dinners, I would be brought out to talk to the press corps, to whom I'd explain the meal we were serving. I would emphasize certain international ingredients and why we had chosen them, and point out the differences between what we were doing and the way it had been done before.

Ann had an impressive ability to keep endless details under control, hire and manage the right people, and make the seemingly impossible come true. In time, she would mastermind the logistics for state dinners several times larger than any previous administration had thrown, as well as events such as the Summit of the Americas in Miami, Florida, that involved hosting world leaders at a variety of locations over a number of days. Though not, at first, a member of the Clintons' inner circle, she quickly established herself as a devoted part of the team, as hard-working and dedicated as any of her colleagues.

A very distinguished and fashionable woman in her mid-forties at the time, with short blond hair, impeccably attired in contemporary, but not flashy, fashion, she had great instincts for how to relate to different people. I was always impressed at how she'd be reserved and deferential toward people like Gary Walters or could flip a switch and be incredibly friendly with people like her Hillaryland colleagues.

In short, she was a very strong manager, motivator, and magic-maker.

She definitely had that effect on me. From the time of our first interview, Ann was constantly pressing me to turn things on their head. Of the Hillaryland team, Ann—by virtue of having spent time in New York City for years—was hands-down the most sophisticated diner, and I always welcomed her input and feedback on dishes, menus, and ideas.

THE CREW

One of the oddities of taking over a department in the White House, even the kitchen, is that tradition holds that the existing staff offer letters of resignation to their new manager. The manager then, often based on an interview, decides whether to accept or decline each employee's resignation.

I kept the steward, Adam Collick, and one of the assistant chefs in the ground floor residence kitchen, John Moeller, replacing the other assistant chef with Keith Luce, who came with me from the Greenbrier. I also kept the one full-time cook currently employed by the residence-staff cafeteria kitchen, hiring a second full-timer to work with him.

The most essential team member was John Moeller. In his early thirties at the time, John was about ten years my junior, a native of Lancaster, Pennsylvania, and graduate of Johnson and Wales College of Culinary Arts who had spent time cooking in France. John had blond-white hair, a matching mustache, and pale skin that turned bright red during the heat of service; I don't know if he knows this, but a few staff members of Spanish and South American heritage referred to him as *jefe rosado*, which means "pink chef."

John and I were very different cooks—I was a big-picture guy whose primary concern was flavor; he was a classically trained European cook who was quite accomplished, but fussed over what I think of as small details, like the precision of vegetable dice—but he was indispensable to me and I'll always be especially grateful for his early assistance. He was a helpful link to how the House worked. He knew where everything was, from large equipment to the stuff stashed in the closets down the hall. He was familiar with each appliance's kinks and how to finesse them, and showed me how to interface with the butlers, how to requisition things, and so on.

In short, in a workplace that put none of its procedures, systems, or information in writing, he was my walking, talking employee manual.

FAMILY MEALS

It was important to not lose sight of my primary job during all of this set-up: to serve the First Family.

During my first several weeks, because I was so immersed in getting my bearings and improving the state of the kitchen, there was just one meal I prepared for the Clintons personally: breakfast. They had been there for thirteen months and a routine had emerged. So while I was there getting ready for the day, a call would come to the kitchen from Mrs. Clinton—identified by an asterisk in the phone's caller ID window—who usually ordered fresh juice (mostly grape-fruit), blueberries or some other fruit, and Quaker brand oatmeal. I'd prepare this meal, and the butler on duty would pick it up and take it to her.

These calls proved to be a valuable opportunity for me to catch up with the First Lady and, more importantly, for her to catch up with me. She'd ask me how planning for this or that event was going and maybe offer some feedback on the previous night's dinner.

At some point in the morning, Chelsea would call for something.

The President almost never ate breakfast. If he did, he'd have it brought to him in the Oval Office from the Navy mess, an on-site commissary for military personnel assigned to the White House. The mess was closer to the office than we were, and having a meal brought up from there was much less of a production than having it prepared in the residence by his personal chef and brought to the West Wing. On the weekends, he'd almost always have breakfast with the First Lady, who would ask for his order while talking to me on the phone, not unlike a couple calling down to room service in a hotel. I could hear her lower the phone and call out, "What would you like, Bill?"

As for their other meals during my orientation time, I let John Moeller and Keith Luce—the cook who came with me from the Greenbrier—see to them, although I'd always approve the planned menu, and always swing by and have a look before they were served. John and Keith had a firm grasp of the Clintons' likes and dislikes, such as 14-year-old Chelsea's go-to dinners of choice, Grilled Chicken Breast with Lemon Pasta and Broccoli, or Kraft macaroni and cheese. (Is there a kid in America who doesn't love that stuff?)

But I did begin to introduce new menu items, and a new approach to serving the First Family.

First of all, after the classic continental style, the First Family was accustomed to two- or three-course meals. One of the first changes I instituted was to pare lunch down to one course modeled on the contemporary American restaurant fashion: two or three ounces of protein (fish or meat) and five or six of vegetables. In a pre-"low carb" era, I also minimized breads and other starches.

Occasionally meals would be even more simple than that, such as when we turned soups into main courses, making them more substantial by stirring in rice or pasta, adding vegetables, or working in protein via a little island of custard or seafood in the center of the bowl.

SEARCHING FOR FEEDBACK

One of the unique challenges of cooking for the First Family was that, although I had intermit-tent access to the First Lady, most of the time my team and I were cooking for a family that mostly existed on the other side of a wall. Accordingly, finding out what was a hit and what wasn't required some creative thinking.

Information came from a variety of sources. One was the morning phone calls from Mrs. Clinton. Another was the butlers, who would often return from the eat-in kitchen or dining room with feedback, letting me know that Mrs. Clinton liked or didn't like something.

Then there was the age-old chef's trick of watching plates to see if they came back clean. This was how I learned that Mrs. Clinton didn't care for frisée; one day, her salad plate come back with everything gone, except for a little pile of frisée off to the side. When she called the next morning, she asked, "What was that strange, frizzy lettuce?"

On occasion, I'd be asked to come to the residence area (second and third floors) because "the First Lady wants to ask you a question." Usually, she wanted to know about a particular ingredient, such as the jícama in a salad, asking me to send her an information sheet about it. Another ingredient she took an instant liking to was Kobe beef. Then there was the time I served her Chilean sea bass and she asked me to come out of the kitchen after dinner. "What was that?" she asked. I told her, and she said "I know I've never had it before. It's very moist and interesting. Can you get me some more information about it?"

There was also a source of bad information. A variety of the Clintons' friends, staffers, and other associates would often pull me aside and offer their advice on the First Family's likes and dislikes. Unfortunately, this guidance was frequently off-base, not that I never read any ulterior motives into bad intel; I just think people like to think they are intimates of the First Family and know something about them.

We never had any real meetings on this subject, but if I and my team stayed attuned to information, there was plenty to be had. To consolidate it all, we kept a log in the kitchen. Whoever was on duty would record what was served, along with any notes. These tidbits could have dramatic ripple effects; for example, one day Chelsea mentioned that she loved Dove bars, so for the rest of the Clintons' time at the White House we kept boxes of them in the freezer.

Feedback was far-reaching and unpredictable. Mrs. Clinton might, for example, send back word that she liked specific chile peppers; through those notes, we adjusted our ordering to include her absolute favorites. Then there was the day she told me that "I really like fresh tomatoes."

On one memorable occasion I made the mistake of sharing one of her predilections with the media, commenting that the First Lady loved hot sauce. This opened a Pandora's box—we received hot sauces from many producers and fans, driving the Secret Service nuts because they had to inspect every package. The First Lady was always looking to expand her palate, so I'd

Grilled Chicken Breast with Lemon Pasta and Broccoli

This was Chelsea Clinton's go-to dinner at the beginning of my tenure. Her roster of pre-ferred meals changed dramatically as she matured, as her palate and tastes became more adventurous and eclectic, and as she committed herself to a vegetarian diet.

I recommend cooking the broccoli and pasta while the chicken is marinating and the grill is preheating, then cooking the chicken as quickly as possible.

FOR THE CHICKEN

2 tablespoons freshly squeezed
  lemon juice
1 tablespoon olive oil
½ tablespoon chopped garlic
1 teaspoon very finely chopped fresh
  rosemary leaves
1 teaspoon very finely chopped fresh
  thyme leaves
Salt and freshly ground black pepper
4 boneless, skinless chicken breasts
  (about 5 ounces each)

FOR THE BROCCOLI

½ pound broccoli florets, cut into 1-
  inch pieces
Salt and freshly ground black pepper
1 or 2 lemons, halved

FOR THE PASTA

¼ cup olive oil
1 tablespoon chopped garlic
¼ cup freshly squeezed lemon juice
2 tablespoons chopped fresh flat-
  leaf parsley leaves
8 ounces dry pasta or 12 ounces
  fresh pasta of your choosing,
  cooked al dente according to
  package instructions and drained
¼ cup freshly grated Parmesan or
  Asiago cheese
Salt and freshly ground black pepper

1. Marinate the chicken: In a small baking dish or other shal-low, dish, stir together the lemon juice, oil, garlic, rosemary, and thyme. Season to taste with salt and pepper. Add the chicken in a single layer, turn to coat, cover, and marinate in the refrigera-tor for 10 to 20 minutes. (You can prepare the broccoli and pasta while the chicken is marinating.)

2. Meanwhile, prepare a charcoal grill for grilling, letting the coals burn until covered with white ash, preheat a gas grill to medium-high, or preheat the broiler.

3. Grill or broil the chicken until cooked through (the juices should run clear when pierced with a sharp, thin-bladed knife). Cooking time will vary based on the power of the grill or broiler and the thickness of the chicken, but should be about 4 minutes per side. Keep the chicken covered and warm until ready to serve.

4. Steam the broccoli: Pour about an inch of water into a small, covered saucepan fitted with a steamer basket. Bring the water to a boil over medium-high heat. Put the broccoli in the basket and steam, covered, until al dente, 4 to 8 minutes, depending on the size of the florets.

5. Transfer the broccoli to a bowl, season with salt and pep-per, and squeeze the lemons over the broccoli to taste, catching the seeds in your hand. Keep covered and warm.

6. Finish the pasta: Heat the oil in a large, heavy-bottomed sauté pan over medium heat. Add the garlic and sauté until soft-ened but not browned, 2 to 3 minutes. Stir in the lemon juice and simmer to reduce for 3 minutes. Stir in the parsley and cook for 30 seconds. Add the pasta and cheese and toss well. Sea-son to taste with salt and pepper and keep covered and warm.

7. To serve, present the chicken, pasta, and broccoli family-style from their own plates, bowls, or platters, or divide among four dinner plates.

introduce her to new hot sauces, such as Indonesian peanut satay sauce or Thai red curry sauce, then wait for a call from her, or check the kitchen log book, to see how it went over.

As for the President himself, he was a very low-maintenance diner, generally happy to eat a lunch from the Navy mess at his desk, and to have whatever his wife, daughter, or their guests desired for dinner.

And so it went, day after day, month after month, an ongoing dialogue—involving the First Family, staff members, ushers, butlers, and cooks—all with one purpose in mind: to hone a White House menu tailored perfectly to the likes and dislikes of the people we served.

KITCHEN LOG

Feedback, recorded in our kitchen log, such as from this week in 1994, helped us shape the meals we served:

➤ **MONDAY, SEPTEMBER 26:** Regarding a lunch for Mrs. Clinton and two guests of a salad followed by a Tartine of Grilled Eggplant and Vegetables with Roasted Yellow Pepper Sauce: "Happy."

➤ **TUESDAY, SEPTEMBER 27:** Regarding a lunch for Mrs. Clinton of a salad and Penne with Bliss Potatoes and Grilled Shrimp (served cold): "Mrs. Clinton liked it, per Buddy" [butler Buddy Carter].

➤ **WEDNESDAY, SEPTEMBER 28:** Regarding a dinner for Chelsea of Grilled Chicken with Green Beans and a Sweet Potato Puree: "Chelsea likes sweet potatoes very much."

➤ **THURSDAY, SEPTEMBER 29:** Regarding a lunch for Mrs. Clinton of Chilled, Curried Cauliflower and Apple Soup and Grilled Salmon Salad with Vegetables: "Cleaned plate; liked soup."

➤ **FRIDAY, SEPTEMBER 30:** Regarding a dinner for President and Mrs. Clinton in the theater of Marinated Vegetables and Foccacia; Salad with Pickled Ginger Vinaigrette; and Grilled Swordfish with Chanterelles, Asparagus, Baby Carrots, Crisp Noodle Pillows, and Fire-Roasted Onion Sauce: "Asked for more salad and noodle pillows."

➤ **SATURDAY, OCTOBER 1:** No feedback.

➤ **SUNDAY, OCTOBER 2:** Regarding a lunch of pizza and salad for the President and Chelsea: "Loved it."

YOU SAY TOMATO

A constant source of amazement to me in my first weeks on the job was how difficult it was to secure raw ingredients of the caliber I expected to serve the First Family. I always ordered ingredients only one to two days in advance of needing them, so I expected them to be in peak condition.

For one day's lunch I had planned a tomato salad. When I opened the box of tomatoes, I was greeted by pale little plum tomatoes that could only be described as pink, not the bright red of a fresh tomato.

With one of the sad, little specimens in hand, I walked across the hall from the kitchen and down a little ramp to the purchasing department. I showed the staff member on duty the evidence. He looked at me with utter confusion. "Yeah?"

"Do you expect me to serve these to the First Family?" I asked, the epitome of a rhetorical question.

"What's the matter with them?"

"They're not ripe."

Without so much as a scintilla of irony, he replied, "Well, if you wanted a ripe tomato, you should have written ripe on the requisition form."

To put it mildly, change comes slowly to a place like the White House. I was developing a real Sisyphus complex, feeling like every day I would push a boulder up a hill, only to have it come rolling back down.

To top it all off, within six weeks, all but two of my beloved monogrammed knives had disappeared.

It wasn't a great start.

A VISIT FROM THE FIRST LADY

We all know that power flows through the White House. But I didn't understand the nuances of power until the day Mrs. Clinton turned my situation around with an almost magical display of her influence.

On a particularly disheartening day—one in which the substandard ingredients, outdated equipment, and unenthusiastic staff were all conspiring to make my professional life less than ideal—Ann Stock paid a visit to the kitchen and asked me an innocent question: "How's it going?"

"Not well at all," I said, going on to explain the resistance I was meeting from the various departments in the House and how it was impeding my ability to meet my mission.

The very next day, Mrs. Clinton made a rare visit to the kitchen and spent a good forty-five minutes standing at my side. We discussed mostly inconsequential things, such as baseball and how I had enjoyed living in West Virginia while at the Greenbrier, but her time and proximity sent a message to the staff: This chef is part of my team; give him the support he needs to succeed.

Her smart and generous gesture made a big impact; by that afternoon, just about everyone on the staff met all requests from the kitchen with enthusiasm . . . and she had done it without flaunting her power or criticizing anyone, either publicly or privately. I was impressed, and grateful.

WEEKLY MEETING

Whenever I talk to people about how the White House runs, I'm always amused at how they think information is conveyed. Many casual observers imagine a complex system of memos, e-mails, and such that circulate constantly, updating all pertinent people on all projects.

In reality, the primary organizational tool was a decidedly low-tech, paper-free tradition know as "The Weekly Meeting."

The weekly meeting took place every Monday at ten o'clock in the morning, when Gary Walters would get together with all of the House department heads and other key personnel for an informal exchange of information.

The meeting included the maitre d' (highest ranking butler), horticulturist Dale Haney, chief florist Nancy Clarke, director of housekeeping Chris Limerick, representatives of the Calligrapher's Office, the Office of the Curator, the housemen (the team who set up and broke down tables, chairs, and other furniture for events), the support facility in Beltsville, Maryland, storeroom, plumbers, electricians, carpenters, Executive Pastry Chef Roland Mesnier, and me.

We also all had access to an internal Web page called "Ushers Information" on which Gary and his team posted news about upcoming events. Most people came to the meeting with an updated printout of this page, and a personal planner of some kind.

Gary would run through his agenda, a roughly one-hour review of upcoming events, including who was visiting the House, what meetings were scheduled, what special meals and functions were planned, on so on.

This was when the carpenter would learn if a stage needed to be erected, the electrician would find out if microphones or special lighting were called for; I would learn of any changes in the foodservice needs of the week, and so on.

After his presentation, Gary would ask "Anything else?" at which point we'd go around the room. Because the needs of any given week were very similar to any other week, there were rarely more than one or two questions from the entire group. Usually, at this point the meeting gave way to chatting and good-natured joking, as this was the only time we were all together and not exclusively focused on our individual responsiblities.

THIS OLD HOUSE

As any homeowner knows, renovation can be fun and rewarding. It can also be frustrating. Similarly, renovating anything in the White House was especially frustrating at first, but by the time we were done it was especially rewarding, because it demanded a real team effort and more than a little ingenuity.

One of the challenges was that you can't knock down a wall in the White House; for historical as well as practical purposes, the footprint of the structure is non-negotiable. In other words, we had to renovate without moving or removing walls, or adding on to the building. The size of individual spaces would remain the same.

Fortunately, there were a few loopholes. For instance, you could add half a wall, which we did—filling in the pass-through for increased privacy and as an added obstacle to any flies that buzzed into the White House.

Our next step was to eliminate inefficiencies. The roughly ten by twelve-foot area that housed the ice machine and fish drawers wasn't at all efficient, so I had those removed and ordered a custom-sized, walk-in refrigerator constructed in their place.

John Moeller, my human White House user's guide, informed me that the deck oven was "a holdover from when Roland was here," referring to the days before the pastry chef had a kitchen all his own. That was all I needed to know. I had the oven eighty-sixed and replaced it with a combi-steamer-oven, a versatile industrial high-speed convection oven that instantly tripled our capacity for how much we could cook in an oven at one time.

Over the course of the next two years, I had the rest of the equipment (by then I had confirmed my initial hunch that most of it hadn't been updated since the mid-1970s) replaced with current models. The older refrigerators were moved to the staff kitchen or simply discarded. The only things we kept were the stainless-steel tables and sinks, and an industrial-size steam kettle, which though more than twenty years old was still capable of boiling liquid quickly.

The next step was to look outside the kitchen and see what space we could commandeer. We performed an audit of broom closets within a reasonable distance of the kitchen and found that many of them housed long-forgotten miscellany. We worked with the Usher's Office to have the old stuff removed and loaded the closets with equipment and supplies we used intermittently, such as an especially large cast-iron pan, the sausage stuffer, wedding cake molds, and the like.

Now came the fun part: to find creative new ways to produce even more usable space within the kitchen itself. To help me in this mission, I asked Dennis Freemyer, Assistant Head Usher charged with among other things, coordinating White House construction and engineering projects, to join me. He brought in a few specialists and we engaged in what I like to call a "free think," brainstorming the possibilities. Dennis welcomed this challenge. In fact, he was energized by it.

We came up with something nifty. At its base, the White House has walls that are about four feet thick. So the window bays in the ground-floor kitchen are four feet deep and ten to fifteen feet tall. We resolved to turn the four kitchen window bays into four storage cabinets—three of which went from floor to ceiling, and one of which was kept one foot shorter to let some precious sunlight into the room.

A few years later, Dennis was also instrumental in solving the kitchen's ventilation problem. Clearly the system had to be retrofitted, but there was a hitch. The chimney, which ran right up through the center of the White House, needed to be relined. But you can't just rip the roof off the White House, and you can't do this kind of noisy work when the First Family is trying to conduct its business.

So, for the summer of that year, I moved my operation down to the staff kitchen, and when the Clintons were away, the team would reline the chimney piece by piece, removing the existing one and adding new tubing in stages, from the roof down to the kitchen, pushing it down as they went.

It was slow, plodding work, but after it was done, you could grill steak all night, and the smoke would be sucked right up and out into the air over the White House. The first time we turned it on, it was so powerful that it rocked in its chamber, prompting Mrs. Clinton to call down and ask me what was going on. We subsequently adjusted the fan, but it still sucked out any smoke in the air; in fact, we began to get visits from the counter-snipers who worked on the roof, wondering what the delicious smell they'd been treated to during their shift was coming from.

Of course, every project created a slew of other projects . . . because while I was working in the staff kitchen, I noticed a number of things I wanted to change there.

And how did we pay for all of this? I had absolutely no idea, although I've subsequently learned that it came from the White House construction and maintenance budget. Though occasionally the Usher's Office would scrutinize a given purchase (such as the previously mentioned combi-oven), once I explained why I needed it, the resistance melted away. I might have been asked to reconsider a given purchase that seemed outlandish to a noncook in the Usher's Office, but I actually never saw a budget in the entire time I worked at the White House. Gary would have me submit a cost breakdown of what I wanted to procure, and then let me know if it was approved—and everything I ever asked for was okayed. Not only that, but early each fall, I'd be told that there was money left in my budget and asked to use it up before the last day of the federal government's fiscal year, which falls on September 30. I'd usually spend it on equipment that would upgrade our kitchen even further, such as a Cryovac machine that vacuum-sealed prepared foods in plastic so they could be heated to order in boiling water.

RE-SOURCING

Next up on my list of improvements was the sourcing of raw ingredients, a problem that had taken on near-comical proportions over the years.

The issues were twofold. One was that very few people who work at the White House are hired for a specific expertise. Many are hired for one job, and move to new jobs over the years as

GOING SHOPPING

I'm frequently asked about how food at the White House is purchased. In the early 1990s, the answer was less mysterious than many would imagine. Everyday staples, food, toiletries, and other household items for the First Family were secured by a member of the Purchasing Office who would visit a local supermarket, or a specialty shop such as a bakery or fish market, in a van driven by a member of the Secret Service.

For receptions, special-event dinners, and other large functions, standard kitchen staples were purchased from one of the large foodservice companies, but they never delivered to us; instead, a Secret Service agent would visit the warehouse to pick them up.

For more esoteric ingredients, my assistant chefs and I would get on the phone to our nationwide network of farmers and farming consortiums to seek out food that was appropriate for the occasion. We'd describe what we were looking for, how much we'd need, and when we'd need it. Our contacts would often then work their networks to procure the requested ingredients from farmers who never found out they were selling (indirectly) to the White House.

We might request wild mushrooms, or an unusual cut of meat, or a hard-to-procure fish. Once we found out what could be had, we'd make arrangements for the food to be shipped to one of the large food companies with whom we did business and have the Secret Service pick it up.

There was one other source of seasonal foods for the First Family. Sometimes it was as simple as when I or one of my assistant chefs passed by a farm or farmstand on a day off in the spring or summer, and saw some outstanding fruits or vegetables: We'd purchase them ourselves, bring them to the White House, and work them into the First Family's meals, the same way we would for our own families.

---

higher level—and higher pay grade—positions become available. As a consequence, many of those charged with ordering fruits, produce, fish, and meats for the White House simply didn't have the knowledge or passion that a foodservice professional would have.

To be clear: All of these people shared a sense of pride in serving the First Family. They just didn't know where to go for the very best foodstuffs, or even how to tell good from bad. Their primary criteria were ease of acquisition and price. Consequently, they procured almost everything from a limited number of purveyors, a fact that also made it easier for the Secret Service to do what they had to do to ensure that all food that came to the White House hadn't been tampered with.

The other aspect of the problem wasn't quite so innocent. Over time, I began to notice that the ordering department paid much closer attention to the food being requested for staff meals than they did to the ingredients for the First Family.

We need to turn this pyramid upside down, I thought to myself, but the resistance I met on this front was shocking. For example, I asked the purchasing guys to get me some lavash, the Middle Eastern bread that has since become popular for making wraps. I was told that they couldn't find any.

"Look in the phone book under Middle Eastern bakeries," I said, and pulled out the book myself. I scanned down the page and saw a name I'd seen in local markets: Mama Lavash. I didn't need to say another word about the subject. Clearly this place sold the stuff I was looking for.

Or occasionally I'd see an article in the paper about an interesting purveyor, and ask the ordering team to track them down. Invariably, this too would prove too taxing.

"We don't know how to reach them," I'd be told.

This was the kind of thing that made me testy.

"Guys, you want to bet a dollar that within five minutes I can not only find them, but can get the president of the company on the line?"

After showing them that it really wasn't that hard to change, the ordering finally got better and better.

Roasted Vegetable Sandwich on Lavash with Peach and Plum Salad

SERVES 4

This vegetarian lunch hit the bull's-eye for what Mrs. Clinton sought in her everyday meals: it was nutritious and flavorful, with international flourishes (lavash, harissa, tahini). Roasting vegetables is a great way to bring out their flavor, which is further distinguished by the contrasts between the heat of the harissa, the smoky smoothness of the eggplant spread, and the sweetness of the accompanying peach and plum salad. The eggplant spread has a deeper, more complex flavor than store-bought baba ghanoush, and doubles well as a dip for crudités or pita chips. Lavash is thin Middle Eastern bread available at most Lebanese bakeries, and even in many supermarkets. You can substitute flour tortillas.

FOR THE EGGPLANT SPREAD
2 medium eggplants (10 to 12 ounces each)
About 6 cloves garlic
Juice of 4 lemons (about ¾ cup)
⅓ cup tahini (see Sources, page 302)
2 tablespoons olive oil
2 tablespoons chopped fresh flat-leaf parsley leaves
About 1 tablespoon harissa (see Sources, page 302)
About ½ tablespoon ground cumin
Salt and freshly ground black pepper

FOR THE VEGETABLE MARINADE
½ cup olive oil
½ cup chopped fresh basil leaves
¼ cup red wine vinegar
¼ cup balsamic vinegar
4 cloves garlic, chopped
1 tablespoon Dijon mustard

1. Make the eggplant spread: Preheat the oven to 350°F. Place the eggplants on a baking sheet and roast until very well done and soft to a knife tip, about 40 minutes, turning them a few times with tongs or a kitchen spoon to ensure even roasting. Remove the pan from the oven and let the eggplants cool. When cool enough to handle, halve the eggplants, scoop the pulp into the bowl of a food processor fitted with the steel blade, and discard the skins.

2. Add the garlic, lemon juice, tahini, oil, parsley, harissa, and cumin to the food processor, and process until the mixture is smooth and the seasonings are well-incorporated. Taste and adjust the seasoning with more garlic, lemon, cumin, and harissa, as desired; add salt and pepper to taste. You should have about 2 cups of spread.

3. The spread can be refrigerated in an airtight container for 2 to 3 days. Let it come to room temperature before using.

4. Make the vegetable marinade: Put all ingredients in a small bowl and stir together until well incorporated. Let sit for 1 hour at room temperature to integrate the flavors, or cover with plastic wrap and refrigerate for up to 24 hours (let it come to room temperature before using).

5. Roast the vegetables: Preheat the oven to 425°F. Lay out the zucchini, squash, asparagus, fennel, mushroom, onion, eggplant, and tomatoes in a single layer on one or two non-stick baking sheets. Stir the marinade to recombine it and

1 medium zucchini, cut crosswise
into ¼ inch slices

1 medium summer squash, cut
lengthwise into ¼ inch slices

12 spears large asparagus, trimmed
and peeled

1 medium bulb fennel, sliced lengthwise, ¼ inch thick

1 medium portabello mushroom,
wiped clean and sliced ⅓ inch
thick

1 medium Vidalia or other sweet
onion, sliced ¼ inch thick

1 medium Japanese eggplant, sliced
¼ inch thick

2 medium plum tomatoes, quartered

1 medium roasted red bell pepper
(see box), peeled and cut into thin
strips

1 medium roasted yellow bell pepper (see box), peeled and cut into
thin strips

TO ASSEMBLE AND SERVE

Four 10 x 10-inch pieces lavash or
12-inch flour tortillas or sandwich
wraps

¼ cup loosely packed fresh basil
leaves

¼ cup loosely packed fresh cilantro
leaves

Peach and Plum Salad (recipe follows)

brush the vegetables lightly with some of the marinade, but do
not soak them.

6. Roast until the vegetables are softened and nicely golden,
10 to 12 minutes, brushing occasionally with the marinade. Do
not cook to the point that they turn mushy. Remove the baking
sheet(s) from the oven and let the vegetables cool to room temperature.

7. Assemble the sandwiches: Lightly spread the lavash from
edge to edge with eggplant spread; you should not use all the
eggplant. Layer one quarter of the vegetables in a row in the
central third of the lavash. Lay some basil and cilantro leaves
over the vegetables, and roll the lavash tightly around the vegetables. Slice the roll diagonally into 3 or 4 pieces. Repeat with
the remaining lavash, vegetables, basil, and cilantro, to make
and cut 4 sandwiches.

8. To serve, arrange the pieces of each sandwich on a plate.
Spoon some more eggplant dip on one side, and pile some
Peach and Plum Salad to the other side.

TO ROAST PEPPERS: Roast peppers by grilling them over an
open flame, or impaling them on a long meat fork and cooking
them over the flame of a gas stove, turning them until blackened
and blistered all over. (You can also do this by broiling the peppers
on a sheet pan, turning them as they blacken and blister.) Transfer
the charred peppers to a heatproof bowl, cover with plastic wrap,
and let steam for 5 to 10 minutes. Remove the plastic wrap and,
when cool enough to handle, remove and discard the skin and
stems, halve the peppers lengthwise, clean out and discard the
seeds, and use as needed. One medium bell pepper or large
poblano pepper will yield about ⅓ cup diced pepper; one medium
jalapeño pepper will yield about 2 tablespoons diced pepper.

Peach and Plum Salad

SERVES 4

This sweet salad with a spicy kick is delicious with the preceding vegetable sandwich, or on its own.

½ cup champagne vinegar, rice wine vinegar, or white wine vinegar
¼ cup honey
¼ cup chopped fresh cilantro leaves
1½ tablespoons olive oil
1½ tablespoons freshly squeezed lime juice
1 teaspoon grated lime zest
1 tablespoon packed light brown sugar
1½ teaspoons seeded, finely diced jalapeño pepper
1 teaspoon hot sauce
1 teaspoon ground cinnamon
½ teaspoon ground star anise
3 ripe peaches, pitted and cut into 10 wedges each
3 ripe plums, pitted and cut into 8 wedges each
Salt and freshly ground black pepper

Put the vinegar, honey, cilantro, oil, lime juice and zest, brown sugar, jalapeño, hot sauce, cinnamon, and anise in a large bowl; stir together until well incorporated and the sugar has dissolved. Gently fold in the peaches and plums and let stand at room temperature for 10 minutes. Season to taste with salt and pepper and serve.

THE FIRST GARDEN

I had made a lot of progress in setting up the kitchen and staff that would enable me to meet the First Lady's mandate. But there were still other action items left to tackle. For example, I had yet to take on one of the more interesting projects she outlined in our interview: to create a vegetable garden on the roof the White House.

Those who know about the history of the White House find her decision to create a garden confusing, because there was already a "First Lady's Garden," a mirror image of the Rose Garden located to the east of the White House along the colonnade. But though this garden did grow herbs, it was after the fashion of an English herb garden, more for show and olfactory pleasure than for actual utility.

Not only would creating the roof garden meet one of the First Lady's wishes; it would also help me solve some of the problems I was facing with sourcing superior produce. There's nothing like something picked straight from a garden, and the roof garden would have an advantage even organic farms couldn't offer: Because it was so high up, way beyond the heights to which most insects traveled, there was no need for pesticides at all—the food grown up there would be one-hundred-percent natural.

There was a greenhouse on the roof for flowers, and the groundskeeping team, I learned, was already growing tomatoes and cucumbers there. But we had bigger things in mind.

At the close of one of our Monday meetings, I made some time with Dale Haney, White House horticulturist, who was in charge of the grounds and gardens. Friendly, always smiling, and exceedingly gregarious with just a bit of a Carolina accent in his voice, Dale's the kind of person I love working with: very knowledgeable and social, but uninterested in networking or climbing.

"I'd be happy to work with you," was Dale's immediate response, despite the already enormous scope of his job, which included maintaining the grounds of the House, much of which have to adhere to certain guidelines due to historical or symbolic significance. He invited me to drop by his office, just down a little ramp and around the corner from the food storage room.

"What would you like to see up there?"

"Missus said she'd like to see some stuff. Can you expand to eight or nine items?"

"I can do anything short of corn," was Dale's answer.

My kind of guy.

This was June, so my first summer would come and go without an expansion of the roof garden. But by the following year, we were growing four varieties of tomatoes, two or three different peppers, and herbs such as chives, basil, thyme, and mint—most of them in ten-gallon planters that could be moved when necessary for security and other purposes. The vegetables were started in the spring at the National Arboretum, then delivered to us when the stalks were about a foot-and-a-half high.

Dale and his team tended the roof garden and I have to say, he and his Park Service staff really knew their stuff. Not only did they know how to grow it, but they had a keen eye for ripeness. When they saw that something was at its peak, they'd bring it to the kitchen and I'd work it into the First Family's meal.

White House Roof Garden Salad

SERVES 4

We made this late-summer dish with items actually grown on the roof of the White House. All items were picked at their peak of ripeness and flavor, and then dressed simply to let their natural flavors shine. When making recipes like this, in which the raw ingredients carry the day, without any cooking or complex preparations to affect their flavors, it is important to have very ripe produce; try to find a local farmers' market, or better yet, grow some of them yourself.

The herbs in the salad are somewhat flexible. The crucial ones are basil, mint, and chives. You could omit the thyme or replace it with tarragon or flat-leaf parsley. Leave out the scallions if you don't have any on hand or don't like them.

½ medium cucumber

2 cups loosely packed of your favorite salad greens, such as arugula, Bibb, or mâche

3 large tomatoes, heirloom if available, cut into ¾-inch chunks

½ medium red onion, sliced very thin

½ cup very thinly sliced yellow bell pepper

½ cup very thinly sliced red bell pepper

¼ cup chopped scallions, green parts only

¼ cup chopped fresh basil leaves

1 tablespoon very thin slices seeded jalapeño pepper

1 tablespoon chopped fresh mint leaves

1 tablespoon chopped fresh chives

1 teaspoon chopped fresh thyme leaves

Garden Salad Dressing (recipe follows)

Salt and freshly ground black pepper

1. Peel the cucumber, halve it lengthwise, scoop out the seeds, and cut it crosswise into ¼-inch slices.

2. Put the cucumber slices, greens, tomatoes, onion, yellow and red peppers, scallions, basil, jalapeño, mint, chives, and thyme in a large bowl. Drizzle with the dressing and gently toss. Let stand for 10 minutes. Season to taste with salt and pepper, toss again, and serve.

Garden Salad Dressing

This is a good everyday vinaigrette.

¼ cup seasoned rice vinegar
2 tablespoons chopped garlic
½ tablespoon Dijon mustard
Juice of 1 medium lemon
1 teaspoon finely grated lemon zest
½ cup olive oil
Salt and freshly ground black pepper

1. Put the vinegar, garlic, mustard, lemon juice, and lemon zest in a small bowl and whisk together. Slowly add the oil in a thin stream, whisking to make an emulsified (thick and creamy) dressing. Season to taste with salt and pepper.

2. This dressing can be refrigerated in an airtight container for up to 3 days. Let it come to room temperature before serving.

CHAIN OF COMMAND

I was making tremendous progress improving the systems and protocols that touched the White House kitchen. But there was one dynamic that was out of my reach and yet affected me on a daily basis: the relationship between the Usher's Office and the First Lady's staff.

My official supervisor was chief usher Gary Walters. As a former military man, Gary was a big believer in the chain of command. To his everlasting chagrin, I was not only hired by Mrs. Clinton, I was also given direct instructions by her staff, especially Ann Stock and Capricia Marshall, on a daily basis. Where previous chefs had been overseen exclusively by the Usher's Office, the Clintons' focus on hospitality led them to take a direct role in managing me themselves.

As if that weren't bad enough for Gary, because the Clintons were so dedicated to a grand vision of entertaining, I was constantly being directed to push the envelope further and further. At all times, I did whatever I could to keep Gary in the loop, but there was distinct and open friction between the Usher's Office and the First Lady's staff, and I often found myself caught in the crossfire. For example, Capricia once asked me if we could put together a reception for five hundred people with just three days' notice. I said "Of course," as I would to any request from the First Lady's team. When Gary heard of my instant agreement, he wasn't happy with me.

"What do you want me to do," I asked him, "tell the First Lady I can't do something when I know that I can?"

Exchanges like these were frustrating to me, but I must say that Gary always had the best of intentions. At a time when we were routinely throwing receptions for two hundred to four hundred people several times a week (several times a day during the holidays), it was crucial to have someone like Gary point out when we were reaching a point where the House and the staff would be overtaxed.

To put it in governmental terms: Though it didn't always feel this way, the Usher's Office in general, and Gary in particular, offered a useful system of checks and balances.

RECEPTIONS

People often ask me if I was ever expected to do the impossible in my role as White House chef. My answer is that when it came to receptions and dinners, my team and I were asked to do nothing but the impossible. That's what we were there for: to bring Mrs. Clinton's almost magical notion of what White House entertaining should be to life. In hindsight, I think that's one of the reasons I was hired, as much as for whatever culinary skills I happened to possess: I had a reputation in the industry for being a good strategic thinker, able to solve any problem put in front of me. Plus, as anyone who's worked with me knows, I never say "no" to the client—in this case, the First Family.

Now, the things we did wouldn't have been "impossible" in other settings. But when you considered the fact that we were working in cramped quarters, with largely temporary staff, and menus that changed from day to day to suit the occasion—or occasions—at hand, every success was seen as a small miracle, all the more so because we were essentially operating in a museum where the furniture, decorations, artwork, and even at times the plates were valuable and irreplaceable antiques.

In addition to the Clintons' hospitality, the big reason our receptions were so well-received was the food itself. The menu was in stark contrast to the platter service that had defined White House gatherings in the past. Where guests to these events were accustomed to helping themselves from platters of smoked salmon, honey-roasted ham, and so on, our receptions featured a variety of about nine styles of hors d'oeuvres and small plates, showcasing the same flavors and techniques that were gracing contemporary American restaurants of the time, such as a Caribbean-themed shrimp canapé.

Depending on their size, receptions would take place in a room or cluster of rooms. Smaller events were confined to the East Room. Larger events would find guests mingling and mulling through the entire State Floor.

But no matter what the occasion, size, or tenor of the event, the kitchen's mission was always the same: to wow guests with a taste of state-of-the-art American cuisine.

SERVICE BY AGREEMENT

If it seems hard to believe that we did everything that needed doing with just a handful of cooks, that's because we didn't. John Moeller, Adam Collick, Keith Luce, the staff-kitchen cooks, and the people who replaced some of them as time went by were my core unit, my professional family, the salaried employees of the White House kitchen. I might have hired more, but House procedures (influenced as much by space and security constraints as by budget) dictated that I was only allowed to have a chef, two assistant chefs, a head steward, and two cooks for the staff cafeteria.

To assist us with the ebb and flow presented by special events—receptions, state dinners, and so on—we enlisted professionals under an arrangement known as "Service by Agreement." Service by Agreement, or SBA, meant that these workers could come and go as we needed them, or as they wanted to work—in other words, a list of approved freelancers to be called on as necessary.

There were two older SBA cooks in place when I began. One of them was in his late sixties, a European gentleman who was a great worker, but who realized, and rightly so, that I was going to take him out of his culinary comfort zone. Figuring he was simply too old to start dealing with exotic ingredients, contemporary techniques, and the like, he quietly left.

Over my years at the White House, I added SBA cooks as we needed them, in time amassing a database of close to forty cooks. The ideal SBA candidate was someone who met the profile—for themselves, for me, and for the White House. Cooks who gravitated to this work tended to be people who for some reason or another didn't want full-time employment. They might be chefs who were between jobs, had lost interest in the standard kitchen brigade, were busy raising money for their next restaurant, or were working on a cookbook, such as frequent SBA team member Leland Atkinson. Some of them had left lucrative careers as executive chefs that had taken them away from the front lines, and they wanted to get back in a kitchen and do some cooking again. Some of them were still in those careers and craved an opportunity to cook as part of a team, rather than function as the leader.

As for the White House, discretion was valued; we didn't want cooks who came in periodically and thought that entitled them to promote themselves as close, personal friends of the First Family. All cooks, even one-timers, had to clear a background check, meaning they had no history of drug use, jail time, suspicious behavior, and so on. Those who were to be supervised by a "hard-pass holder" like me could be enlisted after a local police background check; those who would be working unsupervised needed to clear a full background check like the one administered to me by my "Lieutenant Columbo."

Following Mrs. Clinton's spirit of trying new foods, I invited all of our SBA cooks to share ideas with me. And good ideas came from all over—from chefs like Glen Adams, who was working with us while he developed his own restaurant concept, and from apprentice cooks who were clearly going to go on to great things. Other SBA-ers included Patrice Olivon, who had been the chef of the French embassy; David Luersen, who was the chef-manager at the British embassy but enjoyed working with us part time; Gordon Marr, of the Washington Hilton, who had been best man at my wedding but whom I hadn't spoken to much while I was working in Florida and West Virginia; and Cristeta Comerford, a real superstar who emerged as a key player in my kitchen over the years.

My little team of merry men and women even had a name. When Leland Atkinson published his book, *Cocina! A Hands-On Guide to the Techniques of Southwestern Cooking*, the acknowledgments included a thank-you to "The Casa Blanca Gang," and that's how I've thought of them ever since.

Jerk-Spiced Shrimp on Corn Cakes with Mango and Black Bean Salsa

MAKES ABOUT 24 SHRIMP-TOPPED CORN CAKES, ENOUGH TO SERVE 4 TO 6 AS AN HORS D'OEUVRE

This hors d'oeuvre is representative of the ethnically inspired foods that started to appear on our reception menus in the mid-1990s. Influenced by both the West Indies and the American Southwest, it has very big, forward flavors.

You can double the recipe and serve this as a first course or light lunch. Make the salsa first as it needs to marinate, then the corn cakes and shrimp close to when you are ready to serve the meal.

The salsa can also be used as an accompaniment to just about any grilled fish.

1½ tablespoons whole allspice berries

½ medium stick cinnamon

¼ cup finely diced Spanish onion

¼ cup finely sliced scallions, white and green parts

¼ cup plus 2 tablespoons Red Stripe or other medium-light beer (you can drink the rest of the bottle)

2 tablespoons freshly squeezed lime juice

½ tablespoon packed light brown sugar

1 teaspoon grated fresh ginger

½ teaspoon dried thyme

½ teaspoon ground cumin

¼ teaspoon seeded, finely diced habanero pepper

¼ teaspoon ground coriander

2 cloves garlic, chopped

Salt

¾ pound jumbo shrimp (ideally, 12 shrimp), shelled and deveined

Vegetable oil for cooking the shrimp

Corn Cakes (recipe follows)

Mango and Black Bean Salsa (page 61)

About 24 fresh cilantro leaves

1. Put the allspice and cinnamon in a medium, heavy-bottomed sauté pan and toast over medium heat, shaking the pan to prevent scorching, until lightly toasted and fragrant, 1 to 2 minutes. Let cool, then grind well in a spice grinder or coffee grinder. (If using a coffee grinder, be sure to wipe out all traces of coffee before grinding spices; then wipe out all traces of the spices before using again for coffee.)

2. Transfer the ground spices to a food processor, preferably a small one, fitted with the steel blade. Add the onion, scallions, beer, lime juice, brown sugar, ginger, thyme, cumin, habanero, coriander, and garlic. Process until thoroughly integrated into a smooth puree. Taste and season with salt.

3. Put the shrimp in a medium bowl, pour the puree over the shrimp, stir to coat, cover, and refrigerate for 6 minutes, but no longer, or the lime juice will begin to cure the shrimp.

4. You may need to do the following in batches: Lightly oil a medium, heavy-bottomed sauté pan and heat over medium heat. Lift the shrimp from the marinade, letting any excess liquid run off and brushing off any marinade solids. Discard the marinade. Cook the shrimp in the pan until firm and pink, 3 to 5 minutes, turning once. As they cook, they should curl nicely into a crescent shape.

5. Transfer the shrimp to a clean, dry cutting board and let cool to room temperature. Slice them in half lengthwise to form crescent-shaped disks. The shrimp can be kept in an airtight container in the refrigerator overnight. Let them come to room temperature before serving.

6. To serve, arrange the corn cakes on a platter. Top each cake with a shrimp half and 1 generous teaspoon of salsa. (You will not use all the salsa.) Garnish with a cilantro leaf and serve.

Corn Cakes

1 ear corn on the cob, shucked
3 tablespoons unsalted butter
Salt and freshly ground black pepper
½ cup all-purpose flour
¼ cup fine, yellow cornmeal
½ tablespoon sugar
½ tablespoon baking powder
½ cup milk
1 large egg, separated
2 scallions, white parts only, finely
  chopped
¼ cup peeled, seeded, and finely
  diced roasted jalapeño (see box,
  page 51)
Vegetable oil, for cooking the corn
  cakes

1. Preheat the broiler.

2. Brush the corn with 1 tablespoon of the butter and season with salt and pepper. Place on a rimmed baking sheet and broil, turning, until nicely golden brown all over, about 10 minutes. Remove the sheet from the oven and transfer the corn to a cutting board. When cool enough to handle, remove the kernels from the cob by standing the cob on its end and running the blade of a heavy knife down the edges. You will have between ½ and 1 cup of kernels. Reserve ½ cup for this recipe, and save the rest for another use, or add it to the salsa in this dish for some additional corn flavor.

3. Melt the remaining 2 tablespoons butter and let cool slightly. In a medium bowl, combine the flour, cornmeal, sugar, baking powder, and ¼ teaspoon salt and stir together until well incorporated. Stir in the milk, egg yolk, and melted butter. Fold in the corn, scallions, and jalapeño. Whip the egg white until soft peaks form, then gently fold the egg white into the batter, but do not overwork the batter.

4. Fry the corn cakes in batches: Lightly oil a large, heavy-bottomed sauté pan and heat it over medium heat. Add the batter in 1-tablespoon portions. Cook until bubbling in center and golden brown underneath, then turn and cook until golden brown on the bottom, about 2 minutes per side. As the cakes are done, gather them on a plate or platter and cover with foil to keep warm.

Mango and Black Bean Salsa

MAKES ABOUT 1 1/2 CUPS

3/4 cup finely diced mango (about 1 medium mango)

1/4 cup finely diced red onion

1/4 cup cooked, drained black beans

1 tablespoon finely diced red bell pepper

1 tablespoon freshly squeezed lime juice

1 teaspoon grated lime zest

2 teaspoons honey

1/2 tablespoon chopped fresh cilantro leaves

1/2 tablespoon chopped fresh basil leaves

1/2 tablespoon finely diced seeded jalapeño pepper

1 teaspoon hot sauce

1 teaspoon ground cumin

1/2 teaspoon ground coriander

Salt and freshly ground black pepper

In a medium bowl, combine the mango, onion, black beans, red pepper, lime juice, lime zest, honey, cilantro, basil, jalapeño, hot sauce, cumin, and coriander. Cover and let stand for 1 hour, then taste and season with salt and pepper. The salsa can be refrigerated in an airtight container for up to 24 hours, but is best served fresh, as we always served it at the White House. Let it come to room temperature before serving.

HITTING STRIDE

I'm told by those who worked closely with me at the White House that the transition from one chef to another seemed like a smooth, seamless, and gradual process. But I have to confess: It took about six months before I felt like we were comfortably achieving our goals on a daily basis. By the time we were easing into fall, I had a pretty usual routine going and it felt great.

I'd arrive at the House between five and five thirty in the morning. There were other people working at that hour—West Wing staffers, some members of the residential staff, and, of course, the Secret Service—but I was always the first member of the culinary team, so I had my office and the kitchens to myself.

This was the only truly quiet time in the day, an opportunity to get my bearings and check my voice-mails, as well as the Ushers Information site.

Next, I'd visit the food storage room to be sure any scheduled deliveries for the day had been logged in, or to see what time they were expected. Then I'd hit both the First Family and staff kitchens, inspect the walk-in refrigerators, and make sure everything looked to be in order.

As I think back on it, I realize that my morning ritual wasn't unlike that of the chef-owner of a small restaurant, doing everything possible to ensure that my "business" was set up for success on the day ahead.

One of the assistant chefs, either John Moeller or Keith Luce, would arrive shortly after me, at eight or nine o'clock, have his breakfast, and begin work. He would prepare the First Family's lunch and, as always, I'd inspect the plates and try to be around for any feedback at the end of the meal. At two thirty in the afternoon, the other assistant chef—the one who would prepare the First Family's dinner—would arrive. Adam Collick, the steward, would come in between one and two in the afternoon.

If we had a reception or dinner that night, both assistant chefs would come in earlier than usual at seven a.m., expecting to "pull a double (shift)" and our SBA colleagues would start to arrive in the late morning and get to work, beginning with the deep prep like peeling and slicing vegetables, and moving on to the creation and composition of salads, meats, fish, sauces, and sides.

During the day, I'd break away to keep all of the various projects under my stewardship moving forward: checking in with the ordering guys on new purveyors and farmers we'd discussed, talking to Dale about ideas for next year's garden, having an impromptu sit-down with Gary Walters to work out some details for an upcoming event, and jotting down ideas for new dishes I wanted to try.

The day would typically end around eleven at night—a long stretch, to be sure, so it was a good thing that it was around this time that I finally felt I could be away one day a week, and began taking Sundays off.

It was all very regimented and wonderfully, delightfully systematized. It felt good. I had created my White House kitchen, and, at long last, could focus on the job I'd been hired to do: cook for the First Family and their guests.

Getting To Know You
First Family Meals and Moments

There were two honors to being the White House chef. One was the honor of bringing contemporary American cuisine to the White House, and by extension, the world. The other was serving the First Family, and getting to know them as people. To be among the very few who were able to nourish them in some fashion, to offer them sustenance first thing in the morning and on those rare occasions when they were able to take time out from their incomprehensibly taxing schedules and workloads.

While I never forgot for a second that I was working for the First Family, there were many occurrences that I remember fondly, the way you might remember moments in time with your own family.

THE DAILY DIET

No matter what else was going on in the White House at any given time, my one constant objective in any week was to prepare three meals a day for the First Family, unless of course they were traveling. Since this was something I could anticipate, and since I had such clear guidelines from Mrs. Clinton, I made it my business to plan seven days' worth of lunches and dinners, from Sunday through Saturday, delivering the menu for the coming week to the Usher's Office each Thursday. The ushers, in turn, circulated a typed copy to the butlers, the First Lady's office, and me. I didn't include breakfasts because all three Clintons adhered to the same go-to breakfast they were accustomed to when I came on board.

Although the menus covered the entire seven-day period, the Clintons were more free-flowing on the weekends. On the one hand, they were apt to prefer a simpler dinner—a main-course Caesar salad, say, or some smoked salmon—over the more substantial meals we planned, such as roast chicken with a variety of vegetables. On the other hand, if they were returning from the Kennedy Center or another function, they might suddenly call over to let us know they were going to arrive with twenty guests in tow.

We always had both options covered. We ordered the necessary ingredients to make more casual meals, and also purchased enough to make twenty or more servings of the scheduled dinner. Whatever didn't get used would be redirected to the staff kitchen on Monday.

While I suppose sharing the week's dishes with the Clintons ahead of time removed some of the "what's-for-dinner" spontaneity that everybody loves from their lives, it also allowed them to anticipate and make any desired changes if they saw something on the roster that didn't appeal to them. They also, obviously, maintained the right to change the day's planned meal whenever they felt like it, and often did. The most frequent type of change was requesting leftovers of a previous day's lunch or dinner, or just one part of it—some cold chicken sliced from a roast, or the vegetables that were served as a side dish—the First Family's way of raiding the fridge.

More than any other cooking or planning I did at the White House, the family menus I created adhered to the priorities Mrs. Clinton and I had hammered out: They were relatively low in carbohydrates and fat (especially from butter, cheese, and cream), included almost no red meat (and if they did, the meat would almost always be lamb, not beef, because Mrs. Clinton much preferred the former), and were positively loaded with fruits and vegetables. Two nutritionists contributed advice, ideas, and guidelines to my efforts. One was Dr. Dean Ornish, with whom the Clintons had a relationship before I arrived on the scene. The other was Cynthia Payne, a registered dietician on staff at the Greenbrier. Based on Mrs. Clinton's mandate, Cynthia prepared a full, written plan that included examples of typical meals with model amounts of protein, carbohydrates, fats, and nutrients. I, in turn, transmitted the key guidance from that plan to my staff via a memo, but always kept the plan to myself lest it get out and the Clinton "diet" become fodder for the gossip pages.

Lunches were mostly for Mrs. Clinton and her staff because Chelsea was at school during the day, or on her own schedule and diet in the summer, and the President typically ate a working lunch in the Oval Office, often asking us to rustle up something simple, or sending a butler to bring him something from the Navy mess, the menu for which was distributed every day, and was viewable on a closed-circuit channel on all White House television sets.

(I have a Navy mess-related memory that never fails to make me laugh. One day, early in my tenure, a butler appeared at my kitchen door in a total panic. "I need the soup from the stewardess. The soup from the stewardess," he said, over and over, like a mantra. I had no idea what he meant. Soup from the stewardess? What stewardess? When we finally got him to calm down, we deciphered that he had been told the President wanted "the soup from the steward from the [Navy] mess," and had misunderstood the instruction.)

MENU FOR THE WEEK OF _____ 3/02 to 3/08 _____ FOR __Mrs. Clinton__

SUNDAY BREAKFAST	1/2 Grapefruit or Fresh Fruit / Oatmeal with Skim Milk and Raisins on the Side / Slice of Toasted Cinnamon Pecan Raisin Bread 350 508		THURSDAY BREAKFAST	1/2 Grapefruit or Fresh Fruit / Oatmeal with Skim Milk and Raisins on the Side / Slice Toasted Whole Wheat Bread 350
LUNCH	Eggwhite Frittata with a Lentil and Celery Ginger Salad / Oatmeal Bread w/salad 486		LUNCH	Potato and Leek Soup, Nofat Cottage Cheese Plate with Fresh Fruit and a Multigrain Bread oatmeal 500 575 675
DINNER	Butternut Squash Soup / Braised Chicken in an Apple Cider Sauce with Baked Sweet Potato w/salad 672		DINNER	Curry Cornish Hen with Basmati Rice, Mango and Onion Chutney with Minted Peas w/salad 650 1180 750 w/chicken Breast 4oz
MONDAY BREAKFAST	1/2 Grapefruit or Fresh Fruit / Shredded Wheat with Skim Milk / Slice Toasted Oatmeal Bread 350		FRIDAY BREAKFAST	1/2 Grapefruit or Fresh Fruit / Shredded Wheat with Skim Milk / Slice of Toasted Cinnamom Raisin Pecan Bread 350
LUNCH	Citrus Salad of Boston Lettuce and Watercress with Hummus and Bagel Chips 382 1147		LUNCH	Roasted Vegetable Sandwich on Whole Wheat Pita and a Marinated Vegetable Salad 322 1390
DINNER	Navy Bean and Vegetable Soup / Broiled Arctic Char with an Orange Tarragon Sauce, Multigrain Rice w/salad 455		DINNER	Grilled Chicken and Lemon Pasta with Herbs and Vegetables, Nofat Caesar Salad and Pane Italiano 726
TUESDAY BREAKFAST	1/2 Grapefruit or Fresh Fruit / Multi Grain Cereal with Skim Milk / Slice Toasted Swiss Farmer Bread 350		SATURDAY BREAKFAST	1/2 Grapefruit or Fresh Fruit / Multi Grain Cereal with Skim Milk / Slice Toasted Landbrut Bread 350
LUNCH	Fresh Artichoke Salad with Dijon Dressing, Tomato Pasta and Bean Soup with Semolina Bread 423 1469		LUNCH	Tuna Melt with Nofat Cheese, Lettuce, Tomato on Sundried Tomato Bread w/salad 465 160
DINNER	Cabbage Rolls with Shredded Turkey and Mixed Vegetables served with a Tangy Tomato Sauce and Parsley Boiled Potatoes w/salad 696		DINNER	Sweet Potato and Orange Soup / Rolled Chicken Breast with Kale, Quinoa and Dried Fruits with Herb Polenta 788
WEDNESDAY BREAKFAST	1/2 Grapefruit or Fresh Fruit / Cream of Wheat with Skim Milk and Raisins on the Side / Slice Toasted Multi Grain Bread 350		COMMENTS:	
LUNCH	Spiced Chicken Quesadillas with Nonfat Cheese, Tomato Salsa and a Blackbean and Corn Salad, Chipolte Chili Bread 722 169		Walter - Could you please calculate calories for the meals that are listed? Thank you	
DINNER	Egg Drop Soup / Vegetable and Tofu Potstickers with a Sweet Chili Sauce, Sticky Rice and Vegetables w/salad 620		Cornish Hen to be replaced by chicken breast HRC	

A weekly menu. Mrs. Clinton's handwritten request for calorie counts in the lower right corner began a policy that would continue into the Bush years. (Courtesy Walter Scheib 3rd)

Lunch dishes for the First Lady included, for example, herbed couscous with garbanzo beans, lentils, and grilled vegetables; roasted vegetable wrap with a peach and plum salad; and grilled vegetable gazpacho soup with turkey sandwiches on whole wheat bread.

Dinners were a bit more substantial and, while relatively light, adhered to the conventional American notion of a plate that was anchored by a big piece of protein with a starch and a vegetable or two. So there might be broiled fillet of sole with black pepper and lemon, herbed orzo and vegetables; whole wheat cannelloni with white beans and low-fat chicken sausage; or lamb tenderloin in a ginger-garlic jus with multi-grain rice.

I felt good about the menus, especially because I wasn't trained as a "spa" chef. The diverse selection was the product of the research I did before starting the job, melded with my culinary sensibility. And there was no cheating: Mrs. Clinton asked to see dietary profiles of all dishes—grams of fat, calorie counts, and so on—which I personally determined, primarily from two resources, the USDA guidebook and an old vegetarian cookbook called *Laurel's Kitchen*, which had nutrition profiles of a wide variety of products, including many common supermarket items.

OFF THE MENU

There were times—many of them—when it struck me that although President Clinton was the most powerful man in the world, his day-to-day relationship with Mrs. Clinton was, almost comically, no different than that between most husbands and wives.

They were like many couples who go out to dinner: The man orders a steak, or a piece of cheesecake, and the wife says, "Honey, you're supposed to be on a diet." Well, when it came to the White House family menus, President and Mrs. Clinton had a similar dynamic: She wanted the focus on healthful food; he wanted to indulge.

So, despite the rigorous focus on good nutrition, there were times when President Clinton would request something way off the menu. Occasionally, a butler would come into the kitchen and say, "Poppa wants a steak and onion rings for dinner." (The residential staff, with the exception of the ushers, often referred to the President and First Lady as, respectively, Poppa and Mama. This was not meant disrespectfully; rather it was a term of endearment. It was also quicker to say than "the President" or "the First Lady.")

Mrs. Clinton traveled a lot, and it quickly became very clear to us that the President was most apt to order off the menu when she was out of town. A man able to impact the economy, veto legislation, send armies into battle . . . and he still felt he had to sneak some comfort food when his wife was away.

Because of this trend, my team and I would regularly check the travel schedule, available to us via the Ushers Information site, and a daily printed itinerary that was circulated to all departments by the Usher's Office, to learn when Mrs. Clinton would be on the road. On those days, I'd make sure to have ground beef, steak, onions for onion rings, potatoes, and all the fixings for chili and nachos in the kitchen.

This type of system-tweaking, based on observation, evaluation, and adjustment, is something that sets the White House chef—at least as I saw the job—apart from a lot of other chefs. It seems to me that many chefs have a not-so-secret affection for the occasional drama in the kitchen, whether it's the chaos of a Saturday night at the stoves in a popular, big-city restaurant, or the improvisational troubleshooting required to pull off an event at a catering hall or private home. A lot of my colleagues find the adrenaline spike that comes with these challenges irresistible, and a fun part of the job.

But I always saw being the chef of the White House as different from that. I considered the kitchen the culinary equivalent of any responsible government department, and my role as the director of that department was to play out scenarios in my head and to make adjustments based on past experience. Sure, there were times when things would arise that I couldn't have anticipated—such as when the First Family would decide to have a large group of friends over for dinner on a moment's notice, or last-second luncheon-meetings for the First Lady and her Hillary-land group—but for the most part, I like to think that I got better and better at anticipating whims and being ready for any impulse that might strike the First Family.

Porterhouse Steak with Béarnaise Sauce and Onion Rings

SERVES 4

When Mrs. Clinton was out of town, we delved into our secret stash of very special steaks that were reserved for the boss only. The weight in the recipe is not a typo; we served 24-ounce cuts to the President, and his plate always came back clean. (If you're serving smaller appetites, use smaller steaks, but make sure they're still at least 1¼ inches thick. Or figure on one large steak serving two people.)

Both the steak and onion rings should be served piping hot, so I suggest frying the onion rings while the steak is marinating, or if you have a helper on hand, have one person grill the steaks while another is frying the onions.

4 dry-aged, prime porterhouse
   steaks, at least 1½ inches thick
   (24 ounces each)
2 tablespoons olive oil
Salt and freshly ground black pepper
Onion Rings (page 71)
Béarnaise Sauce (recipe follows)

1. Preheat the boiler, or prepare a charcoal grill for grilling, letting the coals burn until covered with white ash, or preheat a gas grill to high.

2. Meanwhile, brush the steaks with oil and let sit for 15 minutes at room temperature. Season the steaks with salt and pepper.

3. Broil or grill the steaks to desired doneness; an internal temperature of 135°F will give a nice, medium-rare steak. Time will vary greatly based on how powerful your grill or broiler is and how thick the steaks are, but it should take about 8 minutes per side.

4. To serve, put one steak on each of four dinner plates. Set a stack of onion rings alongside and pass the béarnaise sauce in a sauceboat or bowl.

Béarnaise Sauce

I f you clarify the butter and make the tarragon-shallot reduction ahead of time (up to one day), you can make the sauce while the meat is resting at room temperature. Refrigerate the butter and reduction in airtight containers until ready to use—a useful trick to time the finished sauce to coincide with the steaks.

¼ cup chopped fresh tarragon
  leaves
3 tablespoons dry white wine
3 tablespoons tarragon vinegar,
  champagne vinegar, or white wine
  vinegar
2 tablespoons chopped shallots
¼ teaspoon freshly ground black
  pepper
2 large egg yolks
1 cup (2 sticks) unsalted butter,
  clarified (see box)
Salt

1. Put the tarragon, wine, vinegar, shallots, and pepper in a small saucepan set over medium heat. Bring to a simmer and let simmer until reduced by half, 2 to 4 minutes. Remove the pot from the heat and let cool slightly to avoid scrambling the egg yolks in the next step. (At this stage, you can also let the reduction cool completely and refrigerate it in an airtight container overnight.)

2. Put the yolks in a medium stainless steel bowl, add the vinegar-shallot mixture to the yolks, and whisk together well.

3. Bring a small saucepan of water to a simmer, place the bowl on top and whisk the yolk and vinegar mixture over the heat until it thickens and becomes frothy. Move the bowl over and away from the simmering water periodically to keep the eggs from scrambling.

4. Once the mixture is frothy, begin pouring in the clarified butter, a little at a time, whisking it in and continuing to periodically remove the bowl from the simmering water. Once all the butter has been incorporated, season it to taste with salt, cover, and keep it warm.

> **TO MAKE CLARIFIED BUTTER:** Put unsalted butter in a saucepan over medium heat, let it melt, and bring it to a simmer. Skim off and discard the froth (whey protein) that rises to the surface. Continue to skim until no further froth is produced. Let the butter rest for 5 minutes so that all milk solids sink to the bottom, then strain the melted butter through a fine-mesh sieve into a bowl or storage container, leaving the milk solids in the pot. You will lose about one quarter of the volume you begin with; so 2 sticks (1 cup) of butter will yield about ¾ cup clarified butter, and so on. I recommend starting with at least 2 sticks of butter (it's difficult to work with any less in the pot). Extra clarified butter can be cooled and refrigerated in an airtight container for up to 2 weeks. Use the extra to dress cooked steaks and shellfish.

Onion Rings

You can liven up the onion rings by seasoning the flour with Cajun spices, cayenne, or anything else you like. Note that the onions need to soak in buttermilk for one hour before being battered and fried.

1 large Vidalia or other sweet onion, cut into ¼-inch-thick slices and separated into rings
2 cups buttermilk
Vegetable oil, for frying the onion rings
1 cup all-purpose flour
Salt and freshly ground black pepper

1. Put the onion rings and buttermilk into a medium bowl and let the onions soak for 1 hour at room temperature, or cover and refrigerate overnight.

2. Fill a deep-fryer with oil according to the manufacturer's directions and preheat to 350°F. (Alternatively, fill a large, deep cast-iron skillet with oil to a depth of 3 inches and heat until a thermometer registers 350°F.)

3. Season the flour with salt and pepper. Drain the onion rings and toss in the flour just to coat, shaking off any excess. Fry in small batches until golden brown, 4 to 5 minutes. Remove with a slotted spoon, drain on paper towels, and season with salt.

"YA'LL WANNA COME UP AND WATCH THE GAME?"

There was another time that the President deviated from the healthful diet Mrs. Clinton had mandated: when there was a ballgame on TV.

The President was a golfer, but when it came to watching sports, his first love was basketball. In particular, he was a fan of the NCAA and of the Arkansas Razorbacks. In 1994, the season the Razorbacks went all the way to the championship, every single night President Clinton would watch the game. If the First Lady was in town, then they would take to the residence, or have guests or friends stick around.

Occasionally, the Clintons would invite between fifteen and twenty-five people over to watch the game, either in the Solarium, at the top of the building, or in the movie theater between the East Wing and the residence (it's situated in the spot that corresponds to the press briefing room's location in the West Wing), where they'd invite up to fifty.

They'd let us know in advance, and we'd prepare a menu of ballgame–appropriate snacks that included tortilla chips with three dips; buffalo chili; chicken enchiladas with chipotle chili sauce; homemade pizzas; pulled barbecue pork turnovers; and blackened shrimp, roasted peppers, and jalapeño jack cheese on flat bread. Beef was even allowed to make a cameo on these occasions, in something like beef "rollups" with ranchero sauce.

If the get-together was more spontaneous, the menu was chef's choice, but I'd do my best to provide the same kinds of things, especially crab cakes, which were among President Clinton's favorites.

On a few rare but unforgettable occasions, when Mrs. Clinton was out of town, the President would holler out to whoever was within earshot to join him, or send word around to the butlers that one and all were invited to gather in the Solarium to watch the game.

This would be on the weekends, so it was very informal. He and the staff would transform into a group not really distinguishable from a bunch of guys at a sports bar. There was beer and soda, and everyone would be hooting and hollering at every big play.

On one particular Saturday afternoon, I brought the President's lunch—a jalapeño–jack cheese quesadilla—to the third floor on the elevator. One of the butlers, Buddy Carter, delivered it to him, then returned to the elevator and told me that the President had invited me to come join them to watch the game. There wasn't another soul in the elevator, but I nevertheless looked over my shoulder. Nope, no one there. Much to my shock, he was talking to me.

I did as instructed and came into the Solarium.

President Clinton just wanted some company, but I realized very quickly that I wasn't able to provide it. I had work to do, and I've never been particularly comfortable socializing with my "employer." And in this case, he was the leader of the free world, the most powerful man on the planet!

So as the President sat there, munching on his quesadilla and rocking back and forth with delight each time the Razorbacks stuffed the basket, I sat there, feigning smiles when he did, applauding when he did, but in sharp contrast to his casual, slumping, guy-on-the-couch demeanor, I simply could not relax.

After about fifteen minutes, I said, "Well, if you'll excuse me, Mr. President, I need to go take care of some things in the kitchen."

"Oh, okay," he said, sounding truly disappointed.

And there I left him, with the crowd of butlers, the White House's very own Saturday afternoon sports bar, in full swing.

Man of the people. President Clinton was always at home with the White House butlers. *(Courtesy William J. Clinton Presidential Library)*

Crab Cakes with Cajun Rémoulade

Crab cakes were very popular at the White House—in fact, I don't think we made more of any other dish. We served fifteen thousand to twenty thousand miniature ones each Christmas season. Though we sometimes called on them as an entrée, we usually served them as snack or as reception food. They showed up at all the fun venues, whether it was a new movie screening in the White House movie theater or when the President and his guests were watching the Razorbacks win the national championship in the movie theater or Solarium.

Over the years we tried various recipes, but we always ended up returning to a variation of this traditional one, based on the crab cakes I grew up eating all over my home state of Maryland. The main thing to remember when making crab cakes is, the better the crab, the better the cake.

1 large egg
⅓ cup mayonnaise
1 tablespoon Dijon mustard
1 tablespoon freshly squeezed
   lemon juice
1 tablespoon chopped fresh flat-leaf
   parsley leaves
½ tablespoon Worcestershire sauce
½ tablespoon Old Bay seasoning
½ tablespoon chopped garlic
1 teaspoon hot sauce
1 teaspoon freshly ground black
   pepper
½ teaspoon salt
1 pound jumbo lump crab meat, well
   picked of shell fragments
½ cup cracker meal
2 tablespoons clarified butter (see
   box, page 70) or vegetable oil
Lemon wedges
Cajun Rémoulade (recipe follows)

1. In a medium bowl, combine the egg, mayonnaise, mustard, lemon juice, parsley, Worcestershire, Old Bay seasoning, garlic, hot sauce, black pepper, and salt and stir together until well incorporated. Add the crab meat and cracker meal and stir to incorporate, but do not overwork.

2. Form the mixture into four ½-inch-thick patties, or into 16 miniature ½-inch-thick cakes. Cover with plastic wrap and refrigerate for at least 1 hour, or up to 2 hours, to set.

3. Heat a large, heavy-bottomed sauté pan over medium heat. Add the butter and let it warm up. Add the crab cakes and pan-fry until golden brown underneath, about 5 minutes, then turn and cook on the other side until golden brown, another 5 minutes. (For miniature cakes, cook about 3 minutes for the first side and 2 minutes for the other side.)

4. Present the crab cakes with lemon wedges and rémoulade alongside.

Cajun Rémoulade

MAKES ABOUT 1¼ CUPS

se this as a dipping sauce for any breaded shellfish dishes.

1 cup mayonnaise

1 hard-boiled egg, chopped fine

1½ tablespoons finely chopped cornichons or other sour pickle

1 tablespoon chopped fresh tarragon leaves

1 tablespoon finely chopped shallot

1 tablespoon hot sauce

½ tablespoon freshly squeezed lemon juice

1 teaspoon chopped garlic

1 teaspoon cayenne

½ teaspoon dried oregano

½ teaspoon dry mustard

Salt and freshly ground black pepper

In a medium bowl, combine the mayonnaise, egg, cornichon, tarragon, shallot, hot sauce, lemon juice, garlic, cayenne, oregano, and mustard and stir together. Season to taste with salt and pepper. The rémoulade can be refrigerated in an airtight container for up to 3 days. Let it come to room temperature before serving.

"CALL ME HILLARY"

Just as I wasn't quite comfortable "hanging out" with the President, I wasn't able to be as informal as the First Lady invited me, and all her staff members, to be.

"Please call me Hillary," Mrs. Clinton said to me shortly after I was hired at the White House.

"Yes, ma'am," I said, not wanting to disagree with her, but I never stopped calling her "Mrs. Clinton" or "Ma'am." I just couldn't bring myself to call her by her first name, despite her request.

I'll never forget the time I saw just how casual Mrs. Clinton was able to be with her staff. One week, we had been honing a special event menu, passing it around from me to Ann Stock to Mrs. Clinton and back to me. Round and round it went and we were all getting pretty tired of it.

At one point, Mrs. Clinton called me in the kitchen. "Hey, Walter," she said, "Why don't you come up to my study and let's hash this thing out and be done with it."

"Great," I thought, and headed up to the third floor, eager to cross this item off my list.

Arriving at the door to her study, I knocked.

"Come in," she yelled.

I opened the door and there before me was a Hillary Clinton I had never seen before: Her hair up in curlers, her feet in flip-flops, she was wearing a T-shirt and gym shorts, and had some kind of facial cream smeared under her eyes.

"Whoa!" I said, almost involuntarily.

"Is there a problem, Walter?" she asked.

"No, ma'am. I'm just used to you, uh, looking a certain way."

"This is me, too, Walter," she said matter-of-factly. "This is me, too."

I recovered my poise and we got down to work and finished that menu.

LUNCH SPECIAL

There's something about the White House that you can't fully appreciate unless you've worked or lived there. Despite all of its history and heritage, despite all of the things about it that never change, there's one element that varies from day to day: the temperature.

Well, "temperature" is the word I used to refer to the tone of the House on any given day—a palpable sense of the prevailing mood within its hallowed walls. You can feel the temperature from the moment you start work in the morning, which in the White House was as early for me in the kitchen as it was for the First Family and their staffs in the residence and West Wing. If there's good news afoot—a positive report on the economy, say, or a visit from an especially well-liked foreign leader—you can all but smell the optimism in the air, see it in the bounce of the staffers as they move about the House, and sense it in the sunny disposition of the First Family themselves.

Then there are days when the temperature runs hot, or even downright feverish. These would be the days when the media's been pounding the administration for one reason or another, a bill is headed for certain defeat, or there's been some awful news, such as the death of service-men and women.

I learned to recognize signs of the House's temperature early in my tenure as executive chef, mostly for my own peace of mind. If there were negative indicators, then I'd keep to myself as much as possible, cooking or working on new dishes and menus. If the House had a healthy temperature, those were the times I'd bring questions and concerns to Ann Stock, Capricia Marshall, or Gary Walters.

One particular day, the House had an odd temperature, like a low-grade fever. The ushers and butlers were performing their duties with a heavy heart; the members of Hillaryland had their heads down, and their shoulders stooped. The place was pervaded by an odd, inexplicable sense of malaise.

Seeing Mrs. Clinton pass by in the late morning, I realized what it was. The First Lady had been traveling quite a bit and was simply exhausted, her usual aura of energy and enthusiasm uncharacteristically diminished. As with many tight-knit groups, the members of her team took their cue from their leader, and they were simply mirroring her demeanor *du jour*.

I got into cooking to give people pleasure. Seeing Mrs. Clinton that day reminded me of this, and the recollection inspired me to do my part to make her day a little better, even if it meant breaking one of the mandates of my job. Despite my instructions to make the White House diet as healthful as possible, everybody needs to have a little fun now and then, and as the lunch hour was approaching I decided to throw caution to the wind and treat her to a midday indulgence.

Having already learned of Mrs. Clinton's fondness for all things Southwestern, I rummaged around the kitchen to see what I might be able to cook up. Inspiration struck when I found some freshly delivered skirt steak, originally headed for the staff kitchen. I snapped my fingers: "Fajitas!"

My next step was to secure a cast-iron skillet, a piece of equipment that we didn't often use in the White House, but which figured prominently in my vision of this surprise; I found one in a closet down the hall that housed our surplus cookware. Then I prepared all the necessary fixings—slicing jalapeños, grilling onions and peppers, making guacamole and salsa—and arranging all of these components on a condiment tray, along with a basket of freshly baked flour tortillas. When the call came to the kitchen that Mrs. Clinton was ready to eat, I seared the steak slices in the skillet, letting them develop a nice, crusty char.

I got into an elevator with a butler and we rode up to the second floor. When we arrived, we turned the corner of the corridor that put us just outside the formal dining room where Mrs. Clinton happened to be seated on this particular day. I squeezed the lime over the pan. On contact, it sent up a huge, sizzling cloud of smoke.

"Go! Go!" I told him, all but pushing him into the dining room.

As the butler entered the dining room, I could see Mrs. Clinton in a reflection in the window, seated at the table as the smoking pan was delivered to her. Her expression instantly transformed from downtrodden to elated.

"Well, what in the world is this?" she exclaimed, laughing.

It's no small thing to contradict the First Lady's missive that fat and red meat be all but stricken from her diet. But I felt I had done the right thing. And about thirty minutes later, I learned for sure that I had when I received a call from the First Lady herself.

I answered it. "Yes, ma'am?"

"Walter, I just want to tell you: That was good." She paused, then added, "Sometimes you just need something good. Thank you."

The temperature in the house returned to normal that afternoon, maybe even a little better than normal. I'm not saying those fajitas were the only reason why, but I know they did their part.

Sizzling Steak Fajitas

SERVE 4

We didn't serve fajitas often at the White House, but they could be a welcome change when a little fun was called for. Fajitas are served everywhere now, but in the early 1990s they were just becoming popular.

You can use different cuts of beef and the ingredients can be marinated with various flavors, but there's just one mandatory element: They *must* be served with a sizzle. Have the condiments ready in serving bowls before you start cooking so that you can present the fajitas hot at the table.

FOR THE FAJITAS

1 cup homemade or store-bought low-sodium beef stock

½ cup dark beer

¼ cup olive oil, plus more for oiling the grill

¼ cup sherry vinegar

2 tablespoons diced jalapeño peppers (remove the seeds for less spicy fajitas)

2 tablespoons very finely chopped garlic

2 tablespoons freshly squeezed lime juice

1 tablespoon ground cumin

2 teaspoons ground coriander

1 teaspoon chipotle puree (see box, page 80)

¼ cup chopped fresh cilantro leaves, plus 8 to 10 sprigs for garnish

1½ pounds flatiron sirloin or well-trimmed skirt steak

1 medium Vidalia or other sweet onion, sliced ¼ inch thick and separated into rings

1 large red bell pepper, seeds and stem removed, cut into ½-inch strips

2 medium poblano peppers, seeds and stem removed, cut into ½-inch strips

1. In a medium glass bowl combine the stock, beer, ¼ cup oil, vinegar, jalapeños, garlic, 2 tablespoons lime juice, cumin, coriander, chipotle, and chopped cilantro and stir them together. Transfer half to another medium glass bowl. Put the steak in one bowl and toss to coat with the marinade. Put the onion and peppers in the other bowl and toss to coat with the marinade. Cover both bowls and refrigerate for 3 hours.

2. When ready to cook and serve, preheat a grill or grill pan to high and lightly oil the grates. Remove the beef from the marinade, brushing off any marinade solids (discard meat marinade), and grill the meat until medium rare (135°F); time will vary based on thickness and cut of meat, but will take 4 to 5 minutes per side for the sirloin; 2 to 3 for the skirt steak. Transfer the meat to a cutting board.

3. Remove the onion and peppers from the marinade, reserving the marinade for use in the next step. In a 12-inch cast-iron skillet over medium-high heat, cook the onion and peppers until lightly charred but still crunchy, 3 to 5 minutes. While they cook, slice the meat across the grain ¼ inch thick, reserving any juices.

4. Assemble and serve the fajitas: Transfer the sliced meat to the cast-iron pan, and toss with the onion and pepper. Add 2 or 3 tablespoons of the marinade and any meat juices to make the pan sizzle, and finish with a squeeze of lime.

5. Serve the steak, peppers, and onion right from the pan, setting it on a hot pad, with the tortillas, condiments, and cilantro sprigs.

(continues)

TO ASSEMBLE AND SERVE
½ lime, for squeezing
8 flour tortillas, warmed
1 cup homemade or your favorite
    store-bought pico de gallo
1 cup homemade or your favorite
    store-bought guacamole
1 cup sour cream
8 lime wedges

TO MAKE CHIPOTLE PUREE: Puree the contents of a can of chipotle chiles in adobo sauce in a standing blender until smooth. The puree can be refrigerated in an airtight container for up to 1 week.

THE FIRST DAUGHTER

During the entire time the Clintons were in office, the White House press corps, and the media in general, were very respectful of the privacy of the First Daughter, Chelsea Clinton.

I was always glad about that, because Chelsea impressed me greatly. I shudder to think how I would have turned out if I were in her position, with a staff at my beck and call and with few adults able to question or discipline me, from age twelve to nineteen. I imagine I'd have been spoiled beyond belief.

Chelsea, however, was never anything but polite and respectful. How she managed to stay so human in her unusual role—the closest thing we have to royalty in the United States—is a mystery to me, but I think it must have had to do with her mother's determination to protect her, and to Capricia's constant attention.

There were times I found her good manners and unassuming demeanor positively disarming. Occasionally, she'd have four or five of her girlfriends to the House for a sleepover and would call down to the kitchen, sounding almost apologetic.

"Walter, if it's not too much trouble, could you make us something to eat?"

I'd assuage her. "Chelsea," I'd say, "This is what we're here for. Now what can I get you?"

This is where it got funny. "Well, we're really not that hungry," she'd say. "We'd like just a couple'a things. Some yogurt, maybe. And some fruit. Some smoked salmon would be good. Eggs Benedict." And on and on she'd go.

Smiling on the other end of the line, I'd say, "That's no problem Chelsea. It might take us about forty-five minutes, so we'll send up the yogurt and fruit and you can pick on that while we get the rest of it ready."

Of all the family members, Chelsea spent more time in the kitchen than anyone. She had an innate curiosity, and seemed to really enjoy seeing what we were up to. I've also privately theorized that the kitchen was one of the few places in the White House where she could go unnoticed; there was nobody there but me and my crew, and we were usually so focused on our work that we didn't have time to scrutinize her.

She also saw the kitchen as a fun place to bring her friends. Sometimes they'd decide to bake cookies; she'd call down and let us know and we'd get all the ingredients and equipment ready and send it up to the private kitchen on the second floor. I gather they had a great time, because inevitably, the next morning there'd be flour, crumbs, and food splotches all over the place.

Chelsea's Chocolate Chip Cookies

MAKES ABOUT 24 COOKIES

Chelsea and her friends would make these cookies during their White House get-togethers and slumber parties, starting the year I got there, when she was fourteen. When I got the call from Chelsea (or the word from a butler) that she and her friends were in a cookie-making mood, I'd assemble the ingredients and hand-write the basic method, sending it all upstairs with a butler. This recipe is adapted from one from the legendary *Fannie Farmer Cookbook*, but I omitted the nuts and added more chocolate chips. The cookies are soft and chewy right out of the oven, then firm up a bit, but don't turn brittle.

½ cup (1 stick) unsalted butter, softened, plus more for greasing cookie sheets
½ cup packed light brown sugar
½ cup granulated sugar
1 large egg
1 teaspoon pure vanilla extract
1¼ cups cake flour
½ teaspoon salt
½ teaspoon baking soda
1¼ cups semisweet chocolate chips

1. Preheat the oven to 350°F. Grease two cookie sheets.

2. In a large mixing bowl, cream the butter, brown sugar, and granulated sugar together for 2 to 3 minutes. Add the egg and vanilla and mix well.

3. Sift the flour, salt, and baking soda together, add to the mixture, and blend well, then stir in the chips.

4. Place the dough in 2-tablespoon portions onto the cookie sheets, leaving 2 inches between the cookies.

5. Bake until lightly golden brown, 8 to 10 minutes. Remove from the oven, let cool briefly in the pans, and serve warm or at room temperature.

THE CHELSEA CLINTON COOKING SCHOOL

One day in the summer of 1997, when Chelsea was seventeen years old, Mrs. Clinton paid me a visit in the kitchen.

"Walter," she said, "Chelsea is leaving for Stanford in the fall. She doesn't know how to cook for herself because we've always lived in places like this," she said, gesturing at the walls of the kitchen and the White House walls beyond them. This was a constant comment for the Clintons, who sometimes jokingly referred to the fact that they had lived "in public housing" for as long as they could remember.

"We don't want her to have to order in, or go to a restaurant, for all her meals. We'd like her to be able to cook for herself. Would you mind teaching her?"

I have to say that this was one of the most unexpected and flattering requests that had been made of me at the White House. Moreover, coming as it did during the summer—our slowest season—the timing could not have been better.

It also enhanced my fondness for Chelsea, who clearly wanted to be prepared to take care of herself, and I felt sure, didn't want to be a drain on anybody out West, where her going to a restaurant would mean mobilizing her Secret Service detail.

By this time, Chelsea had become a full-fledged vegetarian. In fact, the weekly menus we provided to Mrs. Clinton included a separate section for Chelsea, who had far exceeded even her mother's penchant for healthful eating.

Before we began the classes, I had to go back to school on vegetarian cuisine myself. Although we had become accustomed to using tofu and tempeh in our White House cooking, I had never really studied these ingredients to the point that I could educate someone else about them. So I spent some time reading through books on vegetarian cooking, and even expanded my own repertoire, turning to the cuisines of India, Japan, and Southeast Asian nations that use vegetables in their everyday meals.

In mid-July I began to teach Chelsea and Nicole Davison, a close friend of hers about the same age, two or three times a week for a few hours each day, typically from one to four o'clock or two to five o'clock.

They'd show up in jeans and T-shirts, but we always gave them chef's coats and aprons so they felt like they worked there. We didn't give them hats because we ourselves never wore them, unless there was a photo shoot or other special occasion.

I modeled my class after the structure of the beginning classes at my alma mater, the Culinary Institute of America. We began with the basics: how to hold and use a knife, how to store foods safely, and so on. We talked about shopping, with a focus on vegetables and how to determine their freshness. And we talked generally about how ingredients like tofu and tempeh could be used as meat substitutes.

Cooking followed a similar, very logical progression. We began by just slicing or dicing whatever vegetables we had on hand that day—onions, potatoes, carrots, whatever—then I'd show her the right way to sauté, heating the pan first, then adding and heating the oil, then adding the ingredients.

We moved on next to simple things, such as vegetable stock and vinaigrettes, then into cooking individual components—beans, for instance—and proper seasoning. We covered how to use a standing blender to make a puree and how to strain foods in a conical-shaped strainer (called a chinoise or China cap), pressing down on the solids to get as much liquid as possible out.

From there, it was on to soups and salads. If she was happy with the way something came out, we'd save it and serve it to the family for dinner that night. I can still hear her, announcing with

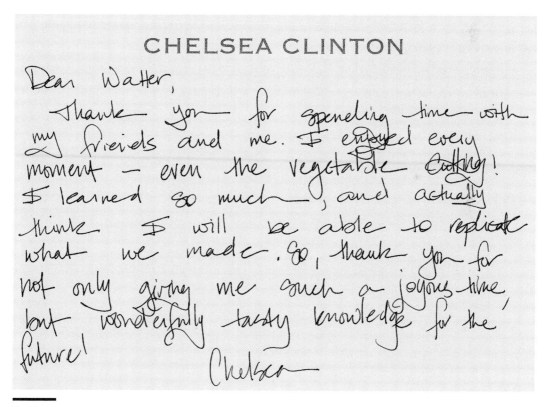

CHELSEA CLINTON

Dear Walter,

Thank you for spending time with my friends and me. I enjoyed every moment — even the vegetable cutting! I learned so much, and actually think I will be able to replicate what we made. So, thank you for not only giving me such a joyous time, but wonderfully tasty knowledge for the future!

Chelsea

The pleasure was all mine: Chelsea's thank-you note for the cooking lessons I gave her. *(Courtesy Walter Scheib 3rd)*

pride as the butlers presented the first course on one particular evening, saying, "This is my zucchini and pea soup!"

Each day, I'd send Chelsea and Nicole off with printed recipes of the dishes we'd prepared that afternoon.

Next came main courses such as vegetarian pizza; buckwheat linguine with lentils, carrots, and Swiss chard; and black bean enchiladas.

Though an avowed vegetarian by this time, Chelsea wasn't particularly thrilled with the soy and tempeh items. In fact, she was just as happy with straight vegetarian cooking, such as dishes that were built on a foundation of rice and beans. So we went in that direction and focused on things such as grilled vegetables with baba ghanoush and hummus, vegetable risotto and lasagna, and anything with sweet potatoes.

Nicole wasn't a vegetarian, so we accommodated her by working some meat into her curriculum, though this caused an occasional misstep; for example, one day we had Nicole's chicken stock in a pot right beside Chelsea's vegetable stock. I had a wooden spoon and after giving the chicken stock a stir, I used the same spoon to stir the vegetable stock. Chelsea protested. "Oh, no! Please don't do that," she said. She was serious about being a vegetarian.

Just before Chelsea pushed off for California in August, we had a graduation ceremony, presenting her with a certificate from the "White House Culinary Program" and had pictures taken. Just as we cooks did for our photo shoots, she wore a chef's toque for posterity.

Egg White and Vegetable Frittata

SERVE 4

Chelsea's diet turned vegetarian during her time at the White House. One of her favorite brunch dishes, especially on the mornings after her slumber parties, was this vegetable-packed frittata.

Salt
¼ cup small broccoli florets, blanched
2 tablespoons olive oil
1 teaspoon very finely chopped garlic
¼ cup thin strips of zucchini, cut from the outer, seedless portion
¼ cup thin strips of yellow squash, cut from the outer, seedless portion
½ cup loosely packed spinach leaves
¼ cup very thinly sliced red bell pepper
¼ cup very thinly sliced yellow bell pepper
¼ cup diced plum tomato
Freshly ground black pepper
16 egg whites
½ cup grated Asiago cheese (about 2 ounces)
2 tablespoons chopped fresh basil leaves

1. Bring a medium pot of lightly salted water to a boil, fill a medium bowl halfway with ice water, and preheat the oven to 350°F.

2. Add the broccoli to the boiling salted water and cook for 1 minute, then drain and transfer to the ice water to stop the cooking and preserve its color. Drain again and set aside.

3. Heat 1 tablespoon of the oil in a large, heavy-bottomed sauté pan over medium-high heat. Add the garlic and cook for 30 seconds, then add the zucchini, squash, broccoli, spinach, red and yellow peppers, and tomato, season with salt and pepper, and sauté until the vegetables are al dente but retain their shape and color, 2 to 3 minutes. Remove the pan from the heat.

4. Put the egg whites in a small bowl, season with salt and pepper, and beat just until frothy.

5. Preheat a 12-inch ovenproof nonstick pan over medium-high heat and lightly oil it with the remaining 1 tablespoon oil. Add the egg whites and cook over medium-high heat until the whites begin to set, about 3 minutes. Sprinkle the vegetables evenly over the whites and top evenly with the cheese; the vegetables and cheese should become embedded in the eggs, but not sink to the bottom. Transfer to the oven and bake until the whites set completely and begin to puff up, and the cheese is melted, 3 to 5 minutes.

6. Slide the frittata from the pan onto a warmed platter, cut into wedges, sprinkle with chopped basil, and serve.

SURPRISE!

The only thing the Clintons loved more than throwing a party was being surprised by a party, and their staffs often threw surprise parties in their honor, generally for a birthday.

For example, there was the time in October 1994, when Mrs. Clinton turned forty-seven, that her staff handed her a poodle skirt. She put it on and came downstairs into the Grand Foyer, where she discovered that the room had been transformed into a 1950s American living room—there was plastic on the furniture, little black and white television sets, and guests dressed in the varsity jackets and jeans of the era. President Clinton himself donned a black leather jacket and blue denim. The entire State Floor, usually the site of formal state dinners, had been converted into a full-blown sock hop, with guests dancing to '50s-era rock and roll.

For Mrs. Clinton's fiftieth birthday, in 1997, the theme was the decades of her life, and I prepared the kind of food from those eras that we would normally never serve in the White House, including meatloaf and other classics of Americana such as peanut butter and jelly, macaroni and cheese, pizza, and barbecued pork butt.

A 1994 surprise party for Mrs. Clinton fashioned after a sock hop; my team and I created menus to match the theme. *(Courtesy William J. Clinton Presidential Library)*

Not even the President was beyond a surprise. For his forty-ninth birthday in 1995, we threw a Western-themed event. One unforgettable sight from that afternoon was Chief of Staff Leon Panetta and Deputy Chiefs of Staff Harold Ickes and Erskine Bowles arriving on horseback. That same afternoon, the staff surprised the President by bringing his 1967 Ford Mustang up from Arkansas, which he then drove around the carport. He literally had not driven a car since he had become President and as he made laps around the driveway, he looked as giddy as a teenager out for his first ride.

Club des Chef des Chef

When I became the chef of the White House, I was immediately invited to join the most exclusive chef's club in the world, the Club des Chefs des Chefs, a group composed solely of chefs to heads of state of countries including England, France, Norway, Spain, South Africa, Canada, and Ireland. The club has about thirty members at any given time, and each year the members get together in a different city. In 1994, they met in Thailand, but I had to stay behind to plan Mrs. Clinton's surprise party. (Because of the nature of our work, I wasn't alone; only about two thirds of the club make it on any given year.) But I did join the group on its annual trip most other years and even served as its president my last few years in the White House.

Largely a social group when I first became a member, the Club des Chefs des Chefs had an increasingly younger membership by the late 1990s, and we began to visit culinary schools and young hospitality professionals in whatever city our annual get-together took place to share our knowledge with young industry hopefuls, giving back something to the profession that had served us all so well.

In 2005, I made one last trip (my favorite) to join the members in Prague in the Czech Republic—actually, just after leaving the White House—and then, since I was no longer cooking for a head of state, relinquished my membership. Curiously, the members rarely spoke to one another outside of this meeting, unless one of our "bosses" was visiting another, in which case we might check in with each other to learn of preferred foods and other valuable information.

The Club des Chefs des Chefs holds a press conference at the Mayflower Hotel in Washington, DC. *(Courtesy Walter Scheib 3rd)*

Smoked Mozzarella and Pepperoni Calzones with Spicy Tomato Sauce

President Clinton threw a surprise birthday party for Mrs. Clinton in 1994, and the theme of the party was the 1950s; the entire State Floor of the White House was transformed into a sock hop. For the event we served diner-type snacks from that era; a big favorite was this calzone with spicy tomato sauce.

There are two schools of thought on whether or not to score the calzones (cut lightly into their tops) before baking. One holds that scoring keeps the dough from puffing up dramatically; the other contends that the dough shouldn't puff up in the first place. Personally, I believe in scoring them so the calzone remains nice and compact, with the dough and filling close to one another.

FOR THE DOUGH
½ cup plus 2 tablespoons warm water
½ cup all-purpose flour
2 teaspoons active dry yeast (not quick-rising)
¼ teaspoon honey
1½ cups bread flour
3 tablespoons olive oil
1 teaspoon salt

FOR THE SAUCE
2 tablespoons olive oil
1 tablespoon chopped garlic
3 cups good-quality canned diced tomatoes
½ cup tomato puree
¼ cup tomato paste
2 tablespoons chopped fresh basil leaves
1 tablespoon red pepper flakes
1 teaspoon dried oregano
Salt and freshly ground black pepper

1. Make the dough: Put 2 tablespoons of the water, the all-purpose flour, yeast, and honey in a stainless steel bowl. Stir together, cover with plastic wrap, and let stand in a warm place until proofed to double its size, about 20 minutes.

2. Add the bread flour, oil, salt, and remaining ½ cup water, stir together until well incorporated, cover, and let proof to double again.

3. Make the sauce: Set a heavy-bottomed medium saucepan over medium heat. Add the oil and let it heat up, then add the garlic and sauté for 30 seconds. Add the tomatoes, tomato puree, tomato paste, basil, red pepper flakes, and oregano, stir, and let simmer for 30 minutes. Season to taste with salt and pepper.

4. If the sauce seems too chunky, puree it in a standing blender or using a handheld immersion blender. You should have about 3 cups. (At this stage, the sauce can be cooled, covered, and refrigerated for up to 2 days or frozen for up to 1 month. Let it thaw to room temperature before proceeding.)

5. Bake the calzones: Put a pizza stone on the center rack of the oven. (If you don't have a pizza stone, use an inverted 12-inch or larger cast-iron pan that's been greased on the bottom with olive oil.) Preheat the oven to 450°F.

FOR THE FILLING

2 cups shredded smoked mozzarella
(about ½ pound)

6 ounces pepperoni, thinly sliced
crosswise

½ medium Spanish onion, thinly
sliced

½ medium red bell pepper, seeds
and stem removed, thinly sliced

1 to 2 tablespoons cornmeal, for
dusting the pizza stone

6. Divide the dough into 2 equal balls, and roll each one out on a floured work surface into a 12-inch circle, about ½ inch thick

7. In a large bowl, toss the filling ingredients with 1½ cups of the sauce and put half the filling on one side of each dough circle, leave a 1-inch rim of dough around the perimeter.

8. Brush the edge of the dough with a small amount of water and fold the dough over the filling, forming a semicircle. Fold and crimp the dough along the edge to seal in the filling. Score if desired.

9. Lightly dust the pizza stone with cornmeal to keep the calzone from sticking. Put the calzones on the pizzas stone and bake until golden brown, 12 to 15 minutes (if scored you will see the sauce bubbling within). If using a cast-iron pan, set a baking sheet on the rack below it to catch any liquids that may drip down.

10. Remove the calzones from the oven and let cool for 10 minutes. Serve with extra tomato sauce on the side for dipping.

THE MOST WONDERFUL TIME OF THE YEAR

There was one time each year that summarized life in the White House kitchen—its unique challenges and the way we overcame them—more than any other. This time also happened to be the most enchanting: Christmastime.

The season made a big impact on all aspects of life at the White House, starting with the House itself, which was transformed into an even more magnificent version of itself.

Every year, there was a theme to the holiday decoration of the White House. The florist, Nancy Clarke, would begin conceptualizing as far back as late spring or early summer, making sketches of what the various rooms would look like for each of her possible schemes and sharing proposals with the social secretary, chief usher, and the First Lady.

Once a design was selected and approved, Nancy would spend months bringing it to life. The heart of her operation was a support facility, a warehouse in suburban Maryland, where her team

Chief Usher Gary Walters escorts Mrs. Clinton on her holiday tour of the White House. That's Chief Florist Nancy Clarke to my right.
(Courtesy William J. Clinton Presidential Library)

Serving the President turkey on Christmas Day. *(Courtesy William J. Clinton Presidential Library)*

of twenty-five or so designers—the White House's own elves, if you will—would congregate to assemble wreaths, bouquets, and other floral elements.

To apply all of this to the house, Gary and his team would essentially close the doors to visitors for two to three days in late November or very early December, and Nancy's team, aided by thirty to sixty volunteers, would decorate the place—an awesome and elegant spectacle.

Every year the themes were different. From year to year they had only one thing in common: They had to appeal to and be approved by Mrs. Clinton. The theme and design could be very traditional, such as "Angels," "The Nutcracker," or "'Twas the Night Before Christmas," or it could be modern or even cutting-edge, as it was in 1999, when a guest designer from New York City, Robert Isabell, built a Millennium wreath that combined lights, vines, and branches, and looked like the mother ship from the movie "Close Encounters of the Third Kind." The First Lady was happy with it, but the staff whispered among themselves that a spaceship had landed in our midst.

In keeping with her mission for the White House to reflect the entire nation, Ann Stock

To Jimmy — Nice to meet you! We're glad to have your father at the White House Hillary Rodham Clinton Bill Clinton

My five-year-old son, Jim, spent all morning rehearsing his holiday greeting: "Merry Christmas, Mrs. Clinton." She was so enchanted, she asked him to repeat it to the President. *(Courtesy Walter Scheib 3rd)*

constantly found new ways to reach out to craftspeople in all fifty states so they could be represented at the holidays. One year, for example, she sent pieces of green velvet to artists and craftspeople asking them to sew the name of their state and the image of something indigenous to the state, such as the state flower or bird. When the pieces came back, they were quilted together into a giant tree skirt.

In other years, Ann solicited tree ornaments—all of which were catalogued and mapped so that they could be located on the tree. After the Clintons' spirit of inclusion, Ann also sent thank-you notes to all people who contributed artwork to the White House, inviting them to come to the White House during the holidays and see it on display. It was a testament to the enduring allure of the White House that thousands accepted the invitation each year, many of them traveling vast distances just for the chance to visit the House and to see their work displayed there.

As soon as the holiday decorations were complete each year, the House was presented to the First Lady in a Decorators' Tour. This event usually took place at twelve noon on a Sunday, with Ann Stock and Nancy Clarke—sometimes with Gary Walters following close behind, as he, or another usher, always did when the First Family was on the State Floor—working in tandem to show each detail and design to the First Lady, not only sharing their work with her, but also enabling her to show off the house to her guests in the coming weeks.

Another point of interest was the oversized gingerbread house, created by Roland and his pastry team, that was set up in the State Dining Room every year, as well as the Christmas tree. (During the Clintons' years in the White House, the tree on the State Floor remained authentic, but because President Clinton is allergic to pine trees, all of the trees on the second floor of the White House were artificial.)

There was a holiday ritual that President Clinton himself engaged in with some of the men on the White House staff, and I was among the lucky few. The President would come see me every December with a selection of ties hanging off his outstretched arm. Word had gotten out that he liked neckties, and he received them from people all over the country.

"Thanks for a great year, Walter," he'd say to me. Then, he'd say, "You wanna pick yourself out a tie?"

I did, every year, and I still have them, my own Presidential Collection, comprising two Arkansas Razorback ties, three saxophone ties, one tie depicting colored orbs that might be Easter eggs or jelly beans, and a Texas tie featuring Texas flags and other icons (such as a clock with semaphore flags and tiny compasses). Most of them stay in the closet, but I occasionally wear the Easter egg/jellybean tie.

I wasn't there for the Clintons' first Christmas in the White House, but I'm told that there were a few hundred people on hand each day for various receptions. But in 1994, with their own chef finally on board, word wound its way down to my office that the First Lady was going to ask between nine hundred and fifteen hundred people to receptions each day. That meant twenty days straight of reception after reception, with the occasional seated dinner thrown into the mix to keep it interesting.

Throughout the nation, Thanksgiving is considered the de facto beginning of the holiday season, but at the White House, the season began with the Kennedy Center Honors, usually the first Sunday in December, and ran until a few days before Christmas.

There was another sign that the holidays had arrived. My team and I developed our own White House eggnog to serve and each year we'd move through the House with a cart, dispensing it to one and all. The "running of the 'nog" became its own tradition that people looked forward to, sometimes too much. One year, I was approached by one of the carpenters, who wanted a batch for a departmental party. I told him he'd need an okay from the Usher's Office for me to give away any alcohol.

Rather than do that, he took it upon himself to raid our refrigerator one night. The next day, he approached me in the kitchen with a look of distaste on his face.

"That stuff was nasty," he said to me.

That's odd, I thought. We're using the same recipe.

"Where did you get it from?" I asked.

He pointed to a large, open tub in the fridge, and I knew what the confusion was. The carpenter had helped himself to a batch of quiche batter, which we had on hand for an upcoming luncheon. But he was correct in one way. A cold mixture of eggs, onions, and garlic, when sipped raw from the refrigerator, was certainly no match for our homemade eggnog.

White House Eggnog

MAKES ABOUT 1 GALLON, ABOUT 32 4-OUNCE SERVINGS

Every year, the holiday season was kicked off with the "running of the 'nog," our playful way of referring to the tour of the House we made with the eggnog (and a riff on the "running of the bulls" from Pamplona, Spain). This recipe replaced one that had been in use at the White House for years. The old one was made with pre-made mix, whatever liquor was around, and melted ice cream. This one uses fresh ingredients and a precise blend of bourbon, Cognac, and rum, which we arrived at by trying a variety of recipes. The result is a smooth, creamy concoction with a carefully balanced combination of liquors that is potent but not harsh.

5 ounces egg yolks (6 to 7 yolks, pasteurized if possible)
1 cup sugar
¾ cup bourbon
¾ cup Cognac
¾ cup dark rum, such as Meyers
7 ounces egg whites (6 to 7 whites; pasteurized if possible)
1 teaspoon salt
2 cups heavy cream
1 tablespoon pure vanilla extract
1 quart milk, plus more if needed
Freshly grated nutmeg, for serving

1. Put the yolks and sugar in the bowl of a standing mixer fitted with the whisk attachment and whip until pale yellow ribbons form, 5 to 7 minutes.

2. Add the bourbon, Cognac, and rum, whip well, scrape down the sides, and mix again. Transfer the mixture to a 6-quart bowl.

3. In a separate, clean mixer bowl using a clean beater, whip the egg whites and salt until very stiff peaks form. Fold into the eggnog mixture.

4. Wipe out the mixer bowl, pour in the cream and vanilla, and whip until very stiff peaks form. Fold this into the eggnog mixture. Add the milk and whisk until smooth, 3 to 5 minutes.

5. Transfer the eggnog to an airtight container, chill in the refrigerator, and serve within 2 weeks if using pasteurized egg yolks and whites, or within 3 to 5 days if not. While the eggnog is refrigerated, foam will rise; simply whisk to reincorporate it before serving. Serve very cold, topped with a sprinkle of nutmeg.

MARATHON MEN (AND WOMEN)

The first holiday season of my tenure was rough. One of the most taxing elements was unique to this time of year. The House was open all day for tours, usually from eight in the morning until two or two thirty in the afternoon, during which time it functioned more as a museum than a home, then turned back into the First Family's residence by sundown, when the first receptions would be ready to commence.

My team and I thought we'd finesse everything we needed to do and just make it all work out. We were all seasoned professionals and surely could handle whatever was coming our way.

Boy, was I wrong. In hindsight, I consider myself lucky to have escaped December 1994 without getting sick or hurt. The kitchen staff was so exhausted by mid-month that many of them became ill, or injured themselves in some way. I myself fell asleep over my paperwork one day, waking up to find a pencil line running down the center of a list of ingredients I was working on when I passed out.

Normally, we could handle almost any scenario with six or eight core people, but by the end of this season it was abundantly clear to me that we had to have between fifteen and twenty. It took that many to handle the constant flow of work: the execution of the day's cooking, the preparation for tomorrow's, and the shortened hours required to enable cooks to make it through the month.

I've often compared my role in the White House kitchen to that of a coach, and that was never more true than during this time of year. Like a hockey coach, I moved players on and off the ice to maintain their stamina and clear-headedness.

The second holiday season I was there for, in 1995, we made some major adjustments that facilitated life in the kitchen. For example, I decided to have one base menu that we would use for as many receptions as possible. Among the items on this menu were smoked chicken with black bean salad on jalapeño corn bread; red-curried butternut squash in bliss potatoes with pepper sambal; seared tuna and barbecued onions with orange-jícama relish; and roasted tomato and couscous salad on garlic pita. Another popular—if uninventive—offering was steamed shrimp cocktail, one of the most popular White House standards thanks to the superlative and gigantic shrimp we used.

The food we served was middle-of-the-road in style, such as carved items like ballotine of turkey or roasted meats, a bit more traditional than what we did the rest of the year, but it was food we were proud of, and the colorful little canapés (usually a selection of four or five) presented on silver tea trays had the same visual flair we were bringing to everything we did.

The holidays begin! Preparing for the first reception of the season, following the Kennedy Center Honors. *(Courtesy William J. Clinton Presidential Library)*

There were certain items that would need to be added or subtracted for specific receptions—for example, the menorah lighting would call for a kosher-style menu; and kid-friendly parties, like those we threw for Chelsea in the early years, would necessitate a less formal type of food. But for the most part, the menu stayed the same.

This approach paid dividends. Rather than prep the food for each party from scratch on a rolling basis, we were suddenly able to get ahead of the game and make a lot of sauces, puff pastry, and so on in advance and freeze them, taking the necessary amount out of the freezer each day.

Ironically, this system—in some ways—created more work for us, because once Mrs. Clinton found out what we were doing, she determined that she could invite even more people; instead of fifteen hundred per day, we found ourselves serving twenty-five hundred. We joked that if we kept at it we would have had ten thousand people out under a pavilion on the south grounds before we were through.

HOUSE GUESTS

And that was just the beginning. In addition to the nightly goings-on on the State Floor, the Clintons had about twenty guests staying in the residence at all times. There were Mrs. Clinton's brothers, Hugh and Tony, each of whom had his own family in tow as well. There was Mrs. Clinton's mother, and President Clinton's mother and her husband, Mr. Kelley. There was the President's brother, Roger, and his wife. Then there were assorted friends of the Clintons, and cousins and friends from Little Rock.

Chelsea also had a number of friends—many of them from grade school back in Little Rock—who stayed at the house, an extended slumber party, so to speak.

These guests began showing up in early December and the group would swell and shrink and swell again during the month. A lot of the time you didn't know who they were, you just knew that they were there. They stayed until the President and Mrs. Clinton left for Renaissance Weekend, a retreat for American and international leaders from all walks of life and their families, the first weekend in January.

So in addition to all of the employees—regular staff and temporary SBA people—required to keep the daily complement of receptions rolling, I assigned two or three people to do nothing but take care of the Clintons and their house guests.

These staff members' days would begin at six thirty or seven in the morning, when they prepared the First Lady's breakfast, and the breakfast period alone would go through until Chelsea, on school break at this time, got up—which was about ten-thirty or eleven. Then Mrs. Clinton would want her lunch around noon, then came the house guests, then Chelsea would want her lunch at about two thirty. Dinner service began around seven o'clock, and went on until around nine o'clock.

To put it another way, during the month of December, the White House essentially became a small inn, and my team was responsible for the room service.

Additionally, we frequently orchestrated spontaneous get-togethers for the First Family and their guests. Mrs. Rodham or Chelsea might drop by the kitchen in the morning and say, "Tonight we're going to have a bunch of people over; can we have a pizza party?" or something to that effect.

(I should add here that all first families are allotted a certain monthly amount to be spent on food. While I didn't deal with budgets directly, I was responsible for tracking how food was used, listing ingredients on pink [First Family], blue [staff], and yellow ["other purpose"] sheets that were used by the Usher's Office and the accounting departments so that they could recoup additional expenses from the First Family themselves, or from third parties whom had agreed in advance to pay for certain events. These expenses were categorized as "reimbursable." In time, this system was computerized and the color-coded sheets were done away with.)

We never said "no" to these requests. Basically, if we were asked for something in the morning for dinner that night, anything—and I mean anything—was possible. If the question was asked late in the day, and we didn't have the desired food in stock, one of the cooks would make a run to the supermarket, or we might send an engineer; if neither was available, we'd improvise, sending out whoever we could enlist, such as an operations staff member. Only if something was impossible to procure would we even entertain the idea of not fulfilling a culinary wish, and even then, we'd always offer to have it for them by the next day.

One of the most taxing aspects of serving the First Family at this time of year was that the day was so very long. We began cooking for them, as we did all year, at six thirty in the morning, and kept going until late at night, well after the public festivities had ended.

The Clintons were always late-night people; often it would be eleven o' clock at night and we still would not have received the "all clear" call from the usher's office or one of the butlers. Accordingly, we kept one cook in the kitchen just for the First Family all day and late into the evening, and if we thought the family might be throwing an impromptu get-together, I might station a second cook there as well. (This was a practice adhered to all year, but evenings tended to run later, and with more guests, during the holidays.)

To staff the kitchen as effectively as possible, we would try to get some intelligence of our own during the day so that we could be set up and ready for anything, like one of Chelsea's slumber parties, for which we'd have salsa, guacamole, and chips and the ingredients for those cookies close at hand.

Once in a while, there would be an unexpected call after we had all gone home for the evening. In those cases, one of the ushers would come into the kitchen and meet the family's requests from the "family box," a small refrigerator where we kept the Clintons' favorite last-minute items. We always knew when there had been a late-night call, and not by looking in the family box; because the cleaning crew was long gone by that hour, all you had to see was the pots and pans in the sinks the next morning.

The public aspect of holiday entertaining at the White House ended around December 23, and it was around that time that we threw a party for the staff. (Each year, when she greeted my wife Jean at this party, Mrs. Clinton would say the same thing: "Thank you for loaning us your husband for the month.") A lot of the SBA cooks fell away after this, and the rest of us went into a more normal working schedule, mostly serving the First Family.

I think that the Christmas season was almost as tough for the Clintons as it was for the chefs. Even with the President's penchant for meeting people, the twenty-five to thirty thousand folks they had to meet and greet during those four weeks must have been exhausting. Occasionally, they would ask that a meal be snuck up to the residence, so they could slip out of a reception, enjoy some peace and quiet, and slip back in.

By Christmas Eve, they were thrilled that it was just the family; that's when it really became the holidays for them. Accordingly, on Christmas Eve the Clintons decorated their own tree in the residence or at Camp David, and always asked us to set up a big family buffet for their family and friends which was served that night or on Christmas Day. For this occasion, we'd combine our own recipes with Clinton and Rodham family formulas for Coca Cola and black cherry Jell-O molds, sweet potato casserole with marshmallow topping, Pepperidge Farm stuffing (it had to be Pepperidge Farm), and other homespun recipes. Though these dishes were a decided break from what we served at the White House most of the time, they were undeniably delicious—what I'd describe as good, guilty pleasures. There was one other tradition the Clintons had—every holiday season, whether on Thanksgiving, or Christmas Eve, or sometimes between the two, they'd visit soup kitchens and shelters, bringing gifts and serving food. To this day, when I think of the holiday spirit, and what it meant at that time, in that House, it's this image that comes to mind.

Gratinéed Parmesan Bites

These savory mouthfuls may remind some of an hors d'oeuvre popular at 1960s cocktail parties. They couldn't be easier to prepare, and they're addictively delicious.

Party Parmesan Spread (recipe follows)

24 ½-inch-thick slices baguette, toasted

Preheat the broiler. Place 2 teaspoons of the Parmesan spread on each crouton and spread about ¼ inch thick. Arrange the croutons on a baking sheet and broil until golden brown on top, 1 to 2 minutes. Serve warm.

Party Parmesan Spread

MAKES 1 CUP

Over the years, I received more requests for this creamy, cheesy spread than any other I prepared while at the White House. I devised it for the unrelenting holiday season and it's the perfect cocktail party standby because it can be made days in advance and lends itself to countless simple uses. In addition to the treatment presented here, you could stir in crab meat and fill mini pastry shells or small potato skins with it, add spinach for an appetizer dip, or add your favorite chopped vegetables and spread it on a variety of breads or crackers.

⅓ cup homemade or best-quality store-bought mayonnaise

⅓ cup very finely chopped Vidalia or other sweet onion

⅓ cup finely shredded Parmigiano-Reggiano cheese (about 1 ounce)

Put the ingredients in a small bowl and fold together with a rubber spatula, but do not overmix or the cheese will become gummy and the onion will give off some of its liquid. At this stage, either use right away or refrigerate in an airtight container for up to 3 days.

The Great Outdoors
Picnics and Other Outside Functions

In their own way, the informal events we orchestrated at the White House were just as challenging as the formal ones. During the Clinton years, we staged a number of enormous functions on the grounds, including congressional and press corps picnics for two thousand to thirty-five hundred people.

My team and I got very creative to devise and prepare the right food to match whatever theme the Clintons had in mind, whether it was an Eastern Shore cookout, a New Orleans celebration, an Arkansas lawn party, a congressional luau, a Caribbean-influenced press picnic, or an honest-to-goodness carnival midway set up right on the South Lawn.

As with so much of my job, at least half the battle wasn't what to serve, but figuring out ways to operate within the spatial and bureaucratic confines of the "people's house."

TAKING IT OUTSIDE

Every spring and summer, the White House stages a number of events outside, mostly on the South Lawn—essentially the backyard of the House—a more-or-less rectangular, approximately ten-acre area surrounded by an elliptical drive that runs around it with two exits, one to the east and one to the west.

A few key events are traditional, held by each successive administration without fail, such as the congressional picnic, the press picnic, and the Fourth of July celebration (with fireworks, of course), and most of them take place in July and August, though sometimes as late as September.

Because each function involves the rental and installation of a large tent, every effort is made to schedule the events only a few days apart, and to host smaller receptions, which change from year to year, in the intervening days, to get as much use as possible out of the tent. For example, one week in June 1996 included a Fulbright dinner, an "environmental reception," an event honoring veterans, and an outdoor state dinner for Ireland at which we served 450 guests.

In years past, anywhere from one thousand to two thousand people would attend the picnics and lawn receptions, and most of the food—the usual selection of burgers, hot dogs, fries, and so on—was prepared by an outside catering company. When I caught wind of this, I chalked it up to the fact that my predecessors had all been restaurant chefs and were probably uncomfortable cooking for such large numbers, partially due to the nature of their training and partially due to the fact that the White House kitchen hadn't been built to accommodate that volume.

As planning for these events began in spring 1994, I told Gary Walters that I wanted my team to do all the cooking, and that I wanted to modernize the menus to bring them in line with what we'd been serving at indoor receptions and dinners.

"If you think you can do it, then go right ahead," was his reply. I thought I detected a healthy dose of skepticism in his voice, but I had no doubt we could pull it off. When I was the chef at the Boca Raton Resort and Club, we regularly prepared the food for parties for twelve hundred to fifteen hundred people, often divided among different locations and venues—one menu for people coming off a boat trip, one for those at the pool, and so on.

THE "KILL THE GRASS" SEASON

The unofficial kickoff to the outdoor season was the Easter Egg Roll, when thousands of children would visit the White House on the Monday after Easter and roll painted eggs across the lawn. John Moeller was the Easter egg champ in the kitchen, overseeing the coloring of approximately twelve thousand eggs donated by the American Egg Board. He'd set up huge steam kettles to hard-boil the eggs, then put them in giant baskets and lower them into different colored dyes.

In 1994, my first year at the White House, I made a number of visits to the South Lawn to walk the site of the upcoming events. On my first reconnaissance mission, I was accompanied by Gary Walters and John Moeller, who explained to me how the area was usually arranged for parties. The west side of the lawn was set aside for the entertainment, bars, and so on. My team was assigned to the east side of the lawn. Guests, John explained, usually started at the west, getting their drinks and then winding their way through the food lines before sitting down at picnic tables in the center of the area.

My plan was to set up our equipment on the roadway, which would be shut down during the event, in order to avoid ruining the lawn. Ann Stock jokingly referred to all picnics as the "kill the grass" events. This was a constant struggle. Plywood was laid down over the President's running track to preserve it, and rolling mats were set over the ground under the tents, where the most people congregated. But all these efforts were in vain; no amount of work saved the grass,

John Moeller preparing Easter eggs for the annual White House roll. *(Courtesy William J. Clinton Presidential Library)*

The set-up for a typical White House picnic; my team served up to 4,000 guests from the column of tables on the right. *(Courtesy William J. Clinton Presidential Library)*

and those mats just left huge, padded-down areas, like the dents you might find in carpeting after removing a piece of furniture that's been in place for a long time.

Over the weeks leading up to the event, I planned out how my team would be arranged. One of my goals was to make our operation as unobtrusive as possible, hiding equipment and grills behind evergreen bushes or trees, and transferring food to buffet stations fifty or sixty yards away when it was ready to be served.

WHAT TO SERVE

I knew that we weren't going to serve only hot dogs, burgers, cole slaw, and so on at the Clintons' picnics. Which only left one question: What else were we going to serve?

My challenge here, as it was so often, was to find the common ground between inspiration and practicality—to come up with food that would surprise and delight, but also which could be prepared substantially in advance and wouldn't wilt or spoil in the sun, an especially important consideration in the dog days of D.C. in July and August, when the heat can be overwhelmingly oppressive.

For guidance, I went a geographical route, looking to regions and countries that are known for their warm weather. I began, for example, to look at cookbooks and magazines that espoused the California style of entertaining, expanding on what I found to devise dishes such as grilled swordfish with papaya and garlic mojo; honey and tamarind glazed pork; and firecracker chicken with pineapple relish. I wasn't looking to reinvent the wheel, just to be interesting and to please the First Lady and her guests. For instance, I didn't mind serving salads at these events, but I didn't want them to be simple lettuce-based affairs; instead I looked for ways to build them around corn, tomatoes, jalapeño peppers, and other seasonal ingredients.

I also researched the foods of North Africa, focusing on couscous salads and vegetables marinated in vinaigrettes that would hold well in the heat. The result of this line of thinking included saffron-cumin braised chicken with couscous salad; asparagus and roasted vegetables with lemon-rosemary dressing; and harissa and garlic–glazed lamb rack.

Serving unpredictable food at these picnics proved successful . . . almost too successful.

My first outdoor event was a themed picnic: The Congressional Crab Feast, on June 23, 1994. Thirteen hundred guests were expected.

In preparation for the party, I made a fact-finding visit to the Eastern Shore of Maryland, tasting signature dishes at crab houses and even a firehouse or two. This was the only time I scheduled a "research" trip of this nature, because it was a fun way to revisit my home state of Maryland. I basically rambled around the area, dropping into restaurants, attending a fundraising chicken and oyster dinner at a firehouse just outside Salisbury, and even following my nose to a club with a big cinderblock pit out back, where they were barbecuing chicken that you could literally smell from miles away. At each of these places, I identified myself to the proprietors, chefs, or firehouse cooks, and told them why I was there. They were only too happy to share their recipes with me.

On the day of the event, we served a menu that included rockfish with Crisfield crab stuffing, Wye River barbecued chicken, and Salisbury Firehouse tomato salad.

Now, when you cook a buffet-style menu for thirteen hundred people, you usually don't make thirteen hundred servings of everything; you make a half-portion of this per person, and a quarter-portion of that per person, and so on, figuring that most people will sample a lot of dishes rather than have a full portion of anything.

The only problem was that people were so surprised by the unconventional White House fare that they piled their plates with much more food than we had banked on. As the lawn filled with thousands of congresspeople and their staffs, I began to see heaping plates go by, and I realized that we'd need to adjust our protocol to account for more servings at all future events.

THE HUMAN TOUCH

No matter how much you plan, fret over details, and communicate, you're only as good as your weakest link. While I always tried to work with only the ushers and butlers I trusted the most, there was one memorable occasion when I let a less-reliable butler into my universe, and I paid the price.

The butler, whom propriety prevents me from naming, was the maitre d' who disappeared with my list of requested supplies on the day of my audition. At the time, I chalked it up to deliberate subterfuge, a test to see how prepared I was for unforeseen obstacles. But after what occurred on the day of the first picnic under my watch, I decided his mistake was the one authentic glitch during my audition.

In preparation for the picnic, I gave the maitre d' a list of all the tabletop supplies we'd need to procure from a rental company: chafing dishes, napkins, salt and pepper shakers, silverware, serving utensils, and so on.

On the morning of the picnic, I went around to all the butlers and asked if they had any questions. To a person, they said "no."

But that afternoon, about two and a half hours before the event, as I walked the grounds looking over the set up of the buffet tables and cooking areas, I noticed that there wasn't one piece of silverware in sight.

"Where's the silverware?" I asked the maitre d'.

"You were supposed to get it," he said to me.

I had the most ominous sense of déjà vu. Just as I had done during my audition day, I produced a spare copy of the agreed-upon work list from my pocket and showed him that "silverware" was indeed his job.

With no time to argue, I whipped out my cell phone and called Gordon Marr, my buddy and occasional SBA chef who was the executive chef of the Washington Hilton, about a mile and a half away.

He put one of his busboys in a cab and sent him to meet me at the northeast gate of the White House with 100 spoons, 100 serving forks, and 150 tongs, all of it arriving just in the nick of time.

As we say in the food business, that's what friends are for.

Later in the day, I told the maitre d' that we weren't going to be able to work together. "I am a singularly organized individual," I said. "Strike one was that audition lunch. Strike two was today. And I'm not waiting for strike three."

I was so mad I couldn't even talk to him. He had been promoted to maitre d' just before I was hired, so I suppose that the chef's deciding to shun him wasn't exactly what he was expecting in his new role, but I didn't care. I was angry. I never forgave him. He kept his job, but became a nonentity in my world. From that day forward, I went to one of the other longtime butlers, George Haney, with all my special requests.

KEEPING OUR COOL

One of our biggest challenges in executing such large picnics was how to keep food cold until it was ready to be served or cooked.

That first summer we decided to do what the Florist's Office often did and rent a generator-powered refrigerator. We parked it out on the South Lawn, behind a big bush.

This was the plan: We would do as much prep work as possible in the kitchen and load the food onto big rolling racks with the names of the stations from which they'd be served scrawled on strips of tape stuck to their sides, such as Buffet One, Buffet Two, and so on.

The only remaining issue was how to get the food all the way from the White House kitchen to the on-site fridge. I decided to rent a refrigerated truck to bring the food out from the House, but this proved to be a disaster because the lift gate at the rear of the cargo area didn't work, and we had to work in teams to hoist several-hundred-pound racks of food up onto the truck, then back down when we reached our destination.

Nonetheless, for the first few years I kept using the trucks. Then one year I rented two eight-by-ten refrigerators and one freezer the same size. These generator-powered boxes were delivered on flatbed trucks and essentially created three walk-in units right at the picnic site. The only problem was that the rental units were in sad condition—not terribly clean, and so old that you constantly had the feeling they might go on the fritz any second.

But they solved one of our big problems, so at the end of that fiscal year, I used my mysterious budget surplus to buy three units of our own—we'd keep them at the White House during the "kill the grass" season, and farm them out to a support facility in Beltsville, Maryland, where they were warehoused the rest of the year, calling on them again during the holiday season when we'd keep them on the periphery of the carport on the west side of the House.

EVERYBODY'S INVITED

As with state dinners and other functions, the Clintons wanted outdoor picnics to be as inclusive as possible. In previous years, only people above a certain rank or position were invited to attend, with their spouses, if they liked.

The Clintons wanted everybody at these summer celebrations—not only was the circle of invitations for the congressional and press picnics expanded to include all staff members from the groups being welcomed down to the assistants, but an invitation meant that you could bring your spouse and your kids. Because this was a new policy, the first press picnic we threw had an extra bit of excitement. Guests would arrive, and a White House staff member would say, "Where are your kids?" Pleasantly shocked at the question, the guests would then run off to call their kids and there was an impromptu security screening set up at the Visitors Gate where arriving children were cleared for admittance.

President Clinton himself was devoted to this spirit of inclusion. If he passed a butler in the hall on a day leading up to the staff picnic, he'd stop him. "Did you know that you were invited to the picnic next week?" he'd drawl.

Most of the time the answer was "Yes, Mr. President," but if the answer was "No," then as soon as he got back into his office he'd call Ann Stock (and in later years Capricia Marshall) and make sure an official invitation was issued.

As with the state and formal dinners, these events grew exponentially over time. We had nine hundred guests at the first picnic we threw, and between three thousand and thirty-five hundred at the last few in 2000.

It was clear that part of the reason the Clintons wanted so many people at these events was to increase the sense of fun, but they also recognized that everybody in attendance was working incredibly hard, and an invitation was a nice way of saying "thank you" by including them in something special.

One of the elements that made the picnics so festive was the entertainment, a nonstop parade of popular music icons including Lenny Kravitz, Eric Clapton, Aretha Franklin, and Stevie Wonder. (My team and I would often sneak out to listen to the sound checks, which were like private concerts for the House staff.)

The burgeoning scale of our picnics led to some creative themes. In 1998, Capricia Marshall oversaw the creation of a carnival midway right on the South Lawn, complete with rides and game booths. The President and Mrs. Clinton went on all the rides, and were especially fond of the Ferris wheel. As for the games, the President enjoyed trying his hand at the carnival institution where you bring a sledgehammer down on a platform in hopes of ringing a bell at the top of a pole. Everywhere you looked somebody was hoisting a stuffed animal he or she had won. The only thing missing was the dunking machine, but it was supposed to be there. Capricia had enlisted several senior staff members to take shifts in the dunking machine, but the truck that was to deliver it to the White House ran into a problem in transit and it never showed up.

For an event of this kind, we served traditional American picnic food, because it was appropriate to the theme. But we still did it ourselves, and searched out special purveyors to provide certain key items. For example, we located an artisan in Baltimore who made superior hot dogs and sausages, and we had beef for the burgers specially ground to our specifications (twenty percent fat; eighty percent lean meat) and delivered fresh on the morning of the event.

MISSION IMPOSSIBLE

Despite the ever-growing crowds and the gusto with which they ate, there was only one time that we actually ran out of food: the press corps picnic in July 1999.

We were expecting approximately twenty-four hundred guests that day, but due to some pressing business on Capitol Hill, they weren't arriving in the anticipated droves. Eager to drum up some excitement, somebody in the White House dispatched a team of volunteers to the Old Executive Office Building, one of the hulking bastions of bureaucracy that dot the neighborhood around the House, with instructions to roam the halls, inviting one and all to the picnic.

The result of this outreach? By the time the expected guests and newly invited guests combined on the South Lawn, we had one thousand people more than were initially expected.

My team and I went into overdrive, raiding the First Family and staff kitchens for anything that could be prepared and served. We were serving vegetable crudités and dip, improvising salads, and grilling any poultry or meat on hand. I even sent a group of SBA guys over to the Navy mess, over which I had no authority, to beg for anything they could spare.

It was during this chaos, when I was standing at the end of one of the buffet lines tossing an improvised slaw with latex-gloved hands, that a butler approached me.

"Walter," he said, "There's someone here who wants to speak with you. Marian Burros from the *New York Times*."

"No!" I shouted. Ms. Burros was the *Times*' key food reporter in the D.C. area, and also had written New York City restaurant reviews for the paper over the years. I had seen her in press conferences, and been interviewed briefly by her when I first got the job, and for a piece she wrote about the first state dinner I prepared, but the prospect of being visited by her in the midst of all this chaos was mortifying.

She marched right over to me with her hand outstretched, but I couldn't return the courtesy, because my hands were buried in vegetables and dressing.

"Hello, Ms. Burros," I said. "I need to ask you a favor."

"What?" she asked.

"Things got a little out of hand today. I'd love to invite you back for a one-on-one chat when my arms aren't buried in cole slaw."

She agreed, and a few weeks later we had a fine interview in the relatively calm, quiet confines of the kitchen.

Summer Vegetable Slaw

SERVES 4

This is a modified, tested, White House–worthy version of the salad I was improvising (and tossing by hand!) when Marian Burros of the *New York Times* paid me a visit at the press corps picnic in 1999. It wasn't the ideal way to be seen by one of the foremost food writers in the nation, but now that some time has passed, I'm able to laugh about it.

FOR THE DRESSING
½ cup olive oil
¼ cup seasoned rice vinegar
¼ cup chopped fresh basil leaves
¼ cup chopped fresh tarragon leaves
¼ cup chopped fresh flat-leaf parsley leaves
1 tablespoon chopped shallot
1 tablespoon chopped garlic
1 teaspoon seeded, chopped jalapeño pepper
1 teaspoon grated peeled fresh ginger
1 teaspoon dry mustard
Salt and freshly ground black pepper

FOR THE SLAW
½ cup shredded Napa cabbage
½ cup julienned seeded summer squash or zucchini
¼ cup shredded carrot
¼ cup julienned peeled, seeded cucumber
¼ cup very thinly sliced red bell pepper
¼ cup loosely packed young spinach leaves
¼ cup very thinly sliced snow peas
¼ cup very thinly sliced red onion

1. Make the dressing: Put the oil, vinegar, basil, tarragon, parsley, shallot, garlic, jalapeño, ginger, and mustard in a standing blender. Blend until thoroughly pureed, 2 to 3 minutes. Season to taste with salt and pepper. This vinaigrette can be refrigerated in an airtight container for up to 3 days. Let it come to room temperature before proceeding.

2. Make the slaw: put the cabbage, squash, carrot, cucumber, red pepper, spinach, snow peas, and red onion into a large bowl. Drizzle the dressing over the vegetables and toss until all vegetables are well coated. Let stand at room temperature for 10 minutes, then serve.

CHELSEA'S GARDEN PARTIES

There was another category of outside event, one that received considerably less press coverage than the large South Lawn picnics.

As she matured into her mid-teens, Chelsea Clinton began to host one or two outdoor parties a year, either on the roof—which guests accessed by walking out through the Solarium's doors onto a tiled terrace, with a great view across the Ellipse to the Washington Monument— or at the White House swimming pool, located south of the Oval Office. In sharp contrast to her informal slumber parties, these were basically her version of her mother's White House parties. She invited anywhere from thirty to eighty people, including not just her friends, but also their parents, and acted like more of an official hostess.

These were fun, festive affairs. While her friend's parents showed a reverence for the White House, her friends themselves were more at ease, and never failed to have a great time.

And, true to form, Chelsea always thanked me the next time we spoke.

One of Chelsea's rooftop parties, this one on the Fourth of July 1996. Few kids could top this setting for a gathering. *(Courtesy William J. Clinton Presidential Library)*

Grilled Artichokes and Roasted Peppers with Oregano and Lemon Dressing

SERVES 4

With respect to Chelsea Clinton's budding vegetarianism, we often served this salad, reminiscent of an Italian antipasto plate, at her rooftop garden parties. It features marinated, grilled artichokes and peppers punched up with lemon and oregano. It's a great take-along dish for picnics and other outdoor events.

FOR THE ARTICHOKES

2 tablespoons freshly squeezed lemon juice

2 teaspoons grated lemon zest

1½ tablespoons chopped fresh oregano leaves

1½ tablespoons very finely chopped garlic

Salt and freshly ground black pepper

6 large artichokes

TO ASSEMBLE AND SERVE

4 red or yellow bell peppers, roasted (see box, page 51), and cut into ½-inch-wide strips

1 lemon, cut into 8 wedges

1 tablespoon chopped fresh oregano leaves

⅓ cup good-quality olives, halved, pitted, and thinly sliced (optional)

⅓ cup (about 1 ounce) crumbled goat cheese (optional)

1. Grill the artichokes: Prepare a charcoal grill, letting the coals burn until covered with white ash, or preheat a gas grill to medium-high, or preheat the broiler.

2. In a large bowl, combine the lemon juice, lemon zest, oregano, and garlic. Season to taste with salt and pepper.

3. Cut off the top two thirds of the artichokes with a heavy knife, then cut off the stem. Pull off the tough, outer leaves, then use a paring knife to trim away the smaller leaves until you get to the yellow heart. Remove the hairy choke with a spoon and discard it. Slice the hearts lengthwise into ⅓-inch-thick slices and transfer them to the lemon-oregano marinade as they are sliced, tossing to coat (this will keep them from turning brown). When you've added all the artichokes to the marinade, let them stand an additional 20 minutes.

4. Drain the artichoke slices, reserving the marinade, and place on a grill-basket on the grill or on a baking sheet under the broiler. Cook, turning once, until they are tender and have taken on a golden color, 3 to 4 minutes. Remove from the heat and set aside at room temperature.

5. Assemble and serve: Arrange the artichoke slices and peppers on a platter and drizzle with the reserved marinade. Garnish with lemon wedges, oregano, and olives and cheese, if desired.

BURN, BABY, BURN

A big element of any outdoor function at the White House, just as it would be at any outdoor gathering in any American home, was the grill.

Just as they did for my predecessors, for our first picnic the Parks Service set up an extended grilling station comprising six to ten huge grills, each of them three feet across and four or five feet wide (the makeup of the line changed from event to event), on the drive along the east side of the south grounds. We filled each of them with charcoal, but didn't light them all at the same time. The plan was to douse them with lighter fluid and light them according to a slightly staggered schedule so that they wouldn't all burn out at once. As the first one went out, we could replenish and light it and have it back in use by the time the one next to it began burning out, and so on down the line.

When it came time to light the first one, I doused the coals with lighter fluid, lit a match, and tossed it into the grill. Instantly, an action movie–worthy fireball shot up over the grill, causing us all to jump back. (I had done a lot of grilling before, but never in grills this deep; the amount of charcoal, combined with the amount of lighter fluid, caused more of a blast than I was ready for.) Even after the initial fire flash died down a bit, there were five-foot flames that took an hour to burn down to the point that we could cook over them; in fact, the heat was so intense that it killed the leaves on nearby bushes. Configured side by side as they were, the grills were overwhelmingly hot. The cooks stationed there were cooking literally thousands of portions of food over the glowing embers, under the hot sun, and it was just too much. They were sweating through their clothes, and chugging as much water as possible to avoid dehydration. They also began wrapping wet towels around their arms and necks, turning themselves into mummified cooks. But nothing helped. One of my SBA guys, Vincent, even began to feel faint, and took off for the hospital.

I'd have struck the grills after that first event, but there was no other way I knew of to cook hot food for so many people. We couldn't even do it in the indoor kitchen and transport it, because it was simply too far away. So we stuck with the grills because guests and—more important—the First Family and the White House event team loved the results.

Grilled Rum and Pepper–Glazed Red Snapper with Tropical Fruit Salsa

SERVES 4

We served this dish at the congressional picnic in 1998 as an innovative alternative to the burgers, ribs, and chicken prevalent at previous White House picnics. It is a spicy and full-flavored dish that is easy to prepare. The marinade can also be used on shrimp, tuna, swordfish, or chicken.

⅓ cup soy sauce
¼ cup seasoned rice vinegar
2 tablespoons honey
2 tablespoons dark rum
2 tablespoons olive oil
2 tablespoons orange juice
1 tablespoon freshly squeezed lime juice
1 tablespoon packed light brown sugar
2 teaspoons grated garlic
1 teaspoon grated fresh ginger
1 teaspoon tamarind puree (see Sources, page 302)
½ teaspoons sambal olek (chili paste; see Sources, page 302)
4 skin-on red snapper fillets (6 ounces each)
Vegetable oil, for brushing the grill
Tropical Fruit Salsa (recipe follows)

1. Prepare a charcoal grill for grilling, letting the coals burn until covered with white ash, or preheat a gas grill to high.

2. Meanwhile, in a medium bowl, combine the soy sauce, vinegar, honey, rum, oil, orange juice, lime juice, brown sugar, garlic, ginger, tamarind, and sambal olek and whisk together.

3. Arrange the fish fillets skin side up in a single layer in a baking dish or other shallow dish, and pour the marinade over the fish. Let marinate at room temperature for 10 minutes, but no longer or the acid in the citrus juices will begin to cure the fish.

4. Remove fish from the marinade, brushing off any solids. Reserve the marinade.

5. Use a long brush to oil the grill. Gently place the fish on the grate, skin side down without crowding. Grill the fish for 4 minutes, basting it with the marinade, then carefully turn the fillets using a spatula and cook on the other side for 3 to 4 minutes, continuing to baste. Remove the fish from grill and keep warm. Discard any unused marinade.

6. To serve, place one fish fillet on each of four plates. Divide the salsa equally alongside. Serve immediately.

Tropical Fruit Salsa

MAKES 1½ CUPS

If you want to avoid having a refrigerator full of leftover fruit, double this recipe and enjoy the remaining salsa cold as part of your lunch the next day.

1 tablespoon olive oil
¼ cup thinly sliced red onion
1 tablespoon chopped garlic
1 teaspoon chopped jalapeño pepper (remove the seeds for a less spicy salsa)
¼ cup diced pineapple
¼ cup diced mango
¼ cup diced papaya
¼ cup diced plum tomato
2 tablespoons chopped fresh cilantro leaves
1 tablespoon freshly squeezed lime juice
2 teaspoons ground cumin
1 teaspoon ground coriander
1 teaspoon hot sauce
Salt and freshly ground black pepper

1. Heat the oil in a medium, heavy-bottomed sauté pan set over medium heat. Add the red onion, garlic, and jalapeño and sauté until softened, 2 to 3 minutes. Add the pineapple, mango, papaya, and tomato, toss, and cook for 2 to 3 minutes to heat through.

2. Add the cilantro, lime juice, cumin, coriander, and hot sauce, toss quickly, and remove from the heat. Season with salt and pepper, and serve warm but not too hot.

PICNIC LIST

Everyone likes to have cookouts, but planning for one at the White House took a good deal of organizing and quite a big food order. For example, the following items were among those ordered for the last press picnic (three thousand guests), congressional picnic (fifteen hundred), and staff picnic (four thousand) hosted by the Clintons on July 26, 27, and 29, 2000, respectively.

4,500 hot dogs	200 pounds haricots verts
5,500 chicken breasts	30 cases miniature lettuces
5,500 hamburgers	160 pounds dry white beans
3,200 ears of corn	100 bags charcoal (30 to 35 pounds each)
15 gallons peeled garlic	50 one-liter containers lighter fluid

REINFORCEMENTS

After three summers, an idea popped into my head. In early 1997, with the spring events on the horizon, it occurred to me to ask Gary Walters, an ex-military man, how the Army fed troops out in the field. I mean, we were just operating on the South Lawn of the White House; how did the Army provide hot meals to soldiers in the middle of a desert?

"They have mobile kitchen trailers," he told me, and the wheels in my head began spinning. Mobile kitchen trailers . . . how can I get me one of those?

"Are they available?" I asked.

Gary directed me to the military aide's office in the East Wing. I strolled over there that afternoon and asked the officer in charge if it would be possible to have a look at one of the mobile kitchen trailers I'd heard about. He called the Military District of Washington Protocol Office at Fort McNair, just across the Potomac. That office, in turn, generated a tasking sheet to Sergeant Denzil Benjamin, the assistant dining facility manager at Fort McNair, who was to be our liaison in this mission.

One day, Gary and I got into his car and drove over to Fort McNair's dining facility (DiFac, for short) where they serve the servicemen and officers. We were greeted by Sergeant Benjamin and Sergeant Brian Williams, the dining facility manager, both of whom were dressed in cook's whites—the apron, chef's coat, and toque (tall, white, cylindrical paper hat) worn in professional kitchens.

We all shook hands, then Sergeants Benjamin and Williams changed into military fatigues and we all got into Gary's car and drove to Fort Myer, near the National Cemetery in Arlington, Virginia. As we drove, they explained their role at the base. They were charged with overseeing the dining facility that fed about five hundred people each day. Additionally, they would go on maneuvers with the troops and they and their crew would be in charge of feeding them. They were cooks by trade who had gone through the quartermasters crew and then been assigned to the feeding area. In army terms, they were food managers, but that's an understatement. I could tell just by talking to them that they both knew food and took a lot of pride in their work.

Once we arrived at Fort Myer, the sergeants led us to the motor pool, a huge outdoor lot, and walked us over to the mobile kitchen trailer (MKT for short)—a trailer that's pulled by a truck. The trailer is about fifteen feet long and twelve feet wide. It was covered by a canvas tarp, which the sergeants rolled back to reveal a self-contained cooking facility with steps leading up the front, and another set of steps leading out the rear. The troops would file in one side, be served cafeteria-style by the cooks, and then exit out the other end.

With an enthusiasm that was barely masked by their military formality, Sergeants Benjamin and Williams gave me more than a tour of the vehicle—they told me everything about it, from how and why it was designed, to how to use it, to what they'd seen cooked on it, even how to refuel it.

Based on their obvious mastery of this equipment, I asked the sergeants if they would be willing to come along to the White House to offer technical support when we used it. They said they'd be happy to, as long as they could get an approval from their commander, which proved to be no problem.

So when the first event outside event of 1997 rolled around, Sergeants Benjamin and Williams arranged for one of the trucks and trailers to be delivered to the White House. The first time we used it, it was parked outside on the driveway on the north side of the House. We cooked the food there and transported it to the picnic, and the trailer performed as I hoped it would, doubling our capacity in one fell swoop.

But there was one more evolution to come. After the event, while the Army guys were cleaning the trailer, they began to take it apart so they could hose down, wipe down, and otherwise clean every side of every piece.

It occurred to me that the components of the trailer were removable.

I asked my army liaisons if it would be possible to use just the guts of the trailer, without parking the whole monstrosity on the White House lawn.

"Oh," Sergeant Williams said, sounding almost disappointed. "Sure. You can use it however you like."

And thus a new approach was born. For future events, such as the carnival midway picnic in 1998, we actually removed the cooking components and used them right at the picnic site. One of the most invaluable pieces of equipment proved to be deep, stainless-steel pans—known colloquially as "squareheads"—that could be used for just about any purpose. They came with their own stands, called "doghouses," but because the ground wasn't quite level, the White House carpenters built stands for the stands to keep them from wobbling. We filled them with oil and used them as deep fryers.

Sergeants Benjamin and Williams always came along when we needed the mobile kitchen trailers, and they began to bring four or five guys with them to help manage the equipment. Those troops were so excited to be serving the White House that they jumped in and helped my crew with the cooking, doing prep work and such.

I was touched, and there's nothing like a few extra sets of hands, so when the following spring rolled along, I asked Denzil and Brian—by then we had dropped the titles—if some of their staff would like to come help us out.

They jumped at the chance, and from then on, they always came with ten to fifteen colleagues who functioned as prep cooks for the "kill the grass" events and other large functions. Over the years, a few of the guys, especially Denzil and Brian, proved so adept at kitchen work that we came to trust them and give them other things to do, such as keeping track of logistics.

Every year, I sent Denzil and Brian's commander a thank-you note, and the men ended up receiving an Army Achievement Medal for their service to the White House.

Southern Fried Chicken

SERVES 4

This is the recipe we used to make fried chicken at White House events, at first in small rented fryers, and later in the supersized "squareheads" we borrowed from the Army's Mobile Kitchen Trailers.

Marinating the chicken in buttermilk serves two purposes: It draws out impurities and tenderizes the chicken. Note that this step requires six hours, or may be done the night before you plan to fry the chicken.

1 chicken, 3 to 3½ pounds, cut into 8 sections (2 breasts, 2 thighs, 2 drumsticks, 2 wings)
2 cups buttermilk
2 tablespoons plus 2 teaspoons salt
Vegetable oil, for frying
1 cup all-purpose flour
2 teaspoons freshly ground black pepper
2 teaspoons garlic powder
2 teaspoons paprika
2 teaspoons dried thyme
1 teaspoon dry mustard
1 teaspoon dried basil
1 teaspoon cayenne

1. Rinse the chicken pieces under cold running water and pat dry with paper towels.

2. Put the buttermilk and 2 tablespoons of salt in a large stainless steel, glass, or ceramic bowl. Add the chicken and turn to coat with the buttermilk. Cover with plastic wrap and refrigerate for at least 6 hours, or overnight.

3. Fill a deep-fryer with vegetable oil according to the manufacturer's instructions and preheat to 350°F. (Alternatively, fill a cast-iron Dutch oven with oil to a depth of 6 inches and heat until a thermometer registers 350°F.)

4. In a medium bowl, combine the flour, the remaining 2 teaspoons salt, the black pepper, garlic powder, paprika, thyme, mustard, basil, and cayenne and stir together until well incorporated.

5. Remove the chicken from the buttermilk, letting any excess milk run off. Dredge the chicken in the seasoned flour until well coated. Carefully place the chicken in the deep fryer and cook until golden brown and the pieces begin to float, 8 to 10 minutes. Remove with tongs or a slotted spoon, drain on paper towels, and serve immediately.

BEST-LAID PLANS

Being outdoors added a factor to our events that never came up at indoor functions. We were at the mercy of the weather, one of the few forces that "outranked" the White House.

One constant nemesis was the wind; we were always hoping for wind that blew from north to south, but inevitably it seemed to blow from east to west, threatening to send embers in the direction of our guests, and forcing us to pay close attention to each and every grill.

But the biggest problem was rain. The grills were so hot that rain didn't put them out, but it made it impossible to cook on them, of course, because the food would get drenched.

Fortunately, we didn't get rained out on too many occasions, but there were a few memorable ones, such as the year that the Olympic torch was scheduled to arrive at the White House during the congressional picnic. As it arrived, carried aloft by a runner, the skies opened up and a torrential downpour began. One of the most memorable sights from that particular day

When a summer storm rolled in unexpectedly, these buffet tables for a White House picnic were moved inside from the South Lawn, with all the food still on them, within 45 minutes. *(Courtesy William J. Clinton Presidential Library)*

was Speaker of the House Newt Gingrich under a picnic table with a tablecloth draped over his head.

On another picnic day, we had the entire South Lawn set up when it began to rain. In forty-five minutes' time, we moved the entire buffet indoors and welcomed picnic guests on the State Floor of the White House.

Then there was the ASCAP (American Society of Composers, Authors and Publishers) event for eleven hundred guests that was interrupted by a storm that felt like a hurricane. Ann Stock and her team ended up shuttling the guests, who were carrying their soggy shoes in their hands, into one of the concert tents that had been erected for this event.

From a food standpoint, the most disappointing event was the reception the White House hosted for twenty-eight hundred Americorps volunteers. It was to be a morning event, but a small plane flew onto the South Lawn of the White House that morning, turning it into a crime scene. Accordingly, the event was pushed back to lunch time. We hadn't planned on serving food to the volunteers, so the Secret Service did something drastic: They ordered McDonald's. So there were a few Big Macs served at the White House after all.

Couscous Salad

SERVES 4

Not all outdoor events were on the scale of a congressional or press picnic. When the season was right, and the weather was welcoming, we also threw the occasional private function outdoors. For instance, in June 1995, Mrs. Clinton's staff threw a surprise birthday party for Ann Stock, whom they got to show up by calling her in to work on a Saturday. This salad, a versatile selection for barbecues, pot-lucks, and picnics because it goes well next to everything from grilled meats and fish to cold cuts and other salads, was one of the dishes we served at that party.

Note that a portion of the salad needs to marinate overnight.

½ cup olive oil
¼ cup canola oil, or more olive oil, if desired
¼ cup freshly squeezed lemon juice
1½ tablespoons chopped garlic
1 teaspoon harissa (see Sources, page 302)
1 teaspoon ground cumin
Salt and freshly ground black pepper
½ cup canned chickpeas, drained and rinsed
½ cup quartered cherry tomatoes
¼ cup chopped scallions, white and green parts
¼ cup chopped fresh flat-leaf parsley leaves
1 cup dry couscous

1. Put the oil, lemon juice, garlic, harissa, and cumin into a small bowl and mix well. Season with salt and pepper.

2. In a medium bowl, combine the chickpeas, tomatoes, scallions, and parsley. Drizzle with the dressing, and toss. Cover and refrigerate overnight.

3. Cook the couscous according to the package directions and fluff with a fork.

4. Put the chickpea mixture and couscous in a serving bowl and toss together. Season to taste with salt and pepper and serve warm, but not too hot.

Honored Guests
State and Formal Dinners

Rarely does the White House chef have the spotlight aimed at him or her the way he or she does during state dinners—star-studded formal affairs that are covered by local, national, and international media like few other events in the world outside of a royal wedding.

Under the Clintons, state dinners—and the almost-as-pomp-filled official dinners—went through a metamorphosis, both in content and in scale. Where they traditionally featured very conservative French/Continental cuisine—such as clear soup with marrow balls; lobster thermidor with Sauternes; roast duckling bigarade; and green beans amandine—presented and served from platters, to about 120 guests, we served restaurant-style contemporary American dishes, plated individually, to ever-larger groups that, by the time President Clinton left office, approached 700 for a state dinner, and up to 900 for an official dinner.

JUST WHAT IS A STATE DINNER?

When I first arrived at the White House, I had no idea what a state dinner was. The first time I remember even becoming aware of the phrase was around the time Jean submitted my resumé to the Usher's Office and I read in the papers that Mrs. Clinton's stock answer to the question of when they would host a state dinner was, "Not until we have our own chef."

Once the phrase registered in my consciousness, I made certain assumptions. A state dinner, it seemed to me, was a formal affair, honoring a foreign dignitary, to which a number of VIPS and celebrities were invited.

I was partially right.

There are a few essential elements required for a dinner to qualify as a state dinner. First of all, a state dinner can only take place when a foreign head of state is in town. (This is obvious when you think about it. The word *state,* in governmental terms, refers to our relationship with other nations, as in State Department and Secretary of State.) A good example is that when Tony Blair, the Prime Minister of Great Britain, is in the United States, that's not a state visit, it's an "official" visit, and a dinner honoring him would be an "official" dinner. If, however, Queen Elizabeth were here, that would be a state visit and a dinner in her honor would be a state dinner.

Having said that, outside of the designation, there's very little difference between a state dinner and an official dinner, at least from the chef's perspective. The preparations were very similar, and there was always politics involved, whether it was a warm and inviting welcome for a close friend of the United States, or reciprocation for an especially grand welcome the President and First Lady had received overseas. Other reasons for a state dinner might be to commemorate the signing of a treaty or an agreement, and those occasions were often planned several months out, sometimes timed to coincide with the news. However, I was not privy to the reasons for individual events; the only information made available on the Ushers Information site was the visiting dignitary, his or her home country, and the anticipated number of guests.

Historically, state dinners typically welcomed no more than 120 guests, although there were exceptions, such as the outdoors, "off-premise" state dinner that the Kennedys hosted in honor of the President of Pakistan, Ayub Khan, at Mount Vernon in 1961, where 138 guests joined the festivities. The Clintons made it clear that they'd be upping the ante right off the bat, when on June 13, 1994, they hosted about 180 guests for a state dinner honoring Emperor Akihito of Japan.

State dinners, as Mrs. Clinton envisioned them, were not just an opportunity to show off American hospitality; they were a chance to parade American food and wine before the world, especially because the dinners were covered so extensively by the media. We take it for granted now, but American cuisine underwent a sea change in the late 1980s and early 1990s. The American lust for innovation and exploration finally found its way into our culinary culture. In restaurants, starting in California and New York and working inward toward the heartland, a bold, new American cuisine was being defined, one which incorporated myriad international influences and featured seasonal and regional ingredients, befitting our melting-pot heritage and the foods grown, raised, or produced right here at home, or fished from our inland and coastal waters.

Mrs. Clinton wanted to see all of that influence reflected at the state dinners, but also wanted it to be measured. This desire was very much compatible with my own point of view that, while much of the food being turned out by American restaurant kitchens was exciting and laudable, distinguished by witty interpretations of classic dishes, or by the seamless weaving together of ingredients from disparate origins, some chefs at that time were overly creative, each one trying to be more outlandish than the next—combining ingredients that had no business being together; composing dishes that were more cerebral than satisfying; and favoring presentations that were often striking but made actually eating the food a logistical nightmare. In light of this sentiment, I was heartened to learn that Mrs. Clinton wanted to maintain a sense of formality, a connection to our culinary heritage, and a respect for the fact that this was still the White House—anything that was served there should be indisputably sophisticated.

After careful consideration, we devised an approach that wove all of these mandates together. One decision was to make at least one course a tip of the hat to the guest country. So in the case of Emperor Akihito, we made the main course Arctic char—a now-popular fish that was all but unknown to the general public at that time—with lobster sausage. Arctic char wasn't a Japanese ingredient per se, but had a Pacific Rim feeling to it thanks to our focus on ingredients from our own Pacific Coast and to our decision to serve fish as a main course. This choice of main course also broke two longstanding White House traditions: We served fish rather than meat as a state-dinner main course, and paired the fish with red wine instead of white (which would be the traditional selection to accompany fish), selecting a pinot noir from Oregon. The wine was an inspired selection by Gary Walters, who is quite knowledgeable about the subject and often—as he did for this event—made selections in collaboration with a Northern California wine consultant named David Berkley, who owned and operated a variety of businesses in the wine and food industries and currently owns a wine and specialty foods shop in Sacramento. Gary and David knew that the red wine was an apt foil for the relatively fatty fish, and that the selection would raise eyebrows and be a subject of conversation and media coverage.

To keep from changing things too quickly, we did serve the main course from platters, both to give the butlers a chance to get used to the new system, and also to hedge our bets and see how the new, plated first courses were received.

For the first course, we presented a distinctly contemporary American starter that sang with Southwestern flavors: Seared Breast of Quail with White Corn Custard, Grilled Vegetables, and a Tomato-Cumin Sauce.

All of this innovation was balanced by adhering to one of the traditional, European-based meal features that had long been in effect at the White House: serving the salad—typically field greens with fruit, cheese, and/or other accompaniments—between the main course and dessert.

Ann Stock did a lot of research as she prepared the first state dinner. With the exception of the arrival ceremony—a series of processions featuring a color guard, honor guard, the introduction of the First Family and the visiting leader and his or her spouse, and so on, the logistics of which were dictated by military protocol—the stylistic flourishes that defined each state dinner were up to the discretion of each administration. Ann read about fifty news articles on past state dinners, and talked to White House staffers past and present—though she did not, it's worth noting, contact any former social secretaries.

It was decided that the Clintons' first state dinner would be a formal, white-tie affair, the first since the Reagan administration. The reason for this was the same as the reason the First Lady chose to have the dinner in the Rose Garden in the hot days of June: The Emperor's father, Emperor Hirohito, had been the guest of honor at a white-tie dinner in the Rose Garden in 1976.

It was also decided that the Clintons would sit at a long table for twelve, elevated slightly above the floor. The other guests, after a model forged by Jacqueline Kennedy, would be seated at round tables.

To ensure that each phase of the evening would proceed smoothly, on the Friday before the dinner, Ann organized a black-tie dinner in the Rose Garden to serve as a kind of dress rehearsal for the kitchen and the butlers. This was welcome news to me, because one of the most challenging aspects of the dinner would no doubt be coordinating my team with the rest of the House staff, especially because state dinners, all four courses, are served in astonishingly fast time—about forty minutes! This is to allow time for the rest of the evening's events, including the military reception, the reception on the State Floor, and the post-dinner entertainment.

The guest list for the state dinner was suitably star-studded. Oprah Winfrey was there, as were Jane Fonda and Ted Turner.

On the day of the dinner, I was introduced to what would become a regular part of my job:

briefing the media on what would be served at state dinners, and why. Mrs. Clinton, Chief Florist Nancy Clarke, Executive Pastry Chef Roland Mesnier, and I took turns describing our roles in the evening to the media (usually assembled for this exchange in the State Dining Room), then answered a few questions.

The dinner seemed to be a success. Ann Stock told me that after dinner, the President and Emperor Akihito walked down a torch-lit lane near the Rose Garden with the Washington Mon-

THE WHITE HOUSE

WASHINGTON

June 15, 1994

Mr. Walter Scheib
White House Chef

Dear Walter:

Congratulations! The food and its presentation at our first State Dinner were wonderful. I am still receiving rave reviews.

I suspect that *The New York Times* article caused a discussion that will have us go to plated service. What do you think?

You have my admiration and appreciation, Walter, for your creative talent. Roland, Franette and you really outdid yourself. Many thanks.

Sincerely,

Ann Stock
Social Secretary

Ann Stock went out of her way to show appreciation for our efforts with thoughtful notes like this one after the state dinner for Japan. *(Courtesy Walter Scheib 3rd)*

ument illuminated against the night sky behind them. Musicians were playing "Autumn Leaves" in the background, and the President began singing the song. The Emperor, who had attended Harvard and was familiar with American culture, started humming along. The next day, she confirmed that the Emperor, and the Clintons, had been delighted with the dinner.

So were the media. Writing in the June 14, 2004, *New York Times*, Marian Burros reported that "there was not a French sauce in the lot. Gone were the saddles of veal, fish mousses in aspic, truffle sauces made from long-simmering stocks. Mr. Scheib served what he described as regional American. . . . "

Ms. Burros also took note of the departure from traditional service. "With French service," she wrote, "the guests help themselves from large platters. American service is the same as restaurant service: the food is served on plates and brought to the individual diners."

The *Washington Post*'s Phyllis C. Richman noted the wine selection: "And contrary to the axiom 'white wine with fish, red wine with meat,'" she wrote, "it was not the quail but the char that was served with pinot noir." She also wrote that wine expert Robert Parker "praised the choices."

We had hit a home run.

State dinners were yet another reminder of how much my job put me in the spotlight. About six months after the dinner for Emperor Akihito, I got a call from a representative of an Icelandic trade organization, inviting me and my family on an all-expense-paid trip to Iceland, as a thank-you for all the attention that had been focused on Arctic char since the dinner. I replied that as a government employee I was not allowed to accept it, and that even if I were, I was much too busy to take such a trip. I told him that he probably wanted to rescind the invitation anyway, because "the char we served was actually purchased from Alaska."

"It doesn't matter," he said. "After all the media coverage of that dinner, sales of char went up ten times."

Roland and Me

There was one component of the First Family's meals and special-event menus that I had no role in: dessert. That was the purview of Executive Pastry Chef Roland Mesnier.

Originally hired by Rosalynn Carter back in 1979, Roland was a French pastry chef straight from Central Casting: A paunchy and expressive figure whose natural accent was still very much intact, and who was technically brilliant and rather witty. Roland's creations were rightfully famous, especially because of the thematic and colorful desserts he'd create using spun sugar, sculpted fruits, and so on.

However, from the time I arrived at the White House, there was friction between me and Roland. I always chalked it up to the fact that he had been the lone White House chef to receive substantial, ongoing media attention for the past fifteen years. I got quite a bit from the moment I was hired, stealing some of his spotlight, so to speak, though I did nothing to promote myself. If anything, I shied away from such attention at the time.

Within two months of my arrival, Roland and I began to keep to ourselves—we didn't fight, but we did little more than peacefully co-exist. To ensure that his desserts would be compatible, and not compete, with my savory courses for special events, the Usher's Office would share a copy of my menus with him and he would determine what to serve after reviewing it.

For one dinner, Roland noticed that we were putting oranges in a salad that didn't have oranges in its name. He approached me and told me that his dessert had oranges in it, but that he would've made something else if he knew the full contents of my salad. From that day forward, in addition to providing a menu to the Usher's Office, I would also scribble the names of any featured fruits not mentioned in the dish name . . . and that's how Roland and I coordinated our menus for everything from a luncheon for ten to a state dinner for hundreds, even though we saw each other all the time.

JUST DON'T CALL IT A TENT

Starting with a state dinner for China in 1997, certain very large functions featured seating in the Rose Garden, on which a pavilion was set up for the occasion. A pavilion is basically a tent, but because of the expense involved in procuring and erecting this one, we were forbidden by the Usher's Office from using that word, a ban that in time became an in-joke among the staff. But in truth, the pavilion was no ordinary tent. It was air-conditioned, and there were chandeliers that appeared to be hanging from its ceiling, though they were, of course, actually suspended from unseen support beams. It also had a wooden floor covered with carpeting.

Grilled Arctic Char with Wild Mushroom Risotto

SERVES 4

This is a simplified version of a dish served at the first Clinton state dinner for the Emperor of Japan. At that time, Arctic char was virtually unknown in the American marketplace, but we managed to have the fish delivered to the White House the day after it was caught.

You can organize your time in one of two ways: Marinate the fish while cooking the risotto, or, if you prefer to divide the cooking into stages, make the risotto up to two hours in advance (see box, page 130), and marinate the fish 30 to 40 minutes before you want to serve the dish.

¼ cup olive oil
1 tablespoon freshly squeezed lime juice
2 teaspoons chopped fresh basil leaves plus 4 whole leaves for garnish
1 teaspoon roasted garlic puree (see box, page 23)
4 skinless 1-inch-thick Arctic char fillets (4 to 6 ounces each)
Wild Mushroom Risotto (recipe follows)
Salt and freshly ground black pepper
Reserved mushrooms from the risotto, for garnish

1. In a small glass bowl, combine the oil, lime juice, chopped basil, and garlic puree. Stir together well. Put the fish fillets in a glass baking dish large enough to hold them in a single layer. Pour the marinade over them, turn once to coat, cover with plastic wrap, and refrigerate for 30 to 40 minutes. At this point, prepare the Wild Mushroom Risotto, if you haven't made it in advance.

2. Prepare a charcoal grill for grilling, letting the coals burn until covered with white ash, preheat a gas grill to medium-high, or preheat a stovetop grill pan or cast-iron skillet over high heat. Remove the fish from the marinade, letting any excess marinade run off and brushing off any marinade solids. Season the fish on both sides with salt and pepper, and grill for 4 to 5 minutes per side, turning carefully with a spatula, or until just opaque in the center. (If the fish is less than 1 inch thick, cook for 3 to 4 minutes per side.)

3. To serve, divide the risotto among four wide, shallow bowls or dinner plates. Put one fish fillet on top of the risotto in each bowl and top with the remaining mushrooms. Garnish each serving with a basil leaf and serve.

Wild Mushroom Risotto

SERVES 4

This risotto can also be served on its own as a first course, as a side dish to roasted and grilled meats, or paired with a simple salad for a perfect lunch.

FOR THE MUSHROOMS

2 tablespoons olive oil

1 tablespoon very finely chopped garlic

1 tablespoon very finely chopped shallot

6 ounces mixed wild mushrooms, such as morels and chanterelles, wiped clean and cut into bite-size pieces (about 1 cup)

¼ cup dry white wine

Salt and freshly ground black pepper

FOR THE RISOTTO

3 tablespoons olive oil

⅓ cup finely diced Spanish onion

1 tablespoon finely diced shallot

1 cup Arborio rice or other risotto rice

¼ cup dry white wine

5 to 6 cups homemade or store-bought low-sodium chicken or fish stock, simmering in a pot on a back burner

2 tablespoons crème fraîche or heavy cream

2 teaspoons grated lemon zest

1 teaspoon roasted garlic puree (see box, page 23)

Salt and freshly ground black pepper

1. Sauté the mushrooms: Heat the oil in a 10-inch, heavy-bottomed sauté pan set over medium heat. Add the garlic and shallot and sauté until softened but not browned, 2 to 3 minutes. Add the mushrooms and sauté until they begin to give off their liquid, 3 to 4 minutes. Add the white wine and let it reduce until nearly dry, 3 to 4 minutes, stirring occasionally. Season to taste with salt and pepper.

2. Transfer the mushrooms to a baking sheet and spread them out so they cool as quickly as possible. Keep at room temperature for up to 2 hours.

3. Make the risotto: Heat the oil in a heavy-bottomed medium saucepan over medium heat. Add the onion and shallot and sauté until softened but not browned, 3 to 4 minutes. Add the rice and cook, stirring, for 3 to 4 minutes to coat the rice with the oil. Add the wine and cook, stirring constantly, until the rice has absorbed almost all of it, 4 to 5 minutes.

4. Ladle 2 cups of stock into the saucepan and cook, stirring constantly, until the stock is absorbed by the rice. Continue to add stock in ½-cup increments, cooking and stirring, and adding more only after the previous amount has been absorbed. Continue until you have used all of the stock, 25 to 30 minutes total cooking time, or until the rice grains are al dente and the risotto is still a bit soupy.

5. To finish, fold in the crème fraîche, lemon zest, garlic puree, and two thirds of the mushrooms. Season with salt and pepper. Serve topped with the remaining mushrooms, or use at this point with the Grilled Arctic Char.

> **TO MAKE RISOTTO IN ADVANCE:** Leave out the last addition or two of stock, transfer the rice to a baking sheet, and spread it out to cool. Transfer it to an airtight container and refrigerate for up to 2 hours. To proceed, transfer the reserved risotto to a clean, dry saucepan, gently warm it over medium heat, and stir in the final addition(s) of stock.

THE HOTTEST TICKET IN TOWN

Just as our holiday receptions continued to grow as we found ways to increase their capacity, Mrs. Clinton wanted to be inclusive and grow the state dinners as much as possible. Every time we cleared a hurdle, we had a new one set in our path.

In October of that same year, 1994, we were to host a state dinner for Nelson Mandela, President of the Republic of South Africa, who had not visited the White House since being set free from prison on Robben Island in February 1990. Since we had managed about two hundred people in the summer, it was decided that this time we would host two hundred twenty guests, an increase of about twenty percent.

To decide who would be invited to state and formal dinners, starting with the state dinner for Japan, Ann and her social office comrades created what they called "the grid"—a chart of who had to be invited, who should be invited, and who wanted to be invited. An invitation to a state dinner is a hot ticket in Washington, and as soon as word broke of an upcoming dinner, people would begin to lobby Ann and her colleagues, explaining why they belonged on the list.

Ann's first step was to ask the various White House departments, and key personnel such as the Chief of Staff, the State Department, the National Security Council, the Press Office, and so on, to recommend people who should be invited. The social office also researched famous Americans from the country of, or connected to the culture of, the visiting dignitary—in the case of Mandela, South Africa. Among the famous African-Americans at this dinner were Whitney Houston, Jesse Jackson, former New York City Mayor David Dinkins, Harry Belafonte, and poet Maya Angelou.

There was also a certain amount of finesse that went into creating the guest list. A real effort was made to be sure the mix of people would create the best, most interesting possible event for the guest of honor. Other decisions were made for the same reason, such as setting the Akihito dinner in the Rose Garden in memory of his father's visit. In the case of Mandela, it was decided that the dinner would take place in the East Room, because it was the room in which President Lyndon Johnson signed the Civil Rights Act of 1964.

Above: From right to left: Patrice Olivon, me, Gordon Marr, and another helpful cook preparing a dish for the Mandela state dinner.
Opposite: Patrice Olivon, right, one of my stalwart Service by Agreement cooks, and I in the kitchen during the state dinner for Nelson Mandela. *(Courtesy William J. Clinton Presidential Library)*

The staging area for the Mandela state dinner. Just one of three courses my team would serve in under forty minutes. *(Courtesy William J. Clinton Presidential Library)*

It was a tall order to cut the Mandela guest list down to size; everybody wanted to be there, including the entire Congressional Black Caucus. By the end of the day, two overflow tables had to be added to the Green Room, and while some key members were invited to the dinner, a separate luncheon with Mandela was arranged for all members of the Congressional Black Caucus.

Although this was only my third state dinner, I realized then and can safely say now that no visiting head of state inspired as much excitement as President Mandela among the White House staff during President Clinton's time in office. For me, it was an honor to serve someone who had suffered so much for his beliefs. After our new protocol of featuring a dish that saluted the guest of honor's homeland, we served a starter of Layered Late-Summer Vegetables with Lemongrass and Red Curry—loosely based on the South African style of food called Cape Malay cuisine, which combines ingredients of South Africa, seasonings of South Asia and India, and cooking techniques of Europe. We also invited a guest chef–collaborator to this evening, African-American chef Patrick Clark, formerly of Tavern on the Green in New York (and before that, the Hay-Adams Hotel across the street from the White House), with whom we conceived the main course, Halibut with a Sesame Crust and Carrot Juice Broth.

Once it became clear that we could serve this many people, the social office began playing with how best to use different room combinations. In the wintertime, for example, we would use the East Room and accommodate any overflow in the Green Room. In time, we'd use the entire State Floor, placing a number of tables in each room, and the President and First Lady would move to different rooms throughout the evening so that all of their guests got at least some time in their presence.

An added logistical concern on these evenings was the serviceware; we simply didn't have enough of any one china pattern to accommodate all the guests, so we'd plate food on different china in each room—the Roosevelt china in one room, the Johnson in another, the Reagan in a third, and so on. (The Clinton china, incidentally, was not commissioned until November 2000, on the occasion of the two-hundredth anniversary of the House. It features a gold rendering of the north side of the House, the first time that official White House china ever depicted the White House itself.)

The Clintons welcome South African President Nelson Mandela; for me, it was an honor to cook for him. *(Courtesy William J. Clinton Presidential Library)*

★ ★ ★

Layered Late-Summer Vegetables with Lemongrass and Red Curry

SERVES 4

In honor of a state dinner we were holding for Nelson Mandela, I created this dish in the spirit of South Africa's Cape Malay cuisine, which blends South African ingredients, South Asian and Indian seasonings, and European technique. Fresh, gently cooked vegetables are set off against a sauce brimming with intense Asian flavors.

You can make this with any vegetables that are ripe and in season, as many or as few types as you like; the secret is to not overcook or over-season them, which will mask their freshness. This dish is best served at room temperature.

You will need four ring molds, 3 inches in diameter and 2 inches high.

1 medium cucumber (about 4 ounces)

Salt

1 tablespoon seasoned rice vinegar

1 tablespoon chopped fresh dill

4 ounces butternut squash, peeled, seeded, and sliced ¼ inch thick (about ⅓ cup sliced)

2 tablespoons olive oil

Freshly ground black pepper

2 to 4 potatoes (4 ounces) small red-skinned potatoes, sliced crosswise ¼ inch thick (about ½ cup slices)

1 medium zucchini (about 4 ounces), sliced ¼ inch thick (about ½ cup sliced

½ tablespoon very finely chopped garlic

¼ cup uncooked corn kernels (fresh or thawed frozen, drained)

¼ cup thinly sliced leek, white part only

1 medium red bell pepper, roasted (see box, page 51), skin and seeds removed, and very thinly sliced

1. Peel the cucumber, halve lengthwise, scoop out the seeds, and cut it crosswise into ¼-inch slices. Put the cucumber slices in a colander, toss with ½ tablespoon salt, and set in a sink to drain for 10 to 15 minutes to extract any excess moisture. Pat dry with paper towels.

2. Stir together the rice vinegar and dill in a small bowl. Add the cucumber, season with salt and pepper, and toss. Set aside.

3. Preheat a 12-inch, heavy-bottomed sauté pan over medium-high heat. Brush the squash slices with ½ tablespoon of the oil, season with salt and pepper, add to the pan, and cook just until tender, 1 to 2 minutes per side. Transfer to a baking sheet and set aside.

4. Carefully wipe out the sauté pan. Brush the potato slices with ½ tablespoon of the oil, season with salt and pepper, add to the pan, and cook over medium-high heat just until tender, 1 to 2 minutes per side. Transfer to the baking sheet with the squash.

5. Wipe out the pan. Brush the zucchini slices with ½ table-spoon of the oil, season with salt and pepper, add to the pan, and cook over medium-high heat just until tender, about 30 seconds. (The zucchini is tender enough that you only need cook the slices on 1 side.) Transfer to the baking sheet with the squash.

6. Wipe out the pan. Add ½ tablespoon of the oil and heat it over medium heat. Add the garlic and sauté for 30 seconds. Add the corn and leek and sauté until just al dente, about 3 minutes.

Lemongrass and Red Curry Dressing
(recipe follows)

Crispy noodles, such as rice noodles,
for garnish (optional; see box)

4 sprigs fresh Thai basil or regular
basil

7. Layer the vegetables into the ring molds, in any order you like, so long as the zucchini is on top. Place each ring mold in the center of a salad plate. Drizzle 2 to 3 tablespoons of the dressing around the ring mold on each plate, then carefully remove the mold. Garnish with crisp noodles, if desired, and basil leaves. Serve.

Lemongrass and Red Curry Dressing

MAKES ABOUT ¾ CUP

½ tablespoon olive oil

1 tablespoon very finely chopped
shallot

2 teaspoons grated garlic

2 teaspoons grated lemongrass
(white base portion only, outer layers peeled off and removed)

1 teaspoon finely grated lime zest

1 teaspoon red curry paste (available in specialty stores and gourmet markets; see Sources, page 302)

1 teaspoon grated fresh ginger

1 kaffir lime leaf (optional; see Sources, page 302)

½ cup homemade or store-bought low-sodium chicken stock

½ cup unsweetened coconut milk

1 tablespoon honey

¼ teaspoon fish sauce (available in Asian markets and many supermarkets; see Sources, page 302)

1. Heat the oil in a small saucepan over medium heat. Add the shallot, garlic, lemongrass, and lime zest, and sauté until softened but not browned, 2 to 3 minutes. Add the curry paste, ginger, and lime leaf, if using, and cook, stirring, for 2 to 3 minutes.

2. Add the stock, coconut milk, honey, and fish sauce. Bring to a simmer and let simmer for 10 minutes. Strain through a fine-mesh strainer set over a bowl, pressing down on the solids with a wooden spoon or spatula to extract as much flavorful liquid as possible. Discard the solids and let the liquid cool to room temperature. (The dressing can be covered and refrigerated for up to 1 week. It will separate; whisk and warm it to reconstitute.)

TO FRY RICE NOODLES (OR WONTON SKINS): Pour vegetable oil into a heavy-bottomed pot to a depth of 4 inches. Heat over medium heat to 375°F. Line a large plate with paper towels. Carefully lower the noodles into the oil in small batches, letting them cook until crispy, about 30 seconds. Immediately remove them with a slotted spoon, drain on the paper towels, and season with salt. Fried noodles can be refrigerated overnight in an airtight container. Let come to room temperature before serving.

THE BIGGER, THE BETTER

And so it went, year after year, the dinners growing bigger and bigger. I don't think that in 1994, there was a member of Mrs. Clinton's staff who said "we're going to do dinner for seven hundred one day," but by the time the year 2000 rolled around, we did just that. It was a dinner for Prime Minister Atal Vajpayee of India, with seven hundred guests.

As dinners grew, logistical challenges presented themselves. One especially memorable one was what to do about the receiving lines. The President and Mrs. Clinton personally welcomed each guest to a state dinner in the East Room, which was not particularly difficult during the first few dinners, although the line that wound through the floor sometimes got in the way of the smooth flow of guests and butlers. As the guest lists approached four and five hundred, however, there was very real concern that a pileup would occur on the State Floor.

Office of the Curator

Located on the ground floor of the White House, the Office of the Curator—home to a head curator plus a group of assistants that fluctuated between three and four in number during my years there—is responsible for maintaining the history of the White House. The art, furniture, and decorative objects in the White House all fall under the auspices of this office, which keeps records about those items, as well as about the history of the House and its occupants. The office is also charged with the study of the House and its history. One might think that this office had existed since the House was first erected, but in fact it was Jacqueline Kennedy who hired the first White House curator, and also created the White House Historical Association.

I typically had two reasons to speak to the Office of the Curator: One was to find out how many pieces of a desired type of serviceware, especially plates, platters, and any antique pieces, existed, and to procure those items for the functions themselves. The other reason was if an accident occurred and one of the pieces was damaged or broken. Breakage is a daily occurrence in most hotels and restaurant kitchens, but because our serviceware was invaluable, the White House cooks and butlers tried very hard not to break anything. If they did, we had to file a written report, and bring all of the pieces to the Office of the Curator. On awkward occasions when a guest broke something, a curator would interview a butler or other staff members who were present, so that a written report could be created for the file.

One added incentive to not break any historical pieces was that this was a pet peeve of Gary Walters. The joke in the White House was that Gary could hear a plate drop no matter how far away he was, and nothing made him angrier. Once, at the start of the holiday season onslaught, he suspended one of my SBA cooks for six months for cracking a wall sconce, recently restored in England, by bumping it with a rolling cart. It didn't matter that losing an extra set of hands at such a crucial time was a major inconvenience to me—he felt that there really had to be very low tolerance for this kind of mishap.

Mrs. Clinton, Chief Usher Gary Walters, Social Secretary Capricia Marshall, and me reviewing plans for the state dinner for China, November 2000. *(Courtesy William J. Clinton Presidential Library)*

The beginning of a solution presented itself when Mrs. Clinton accompanied the President to a G8 Summit (a meeting of the seven leading industrial nations plus Russia) overseas. At a dinner one night, Mrs. Clinton was impressed with the very orderly way a receiving line had been arranged separate from the party proper. After some brainstorming, she devised a new way to be sure each guest was personally greeted by the First Family.

Upon arrival, guests would be handed a card that told them what time to report to the Green Room, where a small group would await their turn before being summoned into the Blue Room, where the First Family would receive them. After meeting the First Family, and having their picture taken, they'd proceed to the Red Room and back out to the party. So that the President and First Lady would know to whom they were talking, the guests would present their cards on their way into the Blue Room and after they left, Ann or one of her team would jot a note about what each person was wearing so that his or her photograph could be identified when it was developed and a print could be sent to the guests to commemorate their visit.

As we grew and grew, we maintained our traditions, such as trying to incorporate a flourish from the guest's country. For the dinner celebrating Indian cuisine, we began with a Chilled Green Pea and Cilantro Soup ladled around Darjeeling Tea-Smoked Poussin. On another occasion, I asked Peter Moutsos, a Greek national who was part of my SBA team, and husband of one of my staff members, for help conceiving a menu for the state dinner for Greece.

In my opinion, our most fluid menus featured Asian influences, and not just at state dinners. I created many other meals that celebrated Asian flavors, such as the luncheon we prepared for the Queen of Thailand that featured Tea-Smoked Breast of Duck with Lemongrass and Basil Infusion; Pan-Roasted Yellowtail Snapper with Coconut Tamarind Sambal; and Asian Greens and Peppered Mango with Ginger Threads, Candied Pine Nuts, and a Champagne-Ginger Dressing.

State dinners also offered a window into the native customs of visiting dignitaries. For example, King Hassan II of Morocco arrived with his own tasters and tea makers in tow. The ever-larger parties caused great excitement in the House, but there was one team that wasn't so enchanted: the curators. To have hundreds upon hundreds of people milling through the White House—which, again, is essentially a museum that's overseen by the National Park Service—brushing up against pictures and lamps, plopping down in chairs, and handling glasses and plates, created tremendous anxiety, but there was nothing they could do about it, and, in time—once they saw that the First Family shared their reverence for the House and its history—the curators began to participate more visibly in White House events. My impression was that they even began to enjoy themselves. Once they saw what could be done, while still preserving the integrity of the House and its history, how could they help it?

THE TIPPING POINT

Just before the Mandela dinner, we hosted Russian Federation President Boris Yeltsin. It was a fun and festive evening, and as usual certain touches were decided upon in honor of the guest, such as a course of Vodka-Marinated Salmon with Cucumber Salad and Kasha Pilaf. President Yeltsin, who enjoys vodka, and plenty of it, had a great time that night . . . almost too great a time. The next morning, the butlers reported to me that at one point during the dinner, they stopped serving him any more alcohol. For the rest of the meal, his wine glass was replenished with pure, unalloyed H_2O.

But that didn't stop the guest of honor from a bit of irreverence later in the evening. The Yale Russian Chorus was the post-dinner entertainment, and when he heard them singing, President Yeltsin rushed over to them and with sweeping, exaggerated gestures, began conducting the group—causing more than a little confusion.

Vodka-Marinated Salmon with Cucumber Salad and Kasha Pilaf

SERVES 4

This spin on traditional gravlax features a little kick of vodka. The kasha pilaf was a tip of the toque to our Russian guest, Boris Yeltsin.

¼ cup sea salt

¼ cup turbinado sugar or packed light brown sugar

1 tablespoon freshly ground black pepper

1 tablespoon grated fresh ginger

1 tablespoon crushed juniper berries

1 pound center-cut boneless salmon fillet, with the skin on

½ cup chopped fresh dill

2 tablespoons vodka

Kasha Pilaf (recipe follows)

Cucumber Salad (recipe follows)

Dill sprigs, for garnish

1. Marinate the salmon: In a small bowl, combine the salt, sugar, pepper, ginger, and juniper. Put the salmon skin side down in a glass baking dish. Rub the spice mixture into the flesh side of the fish, making sure to use it all. Pat the dill onto the flesh side of the fillet, and sprinkle with vodka. Cover the salmon with a sheet of plastic wrap and set a heavy object (such as a plate or small casserole topped with canned goods) on top of the salmon to weight it down.

2. Refrigerate for 48 hours, basting every 12 hours with the brine that forms in the dish.

3. After 48 hours, remove the salmon from the pan, scrape away the marinade solids and excess salt, and pat dry with paper towels. The salmon will keep, wrapped in plastic and refrigerated, for up to 2 weeks.

4. Divide the kasha pilaf among four salad plates. Slice the salmon and arrange thin slices of salmon on top of the kasha. Spoon some cucumber salad to the side. Garnish with dill sprigs and serve.

> **TO SLICE SALMON:** Using a very sharp, thin-bladed knife, ideally a slicing knife with at least a 10-inch blade, slice the fish against the grain into paper-thin slices, starting at the peak of the fillet and slicing down toward the edges. Periodically rinse the blade under cold running water and wipe dry to ensure it stays cool and clean, which will provide the cleanest cut.

Kasha Pilaf

1 cup kasha (buckwheat groats)
4 tablespoons olive oil
⅓ cup diced Spanish onion
1 tablespoon chopped garlic
2 cups homemade or store-bought
    low-sodium chicken stock
¼ cup pine nuts
¼ cup freshly squeezed lemon juice
¼ cup finely chopped dried apricots
¼ cup chopped fresh dill
3 tablespoons chopped scallions,
    green and white parts

1. Heat a medium, heavy-bottomed sauté pan over medium heat. Add the kasha and toast about 2 minutes, shaking the pan to prevent scorching, until fragrant. Remove from the heat.

2. Heat 1 tablespoon oil in a medium saucepan over medium-high heat. Add the onion and garlic and sauté until softened but not browned, about 2 minutes. Add the kasha and cook, stirring, for 2 minutes. Add the stock, bring to a simmer, cover, and let simmer until the kasha is fluffy and the grains are separated, about 15 minutes. Transfer the kasha to a bowl and fluff with a fork. Let cool to room temperature.

3. Heat a medium, heavy-bottomed sauté pan over medium heat. Add the pine nuts and toast about 2 minutes until fragrant, shaking the pan to prevent scorching. Transfer to a large bowl and let cool. Add the lemon juice, apricots, dill, remaining 3 tablespoons oil, and scallions, and stir well. Add the kasha mixture and toss. Let cool and serve at room temperature.

Cucumber Salad

1 small cucumber (about 6 ounces)
Salt
2 tablespoons Dijon mustard
1 tablespoon freshly squeezed
    lemon juice
1 teaspoon dry mustard
1 teaspoon sugar
1 egg yolk
¼ cup olive oil
3 tablespoons chopped fresh dill
Freshly ground black pepper

1. Peel the cucumber, halve it lengthwise, scoop out the seeds, and cut it crosswise into ¼-inch slices. You should have about ½ cup. Put the cucumber slices in a colander, toss with ½ tablespoon salt, and set in a sink to drain for 15 minutes to extract any excess moisture. Pat dry with paper towels.

2. In a medium bowl, whisk together the Dijon mustard, lemon juice, dry mustard, sugar, and egg yolk. Slowly add the oil in a thin steam, whisking to make an emulsion. Stir in the dill and season with salt and pepper. Fold in the cucumber and let marinate at room temperature for 30 minutes or up to 2 hours in the refrigerator. If refrigerating, let come to room temperature before serving.

GUESS WHO'S COMING TO DINNER

The guest lists at state dinners were always a who's-who of the governmental, business, diplomatic, and military communities, plus a mix of famous faces from the worlds of the arts, entertainment, and the media. Being invited to a state dinner is an honor. They're very glamorous affairs.

Some of the biggest names to attend the state dinners for which I was the chef included, from the political realm, Vice President Al Gore, and his wife, Tipper, who attended just about every state dinner; former Secretary of State Henry Kissinger; and all of the most well known senators and congresspeople. From the worlds of arts and entertainment there were Gregory Peck; actresses Goldie Hawn, Mia Farrow, and Candice Bergen; authors John Grisham, Kurt Vonnegut, and Amy Tan; architect I.M. Pei; producer-director Steven Spielberg, then-Miramax chief Harvey Weinstein, newswoman Diane Sawyer, and designer Vera Wang.

I was never introduced to these guests, given that I was mostly behind closed kitchen doors. And while that was fine with me, I'd be lying if I said that my crew and I didn't frequently throw open those doors to take in some of the star power.

FRENCH TOAST

It seems that no matter how far our national cuisine comes, we'll always be compared to the French and their food.

I usually learned about state dinners from the social secretary, then the Usher's Office. But late in 1995, Mrs. Clinton paid me a visit and personally put an upcoming dinner on my radar.

We were going to be hosting French President Jacques Chirac who, although he had visited the White House, had not yet been honored with a state dinner by President Clinton. It was the only time I had ever seen the First Lady the least bit skittish about a visiting head of state.

"Walter, this is very important to me," she said, the seriousness evident in her tone of voice, the look in her eyes, and her posture. "I want us to put our best foot forward." The message was plain: Don't screw this up.

"Yes, ma'am," I said.

A number of decisions were made to ensure the dinner's success. Though by this time we were hosting events for hundreds of people, only 130 were invited to this one, with more invited to join them for a reception after the meal. The media didn't help us relax about our mission, whipping up stories that French food was making a return to the White House.

Despite all the anxiety about the event, the evening was quite a fun one. There was some

A toast to French President Jacques Chirac at the state dinner in his honor, February 1996. *(Courtesy William J. Clinton Presidential Library)*

especially memorable clowning around with actor Michael Douglas, who had recently starred in the movie *The American President*. When Mr. Douglas made his way to the East Wing entrance, Ann Stock introduced herself to him, saying, "Hi, I'm your social secretary."

When Mr. Douglas met the President, President Clinton said, "Hey, I think I'm standing in your place."

The President then traded places with Mr. Douglas, positioning the star next to Mr. Chirac and taking his place on the guest side of the line. Mr. Douglas seemed both stunned and amused.

For my part, the menu was among the most restrained we had ever served; Mrs. Clinton and I decided that we would present a regional American menu—less cutting edge than most of our state dinner menus, but still brimming with big, bold flavors, and complemented by incredible American wines. We decided not to offer an overt nod to the visiting country, although the salad—Layered Artichoke, Leek, and Herbed Cheese with Young Greens and Endive and Balsamic Dressing—featured French accents.

Some of the dishes included some of Mrs. Clinton's favorite foods. There was Lemon and Thyme–Scented Lobster with Roasted Eggplant Soup—the First Lady adored eggplant—to start, and for the main course, Rack of Lamb with Winter Fruit and Pecans, Sweet Potato Puree, Root Vegetables, and a Tarragon-Huckleberry Sauce.

That's a seemingly subtle selection, but there's a lot going on there. President Clinton upped the ante when, during his toast, he named me, saying, "I feel compelled to make a full disclosure: Our chef at the White House, Walter Scheib, is an American." I was relieved to learn that, at the end of the dinner, President Chirac stood up and said, "I've heard a lot about American food. Well, if this is American food, it's okay with me."

The evening was a hit. The next morning, the *Washington Post* covered it under the headline, "Haute Boy! A Classy Bash," and described the toasts of both President Clinton and President Chirac. When I checked my mailbox at the White House, there was a handwritten note from Mrs. Clinton:

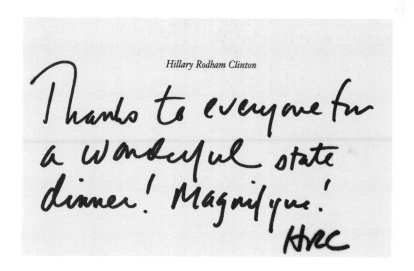

Hillary Rodham Clinton

Thanks to everyone for a wonderful state dinner! Magnifique!
HRC

(Courtesy Walter Scheib 3rd)

Daniel Shanks
Assistant Usher

In 1995, at the behest of Mrs. Clinton, the Usher's Office hired a new assistant usher. But this wasn't just another member of the team. This new person was to be an expert in wine and service who could select American wines on a par with the food we were serving, and help nudge the butlers' service skills up to a new level, bringing them more in line with contemporary American standards.

The person hired for this job was Daniel Shanks, a young veteran of the Napa Valley wine community who had worked there since 1974 including most recently as the sommelier for the very fine restaurant at the Domaine Chandon winery, where he had been for eleven years. He came with a golden Rolodex and an insider's knowledge of the American wine scene, especially Pinot Noir. Accordingly, he knew whom to call to secure rare and very limited bottlings that added even more flair to state dinners and other special occasions. This was an especially useful gift because the White House does not have a wine cellar; there's no warehoused collection of wines to call on spontaneously, so Daniel's expertise and contacts were essential to getting wines for state dinners and other functions on very short notice. Though Gary—who in conjunction with David Berkley and myself—had selected all wines up to this point in time, and continued to make the final decision, Daniel became his close and trusted advisor on this front and in time Gary's approvals became a mere technicality.

Daniel's superior knowledge allowed him to elevate the role of wine in state dinners, selecting wines that saluted the visiting dignitary while still celebrating America, the same way I did with the food. For example, for the dinner honoring Jacques Chirac, he selected wines produced by vintners of French origin who had emigrated to the United States and set up shop here.

On the service front, Daniel was a stickler for detail. For example, he would routinely canvas the dining area scrutinizing the table settings to make sure that they were properly aligned.

Daniel's enthusiasm for his work, and for food and wine, was contagious. The butlers took his cue, and began delivering dishes to their tables with more formality and pride. They also made a point of brushing up on what food and wine we were serving so that if a guest were to ask a question, they were likely to be able to answer it. In short, Daniel turned the butlers from accomplished domestic staff into knowledgeable waiters.

Lemon and Thyme–Scented Lobster with Roasted Eggplant Soup

SERVES 4

I devised this soup for the France state dinner in order to combine one of Mrs. Clinton's favorite vegetables, eggplant, with luxurious lobster. The earthy smokiness of the eggplant here is countered by refreshing citrus and herb. This dish can also be served as an entrée by thinning the soup with more stock to a sauce consistency, and serving a full lobster per person. Grilled pita or other flat bread is a natural accompaniment to this dish, allowing guests to mop up every drop of the soup.

2 live lobsters (2 pounds each)
2 tablespoons olive oil
2 tablespoons sliced shallots
1 tablespoon very finely chopped garlic
¼ cup dry white wine
3 tablespoons freshly squeezed lemon juice
4 teaspoons finely grated lemon zest
1 tablespoon chopped fresh thyme leaves plus 4 sprigs for garnish
Salt and freshly ground black pepper
Roasted Eggplant Soup (recipe follows)

1. Preheat the oven to 375°F.

2. Kill the lobster by driving a heavy kitchen knife right between their eyes, and pulling it down and away like a lever. Remove the tail and claws from the lobsters. Split the tails lengthwise and crack the claws but do not extract the meat; remove and reserve the tomalley (the green liver) from the lobster bodies as well as any juices. Put the cracked claws and split tails on a wire rack set over a baking sheet.

3. Heat the oil in a small sauté pan over medium heat. Add the shallots and garlic and sauté until softened but not browned, 2 to 3 minutes. Add the wine, lemon juice, 2 teaspoons of the lemon zest, and the chopped thyme, bring to a simmer, and reduce by one fourth, 2 to 3 minutes. Remove the pan from the heat and let cool to room temperature. Whisk in the tomalley and season with salt and pepper. Spoon this mixture into the lobster tail sections and onto the cracked claws.

4. Roast the lobster in the oven just until done, 10 to 12 minutes. Do not overcook or the meat will toughen. Let the lobster cool for 15 to 20 minutes, then remove the meat from the tail and cut it into 1-inch pieces. Remove the claw meat in one piece if possible and remove the cartridge from the claws and discard it.

5. Divide the meat among four wide, shallow soup bowls, putting one claw in each bowl. Ladle some soup around the meat in each bowl and garnish with the remaining 2 teaspoons of lemon zest and a thyme sprig.

Roasted Eggplant Soup

SERVES 4

3 tablespoons olive oil

2 medium eggplants (about 10 ounces each)

1 medium Spanish onion, chopped

1 tablespoon chopped garlic

1 tablespoon balsamic vinegar

1 tablespoon freshly squeezed lemon juice

½ teaspoon chopped fresh thyme leaves

About 4 cups homemade or store-bought low-sodium chicken stock

Salt and freshly ground black pepper

1. Lightly oil a cast-iron pan by pouring 1 tablespoon of the oil into it and rubbing it in with a paper towel. Heat the pan over medium-high heat, then add the eggplants to the pan, one at a time, if necessary, and cook, turning, until well charred, but not burnt, all over, about 20 minutes per eggplant. Transfer the eggplants to a colander and let cool. Once cool, halve the eggplants and scoop out the pulp and juices. Discard the skins.

2. Heat the remaining 2 tablespoons oil in a medium saucepan over medium heat. Add the onion and garlic and sauté until softened but not browned, 3 to 4 minutes.

3. Add the eggplant pulp and juice, the balsamic vinegar, lemon juice, and thyme and cook, stirring occasionally, for 2 to 3 minutes.

4. Add 4 cups of the chicken stock, stir, bring to a simmer, and let simmer for 5 minutes.

5. Transfer the contents of the pot to a the bowl of a food processor fitted with the steel blade and puree until smooth. (Be sure to leave the top of the feeding tube off to allow heat and steam to escape.)

6. Return the soup to the pot and add more stock, if necessary, to attain a medium soup consistency, a bit thinner than split pea soup. Taste and season with salt and pepper. The soup can be cooled, covered, and refrigerated for up to 2 days, or frozen for up to 1 month. Reheat gently before serving.

HOW LOW CAN YOU GO?

When the President of the Czech Republic, former playwright Vaclav Havel, visited the White House in September 1998, it was a source of great excitement, especially because of the musical entertainer he had personally requested: rock-and-roll legend Lou Reed. Things got a bit tense, however, during the dress rehearsal for the dinner. Mr. Reed had his amplifier turned up so loud that the chandeliers were shaking.

Capricia Marshall, who by this time had been promoted to social secretary, asked him to turn it down.

"You'll kill whoever's sitting in front of this speaker," she said.

Mr. Reed refused, saying, "This is my art, my music," and letting her know in no uncertain terms that he wouldn't turn down the volume.

A few hours later, he approached Capricia, and said, "By the way, I have a few friends coming and I'd like them seated right up front."

Capricia saw her opportunity and seized it. In a tone dripping with sarcasm, she replied, "Oh, Mr. Reed, you don't understand, these tables are my art. I can't just move people around like that." After a bemused you-got-me chuckle from Lou Reed, a deal was struck—a lower decibel level in exchange for a few front-row seats.

Vaclav Havel, with the microphone, makes a few remarks as the Clintons, rocker Lou Reed (third from right), and others look on. *(Courtesy William J. Clinton Presidential Library)*

Gingered Pheasant Consommé with Chanterelle and Sweet Potato Ravioli

SERVES 4

This dish was custom-designed to suit guest of honor Vaclav Havel. His staff requested that we serve fish as a main course, so we turned to poultry for our first course. In order to make something state dinner–worthy, we fashioned an elegant, and rare, pheasant consommé, an unexpected twist on the classic, clarified broth.

This recipe is one of the more technically challenging in the book. It incorporates a number of classic techniques: preparing a stock, clarifying a consommé, making and rolling out pasta dough, and cutting and filling ravioli. While we made everything from scratch in the White House, you can certainly turn to alternative poultry for this dish (see ingredient list), or use wonton skins for the ravioli. If you're up for the challenge of preparing every component, spread it out over several days, to ease the production.

FOR THE PHEASANT STOCK

1 pheasant, 2 to 3 pounds, washed, trimmed of excess fat, and cut up (2 Cornish hens can be substituted)

2 pounds chicken drumsticks, washed, trimmed of excess fat and hanging skin, and chopped into 1-inch lengths

3 celery stalks, diced

2 medium carrots, chopped

1 medium Spanish onion, diced

2 medium leeks, white parts only, chopped

2 cloves garlic, smashed and peeled

2 bay leaves

1 tablespoon grated fresh ginger

1. Make the pheasant stock: Put the pheasant, chicken, celery, carrots, onion, leeks, garlic, bay leaves, ginger, and 5 quarts water in an 8-quart soup pot. If the water does not cover the solids, add enough water to cover by 1 inch.

2. Bring the water to a boil over medium heat, then lower the heat and let simmer for 3 hours, skimming off any scum that rises to the surface during this time.

3. Strain the stock through a fine-mesh strainer set over a large bowl, discarding the solids. You should have about 2 quarts of stock. Let cool, then cover and refrigerate overnight. The next day, spoon off any fat that has risen to the surface.

4. Clarify the stock into a consommé: Put the carrot, celery, onion, leek, ground pheasant, egg whites, tomato, ginger, and scallions in the bowl of a food processor fitted with the steel blade and chop to medium-fine dice.

5. Transfer the mixture to a clean 8-quart soup pot and add the cold stock. Stir it up and bring to a slow simmer over medium heat, lightly stirring to prevent the solids from sticking on the bottom of the pot.

FOR THE CONSOMMÉ CLARIFICATION

¼ cup diced carrot

¼ cup diced celery

¼ cup diced Spanish onion

¼ cup diced leek, white part only

1 pound ground pheasant, game hen, or chicken thigh meat (ask your butcher to do the grinding)

4 large egg whites

½ cup diced plum tomato

¼ cup grated fresh ginger

¼ cup chopped scallions, white part only

2 quarts pheasant stock from preceding step

Salt and freshly ground black pepper

¼ cup sherry, sake, or Madeira

TO SERVE

Chanterelle and Sweet Potato Ravioli (recipe follows)

Sliced scallions, green parts only, or fried wonton skins (optional; see box, page 137)

6. At some point the mass will rise to the surface; this is called the "raft." Once it forms, do not stir; it is drawing the solids and impurities out of the stock, "clarifying" it. Let simmer for 1 hour.

7. Set two sheets of cheesecloth over a large bowl. Use a ladle to carefully scoop a hole in the center of the raft. Ladle the clarified stock out through this hole, and pour it through the cheesecloth into the bowl. After all of the stock has been ladled out, discard the raft. Cover and chill the consommé overnight. Spoon off and discard any fat the next day.

8. When ready to use the consommé, transfer it to a pot, gently reheat it, and season with salt and pepper. Stir in the sherry to fortify the flavor.

9. To serve, use a slotted spoon to divide the ravioli among four wide, shallow soup plates. Ladle about 1 cup of hot consommé around the ravioli in each bowl and garnish with scallions or wonton crisps, if desired.

Chanterelle and Sweet Potato Ravioli

MAKES 12 MEDIUM RAVIOLI

These ravioli can be served on their own dressed with butter, or floating in a shallow bowl of chicken broth. They can also be made with wonton skins rather than home-made pasta.

FOR THE PASTA DOUGH
½ cup semolina flour
3½ cups all-purpose flour, plus more
    for kneading
3 large eggs
2 teaspoons olive oil

FOR THE RAVIOLI FILLING
1 tablespoon olive oil
1 tablespoon very finely chopped
    shallot
1 tablespoon very finely chopped
    garlic
2 teaspoons very finely chopped
    peeled fresh ginger
3 ounces chanterelle mushrooms,
    wiped clean and very finely diced
    (about ½ cup diced)
½ cup finely diced sweet potato
2 tablespoons dry white wine
2 ounces soft goat cheese (about ½
    cup)
2 ounces ricotta cheese (about ½
    cup)
¼ cup freshly grated Parmesan
    cheese (1 ounce)

TO ASSEMBLE THE RAVIOLI
2 eggs
Salt

1. Make the pasta dough: In a large bowl, sift together the semolina and all-purpose flours.

2. Put the eggs, oil, and ¼ cup water in the bowl of a food processor fitted with the steel blade. Add the flours and pulse to incorporate, but do not overmix; the dough should just form a ball.

3. Turn the dough out on a floured surface, and knead for about 3 minutes; if the dough is still sticky, add a bit more flour and continue to knead. Cover the dough with a damp cloth and let it rest for 1 hour at room temperature.

4. Make the ravioli filling: Heat the oil in a small sauté pan over medium heat. Add the shallot, garlic, and ginger and sauté for 2 to 3 minutes, until softened but not browned. Add the chanterelles and sweet potato, and sauté just until tender, 3 to 5 minutes. Add the white wine and reduce until almost dry, 2 to 3 minutes. Remove the pan from the heat.

5. Let the mixture cool, then stir in the goat cheese, ricotta, and Parmesan.

6. Assemble and cook the ravioli: In a small bowl, make an egg wash by beating together the eggs and ¼ cup water.

7. Divide the dough into two equal balls. On a floured surface (ideally marble), roll them out as thin as possible into two simi-lar-size sheets, about 18 inches square, using a rolling pin and turning the sheets after each pass of the pin to ensure an even thickness. You want the dough to be as thin as possible.

8. Lightly brush the surface of the pasta sheets with the egg wash.

9. Divide the filling into 12 small balls and arrange them on one of the pasta sheets, about 2 inches apart.

10. Lay the second sheet of dough over the first, egg-washed side down, and use a 2-inch ring cutter to cut ravioli from the dough.

11. Use your fingers to press the air out of the ravioli, then seal the edges, being sure the filling is completely sealed. The ravioli should be about 2 inches across and ¾ inch high. (At this stage, they can be kept at room temperature for up to 2 hours, covered with a damp paper towel, or clean lightweight cloth. They can also be frozen: Dust a baking sheet with cornmeal and put the ravioli on the sheet. Freeze until the ravioli are cold and hard, then transfer to freezer bags and freeze for up to 2 months. There's no need to defrost them; transfer them directly to the boiling water when cooking.)

12. In an 8-quart soup pot, bring 6 quarts water to a boil. Add 2 tablespoons salt, lower the heat to medium so the water is simmering, and gently lower the ravioli into the water. Cook for 3 to 4 minutes, until they float to the surface. Remove using a slotted spoon and serve immediately.

A NEW YEAR'S EVE TO END ALL NEW YEAR'S EVES

There were many festive parties thrown during the Clinton years, but one of the most incredible ones, even by White House standards, was the Millennial New Year's Eve.

About a month before New Year's Eve, I was summoned to a meeting with Capricia Marshall and Mrs. Clinton at which they told me what they envisioned: two dinners, one a seated meal for 370 people hosted by President and Mrs. Clinton in the East Room and State Dining Room; and another, buffet-style dinner in the Rose Garden for 240 people, to be hosted by Chelsea. The dinners would be followed by a break to watch the fireworks, then by a reception for 1,100 guests in the Rose Garden from midnight to 2:00 a.m., which would transform into a breakfast buffet from 2:00 a.m. until 5:00 a.m.

This was clearly going to be a lot of work, but I was up for it, and flattered that Mrs. Clinton and Capricia had enough faith in me to know that we could pull it off. I was also excited by the prospect of guests being able to spend time savoring their food, as opposed to the somewhat rushed schedule of a state dinner.

The menu for the White House Millennium Dinner; a real collaboration between Mrs. Clinton and me. *(Courtesy William J. Clinton Presidential Library)*

I began drafting menus for these events and sharing them with Mrs. Clinton. The brainstorming process was guided by two overriding criteria: One, to incorporate luxury ingredients appropriate to New Year's Eve, such as lobster, caviar, and foie gras; and two, to create as many efficiencies as possible by using the same ingredients and preparations in more than one place, although not under the same name.

This recipe development was a fun and creative exchange with Mrs. Clinton. I proposed three possible starters: a soup, a foie gras, and a caviar dish. Mrs. Clinton responded by suggesting that we have a sampler featuring all three, and that's what we did. The first course was A Tasting of Beluga Caviar, Lobster, Foie Gras, and Oyster Velouté. That was followed by Truffle-Marinated Rack of Lamb, Roasted Artichoke and Pepper Ragout, and Crispy Garlic Polenta; and a Salad of Winter Greens, Golden and Red Beets, and Blue Cheese Tartine.

As for the buffet-style reception in the Rose Garden, it featured a more extensive menu, the highlights of which were Saffron-Poached Lobster with Preserved Lemon, Couscous, and Julienne Vegetables; Basil Scallops, Oven-Dried Tomatoes, and Balsamic Onions; Truffle-Marinated Rack of Lamb with Roasted Artichoke and Pepper Ragout and Crispy Garlic Polenta; and a Salad of Winter Greens with Golden and Red Beets and Blue Cheese Tartine.

Though a domestic affair, from a logistical standpoint this evening was essentially two official dinners in one, followed by a cocktail reception and then a brunch reception that featured tomato, leek, and gruyere quiche; eggs benedict; almond French toast with maple-pecan compote; and a Spanish omelet.

I ordered the ingredients for the dinners eight days in advance, putting all of them on one requisition form, with different requested arrival dates for different items. Garlic, onions, heavy cream, and other essentials that would be used all week could come as early as December 28; fish, meats, and greens were requested to arrive as close to the day of the dinner as possible for maximum freshness. I also made up a list of rental equipment such as china, glass, and silver that would be required to serve the foods we had planned.

Working off of a prep list that outlined a plan of attack for making the components of each dish as early as possible, on Monday, December 27, we began preparing the elements of the dinner that could be made that far in advance without sacrificing quality, such as croutons, tartlet shells, and a winter fruit compote. On Wednesday, we began making sauces and dressings, and so on.

One blessing was that because Christmas had come and gone, the crush of the holidays—all those receptions—was past us, so other than feeding the First Family, every cook in the House was devoted to preparing for this event.

On the day of the party, I operated with a crew of about twenty-five people. Most of them began the day at seven in the morning, but some (like my friends from the Army and Navy who had helped us with the mobile kitchen trailers) came in at three thirty or four o'clock in the afternoon. We prepped all day, then I sent about a dozen people, led by John Moeller, to get Chelsea's party up and running at six thirty. Once it was in full swing, half of those people stayed on to keep fresh food on the buffet, while the other half joined the team that was readying the President and First Lady's party, which began at 7:30 p.m. and was overseen by Cris Comerford. And me? I shuttled from room to room, keeping tabs on how things were going with each team and event.

There were literally thousands of guests that night, and the kitchen and butler staffs worked like champs, some of them pausing on occasion to nap in chairs set up along the corridors.

There were also other incredible logistics to contend with that night. For instance, during the fireworks display, Daniel Shanks and his team converted the Rose Garden, where Chelsea's dinner had been served, into a discothèque, as all the tables were moved out and a dance floor was set up.

For us, the most challenging aspect of the evening was that we had to pull all of this off in the same thirty-by-twenty-six-foot kitchen in which we did all of our cooking. There was absolutely no room for spontaneity or improvisation; I had every task assigned to a specific cook and knew who was going to do what and when for the entire twelve-hour stretch. My carefully orchestrated plan allowed for an ebb and flow of cooks in and out of the kitchen—anywhere from sixteen to twenty-four at one time. With an eye toward the first day of the new millennium, I also dismissed some cooks by midnight so they'd be fresh when they returned to work in the morning, both to the residence and to the staff kitchen.

There was a dinner being made by one group, a reception being made by another group and a breakfast being made by a third group. Every team was operating independently, with the only common factor being my checking on everything.

I brought in a lot of extra help for this evening, including my wife, Jean, who made a rare White House appearance for the occasion. A lot of the other cooks' spouses signed on for the day as well, and it was a good thing because otherwise we'd have rung in the new millennium without our significant others. All the SBA workers were paid top dollar for their efforts because there was such a shortage of workers available due to all the parties in D.C. that night.

My Army and Navy buddies really stepped up on this occasion. They carried out all sorts of culinary and logistical tasks, and did so as though it were a military exercise. Many of them also had very finely tuned radars and could simply smell trouble coming. If, on their rounds, they noticed a burgeoning problem, such as a butler putting a hot pan down directly on a buffet table instead of into a chafing dish, or items not being combined properly, they'd come over and whisper in my ear. They'd also alert me to employees who had fallen asleep, tipping me off in time to head off any potential "situations." (In time, I became so friendly with one of these guys, Brian Williams, the same man who had introduced me to those mobile kitchen trailers, that when he earned his lieutenant's bars he asked me and his father to pin the stripes on him at the ceremony.)

It was the longest night any of us had ever worked. I myself had been at the House for twenty-nine straight hours, and hadn't slept a wink in all that time. As soon as it was over, Jean passed out on a couch in the ladies' locker room. We did get to enjoy some of the evening though: Jean and I and all the cooks did stop our work—I confess, the break was preplanned and timed—to watch the fireworks from the Blue Room during the eye of the New Year's Eve operational storm.

As I drove home that New Year's morning, there was a low-lying fog blanketing all of D.C., creating a dreamlike mood that was the perfect backdrop for the combination euphoria-exhaustion that I felt after the most challenging single night of my professional life.

I went home from that event, slept from nine in the morning until two in the afternoon, and then returned to the White House to make sure the regular, daily service was up and running for the First Family and their guests.

It wasn't until a few days later, when we returned from the holidays with new perspective that we realized what we had pulled off. During that first week of January, when much of the staff was away on vacation, after all the party activity, it was almost eerie how empty and quiet the White House corridors were. Those of us who were still there acknowledged each other with knowing "I Survived the Millennium at the White House" looks.

Oven-Roasted Tomatoes and Maytag Blue Cheese on Crispy Polenta

MAKES 16 CANAPÉS

This hors d'oeuvre was served at many winter parties, but none more memorable than the Millennium celebration in 1999. The warm crunchiness of the roasted polenta and the savory blue cheese (ours came from Iowa) made this a cold-weather favorite.

Polenta (recipe follows), chilled
1 teaspoon olive oil
Oven-Roasted Tomatoes (recipe follows)
½ cup crumbled Maytag blue cheese (6 ounces)
1 tablespoon chopped fresh basil leaves

1. Preheat the oven to 250°F.

2. Cut the polenta into 16 circles using a cookie cutter or the mouth of a glass 1½ inches in diameter.

3. Heat the oil in a 12-inch, heavy-bottomed sauté pan over medium heat. Add the polenta circles, in two or three batches, and cook quickly until golden on each side, 2 to 3 minutes per side.

4. Gather the polenta circles in one layer on a baking sheet (it can be the same one in which the polenta was refrigerated, wiped clean). Top each with a piece of the roasted tomato and some crumbled cheese and bake in the oven until the cheese just begins to melt, 1 to 2 minutes.

5. Using a spatula, carefully transfer the canapés to a platter, sprinkle with chopped basil, and serve.

Oven-Roasted Tomatoes

4 ripe Roma (plum) tomatoes
2 tablespoons balsamic vinegar
1 tablespoon olive oil
1 tablespoon chopped fresh basil leaves
1 teaspoon chopped garlic
Salt and freshly ground black pepper

1. Preheat the oven to the lowest possible temperature, ideally 200°F.

2. Halve the tomatoes lengthwise and arrange them, cut side up, on a wire rack set over a baking sheet.

3. In a small bowl, stir together the vinegar, oil, basil, and garlic, and season with salt and pepper. Spoon a little of this mixture over each tomato half.

4. Roast the tomatoes in the oven, leaving the door slightly ajar to help them cook as slowly as possible, until they have shrunk to about two thirds their original bulk, 6 to 8 hours. When they are done, let them cool at room temperature, then remove and discard the skins and cut each piece in half to make 16 pieces total. Use them right away, or pack tightly into an airtight container, cover with olive oil, and refrigerate for up to 1 week.

Polenta

1 tablespoon salt
1½ cups polenta (yellow cornmeal)
½ cup grated Asiago cheese (2 ounces)
1 tablespoon roasted garlic puree (see box, page 23)

1. Combine 4½ cups water and the salt in a medium saucepan and bring to a boil over high heat. Lower the heat so the water is simmering and gradually add the polenta, whisking to avoid forming any lumps. Cook, whisking often to prevent sticking and scorching, until thickened, 20 to 25 minutes. Remove from heat and stir in the cheese and garlic puree.

2. Pour the polenta into a rimmed baking sheet and spread it out to a thickness of about ½ inch. Let cool, cover with plastic, and refrigerate overnight to firm it up.

The Clintons toast the new millennium. The woman on the left, with her back to the camera, is screen legend Sophia Loren. *(Courtesy William J. Clinton Presidential Library)*

On The Road Again
Cooking Around the Country

In order to ensure consistency and quality, the Clintons frequently brought me and my staff along with them when they traveled as part of their regular on-the-road contingent.

As any chef can tell you, being away from your home kitchen never fails to produce a mishap or two, or at least the *possibility* of a mishap. This dynamic is compounded exponentially when you travel with the President and First Lady, because cooking for them anywhere means dealing with all the same security and logistical issues as are present at the White House, and the cooks and support staff at hotels and other venues often get star-struck to distraction when they're serving such luminaries.

Succeeding on the road was a challenge to be sure, but it also brought with it some rewarding opportunities, especially being able to show off regional American ingredients and cooking styles.

ALONG FOR THE RIDE

When I accepted the job of White House Executive Chef, I assumed that there would be some travel, but nowhere near the amount that actually came to pass. There was plenty of precedent for the chef traveling with the First Family—previous chefs had cooked at the presidential retreat Camp David, and as far away as Russia. But while the occasional trip had been part of the job description for my predecessors, it was far from the norm.

This changed dramatically when the Clintons finally hired their own chef. They were so thoroughly devoted to maintaining their standard of cuisine for both themselves and their guests that either I or one or more members of my team cooked for them in locations as diverse as Camp David, New York City, Denver, Colorado, and Miami.

One of the benefits of having a trusted crew working for me was that I sometimes opted to stay behind at the White House, sending one of my assistant chefs along with the First Family. For instance, when they vacationed on their beloved Martha's Vineyard, one of my cooks would accompany them.

Cooking at Camp David. Me in the glasses, and assistant chef Cristeta Comerford, who would become my successor as White House Executive Chef. *(Courtesy William J. Clinton Presidential Library)*

Bringing a chef along to the Vineyard wasn't done for show; just the opposite, in fact. Eager to maintain some semblance of a normal family vacation, the Clintons kept the cook out of sight—he or she would cook the food, and a staff member would present it, but there was no interaction with the kitchen the way there was at the White House.

We sent as many kitchen basics along with the cook as possible: stocks, vinaigrettes, and so on. The rest of the food was purchased from local markets by the cook or by a Navy valet.

While the Clintons were away, I'd take the downtime in the White House to do some annual cleaning, working with my other chefs to empty and deep clean the refrigerators and other kitchen equipment.

Once all that was done, I'd do something I try to do every summer: take a ten-day to two-week vacation, usually to my wife's family's vacation home in the Muskoka region of Canada, where I'd boat, fish, hang out with my kids, and generally decompress.

Shrimp and Vegetable Quesadillas with Avocado and Grapefruit Salad

SERVES 4

When one of my cooks was on Martha's Vineyard with the Clintons, he or she usually prepared the First Family's meals in the guest house where he or she was staying, then have them brought to the main cottage where the Family was staying. The quesadillas would be preassembled and then actually cooked by the Clintons themselves at mealtime. The salad was premade as well and then dressed at the last minute. You can do the same at home, using this as a make-ahead dish to suit especially busy days.

6 tablespoons olive oil
1 tablespoon freshly squeezed lemon juice
1 tablespoon chopped garlic
Salt and freshly ground black pepper
¾ pound medium or large shrimp, peeled and deveined
½ cup ¼-inch-thick zucchini slices
½ cup ¼-inch-thick Spanish onion slices

1. Preheat the broiler.

2. In a medium bowl, whisk together 2 tablespoons of the oil, the lemon juice, and garlic. Season to taste with salt and pepper. Add the shrimp and let marinate for 6 hours, but no longer or the acid in the lemon juice will cure the shrimp. Remove the shrimp from marinade, wiping off any marinade solids.

3. Broil the shrimp for 2 minutes per side. Transfer the shrimp to a cutting board, let cool until warm enough to handle, and halve them lengthwise. Set aside.

¼ cup thinly sliced red bell pepper strips
¼ cup thinly sliced poblano pepper strips
Four 12-inch flour tortillas
¾ cup shredded jalapeño Jack cheese
¾ cup shredded Cheddar cheese
1 teaspoon ground cumin
1 teaspoon ground coriander
¼ cup chopped fresh cilantro leaves
Avocado and Grapefruit Salad (recipe follows)
Homemade or your favorite store-bought salsa (optional)
Homemade or your favorite store-bought guacamole (optional)
Sour cream (optional)

4. Heat 2 tablespoons of the oil in 12-inch sauté pan over medium heat, add the zucchini, and sauté until tender, 1 to 2 minutes. Transfer the zucchini to a medium bowl and set aside. Return the pan to the heat and add 1 tablespoon oil. Once the oil is hot, add the onion and sauté until softened but not browned, 3 to 5 minutes. Transfer the onion to the bowl with the zucchini. Add the remaining 1 tablespoon of oil to the pan. Once the oil is hot, add the red pepper and poblano pepper and sauté until tender, 2 to 3 minutes, and transfer to the bowl with the zucchini and onion.

5. Heat a 12-inch sauté pan over medium heat. Place 1 tortilla in the pan, and arrange one quarter of the vegetables, shrimp, cheese, cumin, coriander, and cilantro over half the tortilla. Fold the tortilla over, and cook until golden brown and the cheese is melted, about 3 minutes per side. Repeat with the remaining tortillas and ingredients.

6. To serve, cut the quesadilla into wedges and serve with the Avocado and Grapefruit Salad alongside. If desired, serve with salsa, guacamole, and/or sour cream on the side as well.

Avocado and Grapefruit Salad

SERVES 4 AS A SIDE DISH

⅓ cup olive oil
¼ cup freshly squeezed lime juice
1 tablespoon chopped fresh cilantro leaves, plus 12 cilantro sprigs for garnish
½ tablespoon chopped garlic
1 teaspoon very finely chopped shallot
1 teaspoon hot sauce
¼ teaspoon ground cumin
2 ripe Hass avocados
2 ripe medium ruby grapefruits
8 leaves of Bibb lettuce (about 1 head), washed and dried
½ small bunch watercress sprigs, for garnish

1. In a small bowl, stir together the oil, lime juice, chopped cilantro, garlic, shallot, hot sauce, and cumin until incorporated. (The vinaigrette can be refrigerated in an airtight container for up to 3 days.)

2. Halve the avocados, remove the seed and peel, and thinly slice the halves lengthwise. Peel and section the grapefruits.

3. Place 2 lettuces leaves on each of four plates and put equal amounts of the avocado and grapefruit on the lettuce. Garnish with watercress and cilantro. Drizzle the dressing over the salad and serve at once.

COOKING AT CAMP DAVID

Cooking at Camp David was substantially more involved than cooking at Martha's Vineyard. The Clintons frequently visited this well-known Presidential retreat just outside Thurmont, Maryland, in the Maryland hills. My chefs and I often traveled to Camp David with the military drivers who transported the food, wine, flowers, and such that were going to the retreat. Then one day, it occurred to me that many of us lived closer to Camp David than to the White House—Cris, for example, lived near Columbia, Maryland—so we began driving there on our own to save time.

Though Camp David was casual—a rustic retreat where the houses are named for trees, like Aspen, where the First Family stayed—the Clintons wanted to maintain their standards there as well.

If it was just the Clintons getting away for a weekend, or for a portion of the holidays, then only one of us would go. But if they were entertaining foreign dignitaries—Great Britain's Tony Blair and his wife Cherie were often there, for instance, and Camp David was of course a frequent meeting spot for Middle East talks with Yasser Arafat, Ehud Barak, and others—then the whole team would make the trip.

Our strategy for Camp David was always the same. We'd prepare as much as we could at the White House, then have it packed up and delivered in a van that went along with the military convoy that trailed the President there.

President Clinton, British Prime Minister Tony Blair, and me. Prime Minister Blair was a frequent visitor to the White House, and Camp David, and often made a point of saying hello to me. *(Courtesy William J. Clinton Presidential Library)*

Chicken, Apple, and Pecan Salad on Autumn Greens

SERVES 4

We served this salad to the Clintons and the Blairs as a light lunch on autumn weekends. To show off American produce, it featured local greens and apples from the southern Pennsylvania area close to Camp David.

FOR THE CHICKEN
1 tablespoon olive oil
1 tablespoon freshly squeezed
   lemon juice
½ tablespoon chopped garlic
½ tablespoon balsamic vinegar
Salt and freshly ground black pepper
4 boneless, skinless chicken breasts
   (3 ounces each)

FOR THE SALAD
1 cup Granny Smith apple wedges,
   cut ¼ inch thick
¼ cup thinly sliced red onion
¼ cup dried currants
1 tablespoon chopped fresh tarragon leaves
1 teaspoon finely grated lemon zest
Port Wine and Tarragon Vinaigrette
   (recipe follows)
2 cups mixed fall greens (such as
   frisée, beet greens, baby spinach,
   endive, or other baby greens of
   your choosing)
⅓ cup chopped store-bought spiced
   pecans or regular pecans
⅓ cup crumbled Stilton or other blue
   cheese (about 1½ ounces)

1. Cook the chicken: Preheat the broiler or a charcoal grill, letting the coals burn until covered with white ash, or preheat a gas grill to high.

2. In a medium bowl, stir together the oil, lemon juice, garlic, and vinegar. Season with salt and pepper to taste. Add the chicken, turning to coat, and let marinate at room temperature for 5 minutes.

3. Broil or grill the chicken until the juices run clear when the breast is pierced at the center, about 5 minutes per side. Transfer the chicken to a cutting board and let cool slightly. Slice each chicken breast diagonally ¼ inch thick.

4. Make the salad: In a large bowl, combine the apples, onion, currants, tarragon, and lemon zest. Drizzle the dressing over the ingredients and gently toss. Add the greens to the bowl and toss again.

5. Divide the salad among four plates. Sprinkle each salad with pecans and Stilton. Arrange the slices of 1 chicken breast over each salad and serve.

Port Wine and Tarragon Vinaigrette

MAKES ABOUT ¾ CUP

½ cup olive oil

2 tablespoons tarragon vinegar or seasoned rice vinegar

2 tablespoons apple cider vinegar

1 tablespoon ruby or tawny Port wine

1 tablespoon chopped fresh tarragon leaves

1 teaspoon very finely chopped garlic

1 teaspoon very finely chopped shallot

1 teaspoon packed light brown sugar

½ teaspoon chopped fresh flat-leaf parsley leaves

½ teaspoon Dijon mustard

¼ teaspoon Worcestershire sauce

Salt and freshly ground black pepper

In a small bowl, combine the oil, tarragon vinegar, cider vinegar, Port, tarragon, garlic, shallot, brown sugar, parsley, mustard, and Worcestershire and whisk together for 30 seconds. Season to taste with salt and pepper. (The dressing can be refrigerated in an airtight container for up to 3 days. Let it come to room temperature before proceeding.)

NEW YORK STATE OF MIND

I also periodically found myself cooking for events in New York State, in part because the United Nations was based there and in part because the Culinary Institute of America was a logical showcase for the contemporary American food we were cooking, not to mention my alma mater.

For example, in October 1995, we worked with a local caterer in New York City to stage a number of meals for the fiftieth anniversary of the United Nations, including a Presidential reception at the New York Public Library for three hundred guests.

On another occasion, Culinary Institute of America President Ferdinand Metz and I were the joint supervising chefs of a lunch honoring Russian Federation President Boris Yeltsin at the Roosevelt family mansion in Hyde Park, New York. This event came with an extra dimension: We also had to prepare 120 boxed lunches for the Secret Service detail covering the lunch.

Loin of Venison with Glazed Shallots and Acorn Squash Gnocchi

SERVES 4

This dish was part of a menu we served to Russian Federation President Boris Yeltsin in Hyde Park, New York, in the fall of 1995. The menu was developed and produced with the assistance of chef instructors and students from the Culinary Institute of America, my alma mater, which is located in Hyde Park. It reflects both the season and the flavors and ingredients of the mid-Hudson River Valley region. Working with the instructors of my alma mater so many years after my graduation was an honor and a pleasure.

FOR THE VENISON

2 pounds boneless venison loin, trimmed of excess fat and silver skin, trimmings reserved (about 6 ounces trimmings)
2 cups dry red wine
1 cup water or homemade or store-bought low-sodium vegetable, chicken, or beef stock
½ cup chopped Spanish onion
¼ cup diced carrot
¼ cup diced celery
¼ cup thinly sliced leek, white part only
1 tablespoon chopped garlic
½ tablespoon crushed juniper berries
½ teaspoon cracked black peppercorns
1 bay leaf
2 tablespoons vegetable oil

FOR THE SAUCE

Reserved venison marinade
1 cup homemade or store-bought low-sodium beef or veal stock
1½ tablespoons red wine vinegar
2 tablespoons crème fraîche
1 tablespoon Cognac
Salt and freshly ground black pepper

1. Make the marinade: Put the venison trimmings, wine, water or stock, onion, carrot, celery, leek, garlic, juniper, peppercorn, and bay leaf in a medium saucepan over medium heat. Bring to a boil, lower the heat, and let simmer for 15 minutes, skimming any scum that rises to the surface. Remove from the heat and let the marinade cool to room temperature.

2. Marinate the venison: Put the venison loin in a high-sided dish and pour the marinade over the venison. Cover and refrigerate at least 8 hours, or overnight. When ready to cook and serve the dish, remove the venison from the marinade, brushing off any marinade solids, and reserve the marinade in the refrigerator.

3. Make the sauce: In a medium saucepan, combine the marinade, stock, and vinegar. Bring to a boil, lower the heat and let simmer 30 minutes, then pass through a fine-mesh strainer into a 1-quart saucepan. Discard the vegetables and trimmings.

4. Bring the liquid to a simmer and reduce to about 1 cup, 20 to 30 minutes; the sauce should be thick enough to coat the back of a wooden spoon.

5. Whisk in the crème fraîche and Cognac. Season to taste with salt and pepper and let simmer an additional 5 minutes to integrate the flavors. Keep the sauce covered and warm while you cook the venison.

6. Cook the venison: Preheat the oven to 350°F. Heat the oil in a large, heavy, ovenproof sauté pan set over high heat. Add the venison and sear until browned all over, 3 to 4 minutes per side.

Glazed Shallots (recipe follows)
Acorn Squash Gnocchi (recipe follows)

7. Transfer the venison, still in the sauté pan, to the oven and roast until an instant-read thermometer inserted to the thickest part reads 145°F, 10 to 12 minutes. Transfer the venison to a cutting board and let rest for 6 to 8 minutes.

8. To serve, gently reheat the sauce, if necessary. Slice the venison crosswise and divide it among four dinner plates. Drizzle the sauce over and around the venison. Place equal amounts of shallots and gnocchi on each plate. Serve immediately.

Glazed Shallots

SERVES 4 AS A SIDE DISH

12 to 16 whole large shallots, peeled
1 cup red wine
1 cup homemade or store-bought low-sodium beef or veal stock
2 tablespoons red wine vinegar
2 tablespoons balsamic vinegar
2 tablespoons unsalted butter
1 tablespoon honey
1 tablespoon packed light brown sugar

1. Preheat the oven to 350°F.

2. Pack the shallots tightly into a small, ovenproof saucepan just large enough to hold them in one layer.

3. Thoroughly stir together the red wine, beef stock, vinegars, butter, honey, and brown sugar in a small bowl. Pour over the shallots, covering them completely. Bring to a simmer over medium heat, cover, and bake in the oven until the shallots are soft to a knife tip, 30 minutes. Uncover and bake for 5 minutes more.

4. Remove from the oven and stir to coat the shallot with the glaze. Keep warm until ready to use.

Acorn Squash Gnocchi

SERVES 4 AS A SIDE DISH

½ cup riced or mashed Idaho or russet potatoes (from about 8 ounces raw potatoes)

1 cup riced or mashed acorn squash (from about 1 pound squash)

2 egg yolks

¾ cup all-purpose flour, plus more for rolling

2 tablespoons olive oil

1 tablespoon chopped fresh chives

1 tablespoon chopped fresh tarragon leaves

Pinch of salt

Pinch of freshly ground black pepper

Pinch of freshly grated nutmeg

2 tablespoons (¼ stick) unsalted butter

¼ cup grated Asiago cheese (about 1 ounce)

1. In the bowl of a food processor fitted with the steel blade, combine the potatoes, squash, egg yolks, flour, oil, chives, tarragon, salt, pepper, and nutmeg. Process until ingredients form a dough, 1 to 2 minutes. Form dough into a cylinder, wrap with plastic wrap, and refrigerate for 2 hours.

2. On a lightly floured surface, divide dough into four equal pieces and roll each into a cylinder ½ inch in diameter. Cut each cylinder into ½-inch lengths.

3. Bring 2 quarts of salted water to a medium boil in a large saucepan over high heat. Working in batches to keep the temperature from plummeting and allow the gnocchi to cook quickly, boil the gnocchi until they float to the surface, 3 to 5 minutes. Use a slotted spoon or skimmer to remove the gnocchi from the pot, letting any excess water run off, and set aside on a large plate or platter to cool.

4. Melt the butter in a large sauté pan over medium-high heat. Add the gnocchi to pan and cook just until heated through. Sprinkle grated cheese onto the gnocchi and toss just before removing from the pan and serving.

MY DAY IN THE BUBBLE

There was just one time that I didn't take a commercial airline, or my own car, to get back to D.C. from an out-of-town event.

On September 22, 1998, we were to serve a lunch hosted by President Clinton in honor of Japanese Prime Minister Keizo Obuchi, again at the Culinary Institute of America. Everything was in place, but an unexpected, low-lying fog rolled in and started to blanket the area. The Secret Service, concerned that they wouldn't be able to get the President out on his helicopter, *Marine One*, as planned, pulled the plug on the lunch, and whisked the President away.

I was instructed to get back to Manhattan and connect with the President's security detail at the Waldorf. I left all of my equipment there, asking one of the chefs to pack it up and ship it to me, then hopped into one of the limousines on hand to transport staffers back to town.

I arrived at the Waldorf and spent a few hours there while the President finished up his business around town. Then we all got into limousines that were to take us down to a secured landing zone at the southern tip of Manhattan.

We pulled away from the Waldorf, slipped right through the clogged streets of Manhattan, and traveled east toward the FDR Drive, the highway named for Franklin Delano Roosevelt that hugs the eastern part of the island fronting the East River. As we turned onto the FDR and up the ramp onto the highway, I looked down to my right over rush-hour Manhattan. The traffic was held at bay three blocks back from the highway and I realized how complicated things get for people driving in a grid system like New York's to have that many streets taken out of commission.

With traffic cleared on the highway too, we continued to barrel down the eerily deserted FDR Drive. Nothing was moving more slowly than us, so I had no way of gauging how fast we were actually going until I glanced at the speedometer and to my shock discovered that we were traveling at well over one hundred miles per hour.

I looked left at the East River and saw a speedboat tracking us, with a soldier training a machine gun over the waters.

I looked up in the sky and saw a helicopter directly overhead.

I asked one of the staffers in the limousine about all of this. "It's a security bubble," he told me, and I realized that this same production takes place every time the President makes a move. We arrived at the landing zone. *Marine One* was parked there, as were a few support helicopters. As the President and his detail got into *Marine One*, the rest of us got into the other helicopters. From the sprint that the first few people went into, it was clear that there was no time to dillydally. Nobody told me this, but it was understood that if you didn't get into the helicopter ASAP, you'd be left behind. We all ran.

It was also essential to get your seatbelt fastened as soon as possible, because they don't even close the doors before takeoff, so if you weren't strapped in, you might slide right out.

We flew across the East River to another secured airstrip where *Air Force One* was idling. We all got dropped off about fifty yards away, and did another mad dash.

Air Force One was astonishing, with the President's and First Lady's quarters up front, and a series of rooms toward the middle and rear. It was more like an apartment than an aircraft. Just as impressive was the altitude we assumed: Where commercial airlines fly at about thirty thousand feet, we soared like a rocket several thousand feet higher than that.

As we all sat around a big table in one of the rooms shooting the breeze, I thought about how surreal the last thirty minutes had been: a car ride at more than one hundred miles per hour, with the city stopped for our safety and speed; a helicopter ride that went by in the blink of an eye, and now this.

That day was the one and only time I experienced the full level of security and deference the President enjoys on the road, and I have to say that I couldn't imagine doing it every day.

TWO FOR THE HISTORY BOOKS

Most of the travel we did for the First Family were in these regions—Martha's Vineyard, Camp David, and New York City or the surrounding area.

But there were two events that far exceeded anything else we ever attempted: the Summit of the Americas in Miami, Florida, in 1994, and the G8 Summit in Denver, Colorado, in 1997. Each of these was actually a series of events, a succession of days in which we cooked for a multitude of world leaders in faraway cities, often using a different cooking facility for each meal.

These were, without a doubt, the most difficult challenges that I had undertaken in my career up to that point. (The Millennium New Year's Eve party in 2000 later turned out to be the Number One challenge.) It all worked out well but there were many obstacles to overcome along the way . . .

MIAMI ON THE MIND

One day in late November 1994, I looked up from my desk to see Ann Stock standing in my doorway. "We're going to Miami to do a site visit for the Summit of the Americas," she told me, a site visit being our equivalent of a movie production team's location scout.

I had heard about the Summit of the Americas. It was to be a three-day gathering of leaders from thirty-four nations, representing every country in the Western Hemisphere, with the exception of Cuba.

"When's the Summit?" I asked her.

"In a week and a half."

SUMMIT OF THE AMERICAS
Leaders in Attendance (in addition to President Clinton)

Prime Minister Lester Bird
  (Antigua and Barbuda)

President Carlos Saul Menem
  (Argentina)

Prime Minister Hubert A. Ingraham
  (Bahamas)

Prime Minister Owen Seymour Arthur
  (Barbados)

Prime Minster Manuel Esquivel
  (Belize)

President Gonzalo Sanchez de Lozada
  (Boliva)

President Itamar Franco
  (Brazil)

Prime Minister Jean Chretien
  (Canada)

President Eduardo Frei Ruiz-Tagle
  (Chile)

President Ernesto Samper Pizano
  (Colombia)

President Jose Figueres Ferrer
  (Costa Rica)

Prime Minster Maria Eugenia Charles
  (Dominica)

President Joaquin Videla Balaguer
  (Dominican Republic)

President Sixto Duran-Ballen Cordovez
  (Ecuador)

President Armando Calderon Sol
  (El Salvador)

Prime Minister Nicholas Brathwaite
  (Grenada)

President Ramiro De Leon Carpio
  (Guatemala)

President Cheddi Jargan
  (Guyana)

Prime Minister Jean-Bertrand Ariste
  (Haiti)

President Carlos Roberto Reina Idiaquez
  (Honduras)

Prime Minster Percival James Patterson
  (Jamaica)

President Ernesto Zedillo Ponce de Leon
  (Mexico)

President Vioelta Barrios de Chamorro
  (Nicaragua)

President Ernesto Perez Balladares
  (Panama)

President Juan Carlos Wasmosy
  (Paraguay)

President Alberto K. Fujimori
  (Peru)

Prime Minister Kennedy Alphonse Simmonds
  (St. Kitts and Nevis)

Prime Minster John G.M. Compton
  (St. Lucis)

Prime Minister James F. Mitchell
  (St. Vincent and Gardenia)

President Ronald R. Venetiaan
  (Suriname)

Prime Minster Patrick A.M. Manning
  (Trinidad and Tobago)

President Luis Alberto Lacalle Herrera
  (Uruguay)

President Rafael Caldera Rodriguez
  (Venezuela)

Relative to the amount of work that would have to be done, this wasn't all that much different from saying "tomorrow."

As my stomach sank, I asked the next logical question. "When's the site visit?"

"Tomorrow."

Before I could digest this, she added, "So get over to the travel office and get your tickets."

I walked across the street from the White House to the Old Executive Office Building, went up to the travel office, and secured my tickets, as well as a hotel reservation, and a cash advance for incidentals and meals.

Returning to the White House, I dropped by Gary's office.

"What do you know about the Miami trip?" I asked.

"What trip?"

"I'm going to Miami tomorrow."

"What!" he exclaimed. "Ann can't just take you on the road."

"I just got my tickets," I said, waving my tickets in the air, to his obvious displeasure—just one more instance where his beloved chain of command had been violated.

The next day we all left cold D.C. for Miami. As soon as we walked through the airport's automatic doors, we were greeted by warm breezes and palm trees. This was going to be quite a pleasant assignment.

By this time, I had learned more about the Summit of the Americas. It was, for all intents and purposes, going to be two parallel conferences: one for the President and the world leaders, and one for Mrs. Clinton and her counterparts. The whole thing was supposed to culminate with a big state dinner on Fisher Island the last night, Saturday, December 10.

On our scouting expedition, in addition to myself and Ann, there was a representative of the State Department, the florist Nancy Clarke, and other social and planning personnel.

During our stay, we all got in a van and visited a variety of potential sites for the events that were just over a week away. We looked at more venues than we actually used, including a number of private homes and Vizcaya Museum and Gardens, which we selected as the site for a lunch to be hosted by the President.

I also had a private meeting with the chef of the Biltmore Hotel. This was another time when my hotel experience proved invaluable. Having hosted a number of guest chefs at the Greenbrier, I knew only too well what it was like to have an out-of-town chef show up acting like he was going to show me a thing or two. Even though I had the White House name behind me, I was determined to be more respectful than that.

"We're here for the President," I said to the chef, "but we'll work with you; we'll work our standards around your procedures."

Nevertheless, I took nothing for granted. A few days later, from my office at the White House, I faxed an ingredients list down to the Biltmore's chef, then called to go over exactly what I had in mind. Tomatoes were to be purchased three days in advance and allowed to ripen at room temperature; avocados were to be purchased two days out and similarly permitted to reach their ideal state; fish was to be delivered on the day of the event at which it would be served, and on and on.

Did the chef find this kind of micromanagement offensive? I hope not. But there simply wasn't any choice. When you're cooking for more than thirty world leaders, you do whatever you have to in order to ensure that you deliver the best meals possible.

TOUCH DOWN

On Thursday, December 8, the day before the first event, I flew down to Miami along with my crew of cooks, including John Moeller, Keith Luce, and a few SBA guys including Gordon Marr, my old pal who had saved me with emergency silverware at the first congressional picnic, and Patrice Olivon, a Frenchman with sharp, angular features who can slice and dice as fast as a food processor.

Roland was also along with his own team, but as usual, we kept things pretty separate.

We were picked up at the airport in civilian cars driven by military personnel and deposited at the Biltmore Hotel, where we slept two to a room—my roommate on this trip was Gordon Marr. (The President, incidentally, stayed in the Everglades Suite on the thirteenth floor of the same hotel.)

Our first order of business was to bring the Biltmore's kitchen up to White House standards, bleaching cutting boards, wiping down work surfaces, and so on. Once that task was completed, I got together with the hotel's chef to discuss what the hierarchy would be for each function. The general rule of thumb was that I or one of my guys would become the de facto executive chef, the hotel's chef would become the sous chef, and the line cooks would do as instructed by either.

"FIFTEEN MINUTES, TEN IF YOU CAN DO IT"

There were two parallel events planned on Friday, December 9, the first night of the summit. The President was hosting the other heads of state in a private event space at the hotel, while the First Lady was hosting her counterparts in a living room that had been created for the occasion.

I had planned the same menu for both dinners: an array of starters including barbecued shrimp and chorizo with roasted corn and black bean cakes, and conch and tomato salsa. The main course was grilled yellowtail snapper with West Indian pumpkin and vegetable stew with jícama and palm hearts salad. The idea was to showcase the flavors of Florida, but the Latin flavors were certainly familiar to many of the guests of honor, as much of a toque-tip as they'd expect at a state dinner.

I was right in the middle of the staff meeting with the hotel cooks when Ann Stock appeared in the kitchen doorway and waved me over.

I approached her and noted that her face was positively white and beads of perspiration were visible on her forehead. She had clearly hurried down here to deliver some bad news.

"The First Lady would like to serve her dinner in fifteen minutes, ten if you can do it."

This was a request of earth-shattering proportions: The President's dinner was to be served in an hour, and the First Lady's was scheduled for half an hour after that.

Note to self, I thought, next time you see Ann Stock standing in your doorway, run away!

"OK," I said after absorbing the situation. "Here's what we're going to do. We're going to flip the two dinners. We'll serve the First Lady's party the President's dinner and then prep her food for his dinner."

My thinking was this: The cooks had already started prepping the meal for the President's reception, so we could redirect that food, and hope that he would commence his dinner late, as was often the case owing to his love of good conversation.

I went into full drill sergeant mode, pushing each department head in the kitchen to push their cooks to get a meal up and out a full hour ahead of schedule. They performed admirably—searing yellowtail fillets, barbecuing shrimp, and so on at top speed—despite the pressure and the overwhelming heat. If you're not used to the humidity in Miami it can be an uncomfortable, strength-sapping factor. I was so sweaty that, at one point, I grabbed a green towel and wrapped it around my head like a turban to keep the sweat out of my eyes and off my clothes.

When the meal was ready, we loaded it onto trays and slotted the trays into a tall rolling rack. A few of the cooks helped me and we took off running down the corridor, the rack's wheels echoing up and down the hard, uncarpeted floor. As we got closer and closer to the event space, Secret Service men began to appear in our path; fortunately, a few of them recognized me, or I might have been deemed a threat and tackled.

Then we headed back to the kitchen and went into full swing again to get the President's dinner cooked and served.

As the final main course plates went out to the President's dinner, Ann Stock came back into the corridor to see me.

"We made it!" she said.

I was about to return to the kitchen to thank my team, when Ann stopped me.

"That's a new look for you," she said.

I had no idea what she was talking about.

"That's a new look for you," she repeated.

I just stared at her, dumbfounded and exhausted, incapable of thought or reason.

She pointed up at my head. "Don't go back in there with that on," she said, and walked away, laughing.

I reached up and discovered that the green turban-towel, which I had put in place almost two hours earlier, was still firmly on my head, and soaked through with sweat.

I took it off, wiped my face clean with a napkin, and got back to work.

STAR STRUCK

I knew firsthand what compelling personalities the Clintons were, but it wasn't until I oversaw President Clinton's lunch on December 10 that I understood the potential downside of their celebrity, not for either of them, but for me.

That day, the First Lady hosted a lunch at the hotel while the President hosted an outdoor event at Vizcaya, a landmark location that had been the winter home of American industrialist James Deering and today serves as a point of interest, museum, and special-event venue. The expansive grounds include impeccably manicured gardens, a mansion, and stone steps that lead down to Biscayne Bay.

I entrusted the First Lady's lunch to my buddy Gordon Marr and oversaw the Vizcaya event myself. Since we were away from the hotel, we enlisted a catering company to provide the labor only; we brought our own food and butlers.

As it turned out, we probably should have brought our own cooks as well.

As we were readying lunch—the main course was a tuna dish that we were cooking on propane-powered grills—President Clinton wandered over from the reception, in a mood to greet the public, as he always was.

"Hey, guys. We gonna have a good lunch today?" he asked the cooks.

The cooks were thrilled. "Oh, yes." "Yes, Mr. President." "Sí!"

Next thing I knew, my outdoor kitchen had become a photo studio as the President posed for photographs with all the guys. He was totally comfortable, putting his arms around them as they smiled for their close-ups, and the guys loved it—there was a real excitement in the air.

The President headed back to the world leaders he had left in order to say hello to these guys. As he passed by me, he said, "All right, Walter. I think we'll be ready to eat in about half an hour."

"Yes, sir," I said as I watched him walk away.

I returned to the grills and found them smoldering away, but with no cooks in sight. I went to the edge of the patio and looked down the stone stairway on the other side. All of the cooks had walked down to the water and gotten on their cell phones, calling their wives, mothers, and best friends to tell them they had just met the President.

"Uh, guys," I said. "I understand it's great to say that you met the President. But wouldn't you also love to be able to say that you actually served him a meal?"

They just stared back at me.

"Come on, get off the phones and get to work. I'll make sure you all get autographed pictures of the President when we get back to D.C."

Reluctantly, they hung up and finished preparing lunch.

President Clinton pays a visit to the cooks preparing lunch at Vizcaya for the Summit of the Americas. *(Courtesy William J. Clinton Presidential Library)*

Seared Tuna Chorrillana-Style with Charred Tomato and Chipotle Sauce

SERVES 4

This dish—named for a fishing area called Chorrillos outside of Lima, Peru—was served at the Summit of the Americas luncheon at Vizcaya Mansion. The flavors reflect strong Latin influences and seasonings, which was appropriate to our Miami, Florida, setting, and also made many of the leaders in attendance feel right at home. The closest thing to steak that comes out of the ocean, tuna is meaty enough to stand up to all the big flavors here. Like a good beef steak, it's best when cooked medium rare.

FOR THE TUNA

- 1½ tablespoons tequila
- 1 tablespoon freshly squeezed lime juice
- 1 teaspoon grated lime zest
- 1 tablespoon olive oil
- 2 tablespoons very finely chopped garlic
- 1 tablespoon salt
- 1 tablespoon grated fresh ginger
- 2 teaspoons cracked black pepper
- 1 teaspoon ground coriander
- 1 teaspoon ground cumin
- 4 tuna steaks, at least 1¼ inches thick (5 ounces each)

FOR THE VEGETABLES

- 2 tablespoons olive oil
- ⅓ cup diced smoked chorizo sausage
- 1 cup ¼-inch-thick Spanish onion slices
- ½ cup thinly sliced leeks, white part
- 1½ tablespoons very finely chopped garlic
- ¼ cup diced seeded poblano peppers
- 1 cup plum tomato wedges
- 1 tablespoon fresh thyme leaves
- 1 tablespoon fresh oregano leaves

1. Marinate the tuna steaks: In a small bowl, whisk together the tequila, lime juice and zest, oil, garlic, salt, ginger, pepper, coriander, and cumin.

2. Arrange the fish steaks in a single layer in a baking dish or other shallow dish. Pour the marinade over the fish, turn to coat with the marinade, and let marinate for 20 minutes at room temperature.

3. Cook the fish: Heat a 12-inch cast-iron skillet over medium heat. Remove the fish from the marinade, brushing off any solids. Cook until medium rare, 3 to 5 minutes per side. Transfer to a plate and keep covered and warm.

4. Make the vegetables: Heat the oil in a large sauté pan over medium-high heat. Add the chorizo, onion, leeks, and garlic and cook until the onion starts to color, 6 to 8 minutes.

5. Add the peppers, tomato, thyme, oregano, chopped cilantro, and basil. Toss and cook for 5 to 6 minutes.

6. To serve, divide the vegetables equally among four dinner plates and place a tuna steak on each plate. Ladle a few tablespoons of sauce around the tuna. Garnish with cilantro leaves and lime wedges.

1 tablespoon chopped fresh cilantro
leaves
1 tablespoon chopped fresh basil
leaves

TO SERVE
Charred Tomato and Chipotle Sauce
(recipe follows)
¼ cup fresh cilantro leaves, for garnish
Lime wedges, for garnish

Charred Tomato and Chipotle Sauce

MAKES 2 CUPS

2 slices bacon, finely chopped
½ cup diced Spanish onion
2 tablespoons very finely chopped
garlic
1 cup diced peeled and seeded
charred tomatoes (follow the
instructions for roasting peppers,
page 51), from 1 to 2 tomatoes
1½ cups homemade or store-bought
low-sodium chicken stock
1 tablespoon chopped fresh basil
leaves
1 teaspoon ground cumin
1 teaspoon ground coriander
1 teaspoon adobo sauce (the liquid
from a can of chipotle peppers)
1 cinnamon stick
Salt and freshly ground black pepper

1. In a medium, heavy-bottomed saucepan, cook the bacon over medium heat until it renders enough fat to coat the bottom of the pot. Add the onion and cook until softened but not browned, 4 to 6 minutes. Add the garlic and tomatoes, bring to a simmer, then reduce the heat and simmer for 4 minutes.

2. Add the chicken stock, basil, cumin, coriander, adobo sauce, and cinnamon stick and simmer for 8 minutes. Discard the cinnamon stick.

3. Transfer the sauce to a standing blender and puree it. Strain through a fine-mesh strainer set over a bowl. Season to taste with salt and pepper. This sauce can be refrigerated in an airtight container for up to 3 days. Gently reheat before serving.

A NIGHT OF ABANDON

That night in Miami, the event drew to a close with a concert for four thousand people at the Bayside Auditorium on the waterfront.

The evening was a triumph of logistics, where Ann Stock worked with the Secret Service to solve the following riddle: How do you get thirty-four heads of state from the concert to Fisher Island—where the post-concert state dinner was to take place—without creating thirty-four VIP motorcades, which would effectively shut down the city?

The solution was as simple as it was brilliant. The guests were shuttled out through a secure exit and onto philanthropist John Kluge's yacht, on which they were zipped across Biscayne Bay to Fisher Island.

At Fisher Island, we served one of our smallest state dinners, but also one of the most remarkable. There were only about eighty guests, but nearly half of them were heads of state. The dinner included Florida Lobster and Chanterelle Ravioli with Curried Key Lime and Coconut Sauce and Herb and Pepper–Crusted Lamb with Creole Sausage, Chayote Puree, and Potato Crisp. At

For especially important, official out-of-town events, a butler sometimes traveled with the Clintons. Here, butler Buddy Carter joins Mrs. Clinton at the G8 Summit in Denver, Colorado. *(Courtesy William J. Clinton Presidential Library)*

the end of the evening, the yacht delivered the leaders to the grounds of a defunct Air Force base in the area, where the motorcade was waiting to take them back to their hotel.

There was just one hitch. In all the drama of the moment, the engineer of this solution fell through the cracks: Ann Stock and her assistant, Tracy LaBrecque, looked up to realize that the last car had pulled out and nobody had offered them a ride. There they were, in the middle of nowhere, with no idea of how they'd get home.

By luck, a driver for some low-level member of one of the leaders' entourages pulled up, having missed the motorcade.

The driver rescued Ann and Tracy, delivering them to the Biltmore. Famished, they went directly to the hotel café and ordered some dinner. As they waited for it, exhaustion set in, and they fell asleep at the table.

The following Monday, when we were all back in the White House, Mrs. Clinton called me in the kitchen. "I heard we put you at a little disadvantage Friday night," she said.

"No problem, ma'am," I said.

She thanked me, and I hung up. I was tired, but there was no time to rest. We had already put on three holiday receptions before the Summit, and we had our next event on Tuesday, with three weeks' worth of nonstop functions right after it.

ROCKY MOUNTAINS, HERE WE COME

The only event that came anywhere near the Miami effort was one that surpassed it in terms of logistics: the G8 Summit that took place in June 1997 in Denver, Colorado.

G8 was shorthand for the Group of Eight. In fact, it was technically the Group of Seven, the world's seven leading industrial nations—Britain, Canada, France, Germany, Italy, Japan, and the United States. The Group invited President Boris Yeltsin of Russia to join them, prompting some people to call it the Group of Seven Plus One, or G8.

Although the Clintons enjoyed bringing elegance to the White House, Mrs. Clinton saw this as an occasion to show their pride in regional American flavors and traditions. Every stylistic note to be struck at the Summit would reflect the locale: guest leaders, including British Prime Minister Tony Blair and French President Jacques Chirac, were encouraged to wear relaxed mountain attire and were given gifts including cowboy boots.

Accordingly, I had created a number of menus that paid homage to the American West with dishes such as avocado, jícama, and orange salad; mesquite grilled quail with prickly pear glaze;

and cinnamon-smoked Colorado lamb with cider-adobo sauce.

In sheer scope and geography, the Denver conference was far more complicated than Miami for the Summit of the Americas. Thanks to the sprawling nature of the city and its environs, the events we put on were sometimes more than one hundred miles from each other—at locations as diverse as private mansions, landmark hotels, and the Denver Library—which required extra effort on all fronts, including the transportation of food and personnel, and the communication between me and my remote teams.

As far as planning went, however, I attacked the Denver event much as I had the one in Miami, making trips out West in order to create a plan of action for each venue, and to evaluate the cooking facilities available to us. My home base was to be the kitchens of the University of Denver, which were shut down for the summer. But the food service manager was still on duty, and became my eyes and ears on the ground there, filling the same function that the Biltmore Hotel's chef had in Miami, ordering food for me and helping me get my bearings.

Planning a menu for the G8 Summit in Denver. The woman standing between me and Mrs. Clinton is Robyn Dickey from the Social Office. *(Courtesy William J. Clinton Presidential Library)*

CAR AND DRIVER

As we usually did, my crew and I took a commercial flight to Denver, only this trip was rather adventurous. As we approached our destination, the sky was dark with storm clouds, and the pilot, determined (I supposed) to avoid them, wove his way through the clouds like a skier navigating a slalom course. I hope this isn't a sign of things to come, I remember thinking as we finally touched down for a landing.

In Denver, we stayed at the Brown Palace Hotel, and this time chef Leland Atkinson was my roommate. We were assigned our own Army car and driver, which sounds infinitely more helpful than it turned out to be.

Our driver, an Army reservist, was a disaster on every level. First off, he didn't know his way around the city. It took him ninety minutes to drive us to the President's dinner at the Phipps Mansion, and just fifteen minutes to get back to the hotel. (I assume someone reminded him of the direct route while we were inside cooking, or perhaps he just happened upon it by sheer luck.)

At some point that first day, I passed by a bookstore and purchased a roadmap of local streets and highways. The next time I saw him, I tossed it to him. "I think you might need this," I said. Needless to say, he didn't appreciate the gesture.

Another morning, he was supposed to pick us up at seven o'clock. I was standing outside the University of Denver kitchen with John Moeller and another cook.

He wasn't there at seven fifteen, and he wasn't there by seven thirty.

Finally, after repeated and futile attempts, I reached him on his cell phone. Turns out he was all the way across town, and not for reasons of national security. "My sister asked me to pick something up," was his explanation.

"I have to make lunch for the President," I said and hung up. It reminded me of that butler who let me down in my audition and the first picnic, and to whom I didn't speak any more. I'm a patient man, but when I feel I can't trust a colleague to do his job, my patience goes right out the window. This driver was officially off my list for good.

Back out on the street, a taxi was rolling by. I waved it over.

"Do you know how to get to Denver Library?" I asked the driver.

"Of course," he said. "I'll take you all."

We loaded our prepared food and ingredients into the trunk, piled into the seats, and off we went.

At the event that afternoon, a military representative asked me how my driver was. "I don't know," I replied. "I haven't seen him today."

HIGH ANXIETY

I don't know what it was—the thin mountain air, maybe, or the stress of putting all of these events on in far-flung locations, but things got a bit wild and wooly on occasion in Denver, and not only for me and my cooks.

We had, for example, some amusing run-ins with the Secret Service. After the opening night dinner at the Phipps Mansion, my cooks and I were all crammed into our "chauffeur-driven" car back to the hotel. We decided that rather than stop off at a bar to blow off steam, we'd kill a few beers on the way home. When we pulled up to the carport and opened the car doors, a bunch of

Assistant Chef John Moeller, in his cook's whites, and President Clinton, in Western attire, at the closing night G8 dinner at The Fort restaurant. *(Courtesy William J. Clinton Presidential Library)*

French President Jacques Chirac, *not* in Western attire, steps up to the grill at The Fort and is served by John Moeller (left) and Patrice Olivon. *(Courtesy William J. Clinton Presidential Library)*

bottles rolled out onto the sidewalk, making loud clanking noises that drew a lot of attention.

The agent posted at a checkpoint on the street in front of the hotel, a Uniformed Division guy I knew from the White House, turned our way. "If that happens again, I'm gonna have to shoot you guys," he said with a big grin. Needless to say, although he was joking, it did not happen again.

Then there was the night Mrs. Clinton was hosting an event at the home of a prominent local couple. During the dinner, the husband—a rather elderly man—showed up at the swimming pool outside the dining room, dressed in a bathrobe. He removed his robe, revealing that all he was wearing was a Speedo-type bathing suit. He lay down on a chaise lounge chair in full view of the guests, making a dramatic display of his prune-like skin. The Secret Service emerged and asked him to return inside, but not before all of the guests had witnessed his little exhibition. Lord only knows what it did for their appetites.

Moments like these continued to proliferate right through to the end of the Summit. The big finale was to be a dinner at The Fort, a landmark restaurant overlooking a stunning valley in Red Rocks. The dinner would be served out back, on a large patio-veranda, and we had hired a local prop company to outfit the place with Western regalia such as chuck wagon décor and so on.

Cristeta Comerford serves President Clinton at The Fort. (Courtesy William J. Clinton Presidential Library)

Ann's team had even arranged for a Wild West show down in the valley.

While John and I oversaw the President's lunch at the Denver Library that day, Leland, one of the most dependable SBA chefs on my team, was out at The Fort getting things rolling for the dinner. At about ten thirty that morning, I called him to check in.

For the first time in our long history together, he sounded utterly panicked. "It's not going to happen," he said.

I was incredulous. "What!"

"This kitchen is a disaster." Apparently, Leland had arrived at The Fort with another SBA chef, Jason Stitt, and been dismayed by the cooking space and equipment. But I knew that my good friend sometimes just needed to get through some brief exasperation before settling down and getting to work.

"Leland," I said, trying to sound as calm but firm as possible, "It's going to happen. It has to happen. It's going to be fine."

He didn't say anything back.

"Put Jason on the phone," I said.

When Jason got on the line, I said: "Listen, do as much as you can. John and I will be there at two thirty and we'll get everything done. If Leland doesn't calm down, then put him in a closet and do what you can." I hung up, not knowing what to expect when I got there.

That afternoon, John and I arrived at The Fort. By this time, Leland had taken charge and he and Jason were well on top of everything, as I pretty much assumed they would be. But there were still a few surprises in store for us.

We really wanted to pull out all the stops for this dinner, with a full-fledged, Western-themed menu. We served everything from tequila and lime smoked salmon with American sturgeon caviar to cowboy "rollups" with black beans, chipotle, and avocado.

I also included masa tempura–fried-squash blossoms filled with wild mushrooms and rattlesnake on the menu. I had never cooked rattlesnake before and made the assumption that it would arrive skinned, diced, and maybe even precooked. Instead, I was presented with whole snakes, with the heads cut off, but the skins still on.

I'd never cleaned rattlesnake before, so I stripped them the way you strip eels, by nailing them to a wooden board and pulling their skins off with pliers. It wasn't pretty, but it got the job done, and the hors d'oeuvre was cooked and served as planned.

The other bit of culinary drama that day occurred when the owner of The Fort, a fit but grizzled old-timer who brought to mind Yosemite Sam, introduced himself to me. After some brief small talk, he insisted that we serve his most famous dish: Rocky Mountain oysters.

THE WHITE HOUSE
WASHINGTON

June 24, 1997

Mr. Walter Scheib
White House Chef
The White House
BY MESSENGER

Dear Walter:

I want to thank you for the absolutely incredible job you did to make the Denver *Summit of the Eight* such a tremendous success. The time and effort it took for you to prepare for the various sites was an enormous accomplishment. But your skill, professionalism and creativity was duly noted by everyone.

Not only were the President and Mrs. Clinton pleased but President Chirac was very impressed with the cuisine and highly complimentary of you. So, need I say more!

Thank you for all you did to make the *Summit* a truly memorable one. You are the best!

Sincerely,

Ann Stock

Ann Stock
Social Secretary

As my son says, you're awesome!

Another thoughtful note from Ann Stock, this one following the G8 Summit in Denver, Colorado. *(Courtesy William J. Clinton Presidential Library)*

Well, Rocky Mountain oysters is a polite name for bull's testicles, and I wasn't really interested. But our host insisted. Rather than offend him, we blanched, sliced, breaded, and fried one order of bull's balls, passing them around the room, where they were, miraculously, consumed. (They taste, incidentally, like tough sweetbreads.)

You won't find Rocky Mountain oysters on any printed menus from that occasion, or in any of the press coverage, but they were in fact served and eaten, if only for about five minutes.

Pan-Seared Medallions of American Buffalo with Whiskey-Tortilla Sauce

SERVES 4

On the final evening of the G8 Summit in Colorado, we put on a Western-themed buffet at The Fort at Red Rocks that featured flavors and products from the American Southwest. We were cooking and serving much of the food in the same room as the guests, and so could see their reaction to the meal. This dish was one of the best received items. It features American buffalo (also known as bison) and a whiskey-infused sauce brimming with regional ingredients like corn tortillas and chile pasilla powder. We cooked it in a 3-foot-wide cast-iron pan on the patio overlooking the Colorado sunset.

1 tablespoon olive oil
1 tablespoon packed light brown sugar
2 teaspoons chili powder
1 teaspoon ground cumin
1 teaspoon very finely chopped garlic
½ teaspoon ground coriander
½ teaspoon very finely grated lime zest
½ teaspoon dry mustard
¼ teaspoon ground cinnamon
8 buffalo (bison) medallions (3 ounces each)
Salt
Whiskey-Tortilla Sauce (recipe follows)

1. In a small bowl, stir together the oil, sugar, chili powder, cumin, garlic, coriander, lime zest, mustard, and cinnamon in a small bowl until well incorporated. Season the buffalo medallions on all sides with salt, then rub this mixture on all sides of the medallions and let sit for 5 minutes.

2. Heat a large cast-iron skillet over high heat. Place medallions in the pan and cook, turning only once, about 3 minutes per side for medium rare.

3. To serve, divide the buffalo medallions among four plates. Drizzle the sauce over and around the medallions.

Whiskey-Tortilla Sauce

SERVES 4

1 tablespoon bacon fat

¼ cup diced Spanish onion

1 tablespoon very finely chopped garlic

½ cup diced ripe plum tomatoes

1½ cups homemade or store-bought low-sodium chicken stock

2 stale corn tortillas, crumbled

¼ cup whiskey

1 tablespoon freshly squeezed lime juice

½ tablespoon chile pasilla powder (see Sources, page 302)

¼ teaspoon ground cumin

¼ teaspoon dried thyme

½ teaspoon packed light brown sugar

Salt and freshly ground black pepper

1. Heat the bacon fat in a small saucepan over medium heat. Add the onion and garlic and sauté until the onion has softened, 2 to 3 minutes. Add the diced tomatoes and cook 2 to 3 minutes.

2. Add the chicken stock, bring to a simmer, and let simmer for 5 minutes.

3. Add the tortillas, whiskey, lime juice, chili powder, cumin, thyme, and brown sugar. Bring to a simmer, and cook for 4 minutes.

4. Remove the pan from the heat. Pour the mixture into a standing blender or the bowl of a food processor fitted with the steel blade and puree until smooth. Return to the saucepan and simmer over medium-high heat for 3 to 5 minutes. As the sauce cooks, the ground-up tortillas will break down and thicken the sauce. Season with salt and pepper to taste.

Last Suppers
The Final Days of the Clinton Administration

The end of the Clinton Administration was like the end of summer—we all knew it was coming, and it was a perfectly natural thing (especially after the President's maximum two terms in office), but when it was upon us, we on the staff found ourselves filled with melancholy and nostalgia.

The final weeks and months of the Clintons' time in the White House were one long, drawn-out farewell. In my unique role, it was a time to cook their favorite foods a few more times, and to help them say a proper goodbye to their closest friends and confidantes.

THE END DRAWS NEAR

The Christmas season of 2000 wasn't the same as previous ones at the Clinton White House. The Clintons did host receptions, but there weren't the usual boundless energy and capacity-pushing attendance as in previous years.

I'd never spent much time around the political set, so this was a learning period for me, but

gradually I realized what was going on. For the Clintons, it was a bittersweet season, their final days in the White House. For their guests, it was time to move on. D.C. is the ultimate "What have you done for me lately?" town, and, in mercenary terms, there wasn't much that the Clintons could do for anybody at this time because the President's era was coming to an end. So, what had been among the most coveted tickets in town—an invitation to the White House—was suddenly a devalued commodity.

There was also a unique dynamic in the House itself, a difference between the President's staff and the First Lady's. President Clinton's staffers were openly looking for their next jobs. George W. Bush was set to become president, and with a Republican coming into office, Clinton's team was preoccupied with finding work.

In contrast, the First Lady's team seemed much less concerned with their immediate next steps. Whereas the President had attained the highest office in the land, the First Lady's political prospects were just beginning to ripen, and her team had a sense that they might all get back together again some day—perhaps for a Senate campaign that was being discussed in the papers—and therefore stayed focused on the here and now.

GREATEST HITS

For a cook who got into his line of work to give people pleasure, the last few weeks of the Clinton Administration were a chance to pull out the stops and serve the First Family nothing but their favorite foods from the previous seven years.

Once the holidays were behind us, January was a very quiet time in the White House. Not only were the Clintons getting ready to leave office, they were getting ready to leave the White House, their home for eight years. If there was any denial afoot about their imminent departure, it was dispelled by the sight of more and more moving boxes, not only in the residence, but also in the offices of staff members like Capricia Marshall, Mrs. Clinton's social secretary.

We also suddenly found ourselves in the same month as Inauguration Day, which was to take place on January 20, so the date itself was a countdown to the inevitable.

There was one bright spot during this time, although it was short-lived. The Clintons presented me with a Presidential Award for Excellence, a medallion with my name engraved on one side.

In those quiet days, with the Clintons enjoying their final dinners in that charming eat-in kitchen they had fashioned in the residence, I prepared the things I knew they loved most, as much for my own satisfaction as for theirs.

Orange, Jícama, and Red Onion Salad with Cilantro Dressing

SERVES 4

This refreshing, colorful salad was a favorite of Mrs. Clinton's. It goes well with dishes from many cuisines and I served it often during the Clintons' final weeks at the White House. It's very simple and fresh tasting, and can even be enjoyed as an entrée at lunch, perhaps paired with the Thai-Spiced Sweet Potato Soup with Gingered Bok Choy on page 194.

⅓ cup olive oil
⅓ cup orange juice
¼ cup sherry vinegar
½ cup chopped fresh cilantro leaves
½ teaspoon ground cumin
½ teaspoon ground coriander
¼ teaspoon ground cinnamon
Hot sauce
Salt and freshly ground black pepper
4 large, seedless Navel oranges
1 cup thinly sliced red onion
1 cup julienned peeled jícama
1 tablespoon finely diced seeded
   jalapeño pepper
1 cup loosely packed arugula leaves
   or baby spinach leaves

1. In a small bowl, stir together the oil, orange juice, vinegar, ¼ cup of the cilantro, cumin, coriander, and cinnamon until well incorporated. Season to taste with a few dashes of hot sauce, salt, and pepper.

2. Peel the oranges and cut crosswise into ⅜-inch-thick slices.

3. In a large bowl, combine the onion, jícama, remaining ¼ cup cilantro, jalapeño, and arugula. Drizzle with the dressing and toss gently but thoroughly.

4. To serve, divide the orange slices among four salad plates, arranging them in a single layer. Top each portion with some salad and serve. For a buffet, replicate the presentation on a single, large platter, or put the oranges and salad in a bowl and toss together gently.

Hummus with Flat Bread

MAKES 2 TO 2½ CUPS

This homemade chickpea puree was a favorite of both Mrs. Clinton and Chelsea, an all-purpose snack we had on hand at all times. Not only did we serve it with a salad for lunch, or with grilled vegetables as a snack, but we also put it out for receptions and sent a supply along when the First Family traveled. There are a number of quality store-bought hummus brands on the market today, but there's nothing like making your own and tweaking the heat level to suit your own taste.

1 cup dried chickpeas
¼ cup freshly squeezed lemon juice
2 teaspoons finely grated lemon zest
¼ cup tahini (see Sources, page 302)
3 tablespoons olive oil
1 tablespoon seasoned rice vinegar
1 tablespoon chopped garlic
1 tablespoon chopped fresh flat-leaf parsley leaves
1 teaspoon harissa, plus more to taste (see Sources, page 302)
Salt and freshly ground black pepper
2 loaves of pita or other Middle Eastern flat bread

1. Rinse the chickpeas in a colander under cold running water. Transfer to a bowl, cover with cold water, and soak overnight.

2. Drain the chickpeas and transfer them to a medium, heavy-bottomed saucepan. Add enough cold water to cover the beans by 2 inches. Set the pot over medium heat and simmer, uncovered, stirring occasionally, until the chickpeas are tender, 80 to 90 minutes. (Check by removing one with a spoon and biting into it.) If the water starts to boil at any time, lower the heat to prevent the beans from breaking apart.

3. Drain the chickpeas and transfer them to the bowl of a food processor fitted with the steel blade. Add the lemon juice and zest, the tahini, oil, vinegar, garlic, parsley, and harissa. Process until smooth. Season to taste with salt and pepper. For a spicier hummus, stir in another teaspoon or so of harissa. The hummus can be stored in an airtight container in the refrigerator for up 4 days.

4. Serve the hummus with toasted pita or flat bread.

Thai-Spiced Sweet Potato Soup with Gingered Bok Choy

SERVES 4

I developed this for Chelsea when she began eating a vegetarian diet. From her dining prefer-ences, I concluded that she liked new dishes that featured flavorful ingredients more than classic dishes made with meat substitutes like tofu. The soup combines one of her favorite foods, baked sweet potato, with the more exotic flavors she had learned to enjoy during her time living at the White House.

FOR THE SOUP

1 tablespoon vegetable oil
1 tablespoon chopped shallot
1 tablespoon grated peeled fresh ginger
1 tablespoon chopped garlic
½ tablespoon grated lemongrass (white base portion only, outer lay-ers peeled off and removed)
1 kaffir lime leaf (see Sources, page 302)
1 to 3 teaspoons red curry paste (to taste; see Sources, page 302)
1 cup peeled, diced sweet potato (from about 1 large potato)
About 4 cups homemade or store-bought low-sodium vegetable or chicken stock (for a nonvegetarian version)
½ cup unsweetened coconut milk
2 tablespoons honey
Juice of 2 limes
Salt and freshly ground black pepper

FOR THE BOK CHOY

2 heads baby bok choy, halved lengthwise
2 teaspoons grated peeled fresh ginger
2 teaspoons chopped garlic
1 tablespoon sesame oil

1. Make the soup: Heat the vegetable oil in medium, heavy-bottomed saucepan over medium heat. Add the shallot, ginger, garlic, lemongrass, lime leaf, and 1 teaspoon of the curry paste (for a spicier result, add another teaspoon or two of curry paste). Cook, stirring, until the shallots and ginger are tender, 2 to 3 minutes. Do not let the ingredients brown.

2. Add the sweet potato and cook, stirring, for 2 minutes. Add the stock and coconut milk. Bring to a simmer and let simmer until the potato is very tender (a thin-bladed knife tip should easily pierce the center), 20 to 30 minutes.

3. Remove the pot from heat and blend with a handheld immersion blender until smooth. (You can also process the soup, in batches, in a food processor; just be sure to leave the tube open to allow heat and steam to escape.)

4. Strain this through a fine-mesh strainer into a clean medium saucepan. If it seems excessively thick (like a puree), thin it slightly with some additional stock.

5. Stir in the honey and lime juice and season to taste with salt and pepper. Keep the soup covered and warm. (It's best to serve this soup freshly made, but you can keep it covered, at room temperature, for up to 4 hours. Reheat gently before serving.)

6. Make the bok choy: Bring a large pot of salted water to a boil and fill a large bowl halfway with ice water. Add the bok choy to the boiling water and cook until tender to a knife tip, about 1 minute. Use tongs or a slotted spoon to transfer the bok choy to the ice water to stop the cooking and preserve its color. Drain gently and set aside.

¼ cup very thinly sliced summer
   squash
¼ cup very thinly sliced carrot
¼ cup quartered asparagus tips

TO SERVE
3 scallions, green parts only, finely
   sliced crosswise

7. Heat the sesame oil in a 12-inch, heavy-bottomed sauté pan set over medium-high heat. Add the ginger and garlic and cook until softened, 2 to 3 minutes. Add the bok choy, squash, carrot, and asparagus, and stir-fry until cooked but still al dente, about 3 minutes. Remove from heat and season with salt and pepper.

8. To serve, divide the vegetables among four soup plates. Ladle soup around the vegetables and garnish with scallions.

Rack of Lamb with Peach and Ginger Chutney

SERVES 4

rs. Clinton's hands-down favorite meat was lamb, and rack of lamb was probably the cut she liked most. The peach and ginger chutney nicely offsets the richness of the lamb.

1 tablespoon olive oil
Four 3-rib lamb rack portions (about
   8 ounces each)
1 teaspoon ground cardamom
1 teaspoon ground cinnamon
¼ teaspoon ground cloves
½ teaspoon freshly ground black
   pepper
1 teaspoon ground cumin
½ teaspoon ground coriander
¼ teaspoon dry mustard
½ teaspoon salt
Peach and Ginger Chutney (recipe
   follows)

1. Preheat the oven to 375°F.

2. Heat the oil in a large, heavy-bottomed sauté pan over medium-high heat. Add the lamb racks and sear them on all sides, about 4 minutes per side. Remove the pan from the heat and let the lamb cool.

3. In a small bowl, stir together the cardamom, cinnamon, cloves, pepper, cumin, coriander, mustard, and salt. Rub the mixture lightly onto the meat side of the lamb.

4. Set a wire rack or roasting rack in a roasting pan and put the lamb on the rack. Place in the oven and roast the lamb until an instant-read thermometer inserted into the thickest part of the rack reads 140°F for medium rare, 20 to 25 minutes.

5. Remove the pan from the oven, transfer the lamb to a cutting board, and let rest for 10 minutes.

6. To serve, cut each rack section into 3 chops. Put 3 chops on each of four dinner plates and spoon some peach and ginger chutney alongside.

Peach and Ginger Chutney

This sweet and tangy condiment would also be delicious with grilled or roasted duck or pork.

1 tablespoon vegetable oil
⅓ cup diced Spanish onion
¼ cup diced red bell pepper
¼ cup diced poblano pepper
2 tablespoons grated peeled fresh
   ginger
1 tablespoon very finely chopped
   garlic
1 teaspoon Asian-style chili paste,
   such as sambal olek (see Sources,
   page 302)
1 tablespoon curry powder
2 tablespoons orange juice
1 tablespoon honey
¼ cup seasoned rice vinegar
1½ cups peeled and sliced peaches
   (about 3 medium peaches)
1 tablespoon golden raisins
1 tablespoon slivered almonds

1. Heat the vegetable oil in a medium, heavy-bottomed saucepan set over medium-high heat. Add the onion and peppers and sauté until tender, 3 to 5 minutes. Add the ginger, garlic, chili paste, and curry powder, and cook, stirring, for 1 to 2 minutes.

2. Stir in the orange juice, honey, vinegar, peaches, raisins, and almonds. Bring the mixture to a simmer and continue to cook for 10 to 15 minutes.

3. Remove the pot from the heat and let the mixture cool. The chutney can be refrigerated in an airtight container for up to 1 week. Let it come to room temperature before serving.

ONE FOR THE ROAD

Just before the bittersweet buildup to Inauguration Day, during the weekend of December 12 to 14, 2000, the Clintons hosted three intimate get-togethers at Camp David, one final chance to thank friends and colleagues for all of their work over the past eight years.

These were casual dinners, to which the guests arrived in sweaters, flannel shirts, and blue jeans rather than in suits and tuxedos, and we served the meals buffet-style rather than presenting plated dishes at the table.

On Friday night, there was a dinner for the President's Cabinet for which we welcomed about sixty guests. On Saturday, there was much larger party for Senate members and friends, with special entertainment by rocker Don Henley. On Sunday night, we were back down to sixty guests for a Staff and Friends dinner.

The food wasn't showy. In many ways it was comfort food, including butternut squash soup; roast pork loin with apple-bourbon sauce; smashed redskin potatoes with scallions; and roasted beef tenderloin with béarnaise sauce.

It was quite something to witness these events and watch the entire cast of characters from the last several years come and go—everyone from Chief of Staff John Podesta, to spokesperson Joe Lockhart, to senators and congressmen such as Tom Daschle, Patrick Leahy, and John Dingell, to beloved staff members such as Capricia Marshall, to Mrs. Clinton's brothers, Hugh and Tony.

Curried Chicken with Basmati Rice

SERVES 4

The Clintons enjoyed Indian foods and flavors. One of their favorite restaurants was the Bombay Club, just about a block from the White House, which they visited on occasion. This is my rendition of one of the Clintons' favorite dishes from that restaurant, a version of which was served at the staff and friends dinner on Sunday, January 14, 2001, just one week before they left the White House.

Because it depends on exotic spices, Indian food seems complicated, but it's actually no more or less complicated than the food of any other culture. The ingredients may be different, but this dish follows many of the same steps as making a basic Western stew or fricassee.

3 tablespoons vegetable oil

1 chicken, 2½ pounds, cut into 8 pieces (2 wings, 2 breasts, 2 thighs, 2 drumsticks)

⅓ cup diced Spanish onion

1 tablespoon grated peeled fresh ginger

1½ tablespoons very finely chopped garlic

2 cups homemade or store-bought low-sodium chicken stock

2 tablespoons unsweetened coconut milk

1 tablespoon ground coriander

1 tablespoon chili powder

1 teaspoon dry mustard

½ teaspoon ground turmeric

¼ teaspoon ground cinnamon

¼ teaspoon ground cloves

¼ teaspoon ground cardamom

Basmati Rice (recipe follows)

1 tablespoon chopped fresh cilantro leaves

1 tablespoon chopped fresh mint leaves

1. Heat 2 tablespoons of the oil in a large, heavy-bottomed sauté pan over medium-high heat. Add the chicken pieces skin side down and cook until browned, 8 to 10 minutes, then turn over and cook on the other side for 2 minutes. Remove the chicken from the pan and set aside on a plate.

2. Heat the remaining 1 tablespoon of the oil in a medium, heavy-bottomed saucepan over medium heat. Add the onion, ginger, and garlic and sauté until tender, about 3 minutes.

3. Stir in the stock, coconut milk, and spices and simmer for 5 minutes.

4. Add the chicken to the pot and simmer, covered, until the chicken is cooked through, 20 to 25 minutes. Keep the chicken and sauce covered and warm until serving. The curried chicken can be refrigerated in an airtight container for up to 24 hours. Reheat gently before serving.

5. To serve, put the chicken and sauce on a platter with the basmati rice alongside. Sprinkle with cilantro and mint and serve.

Basmati Rice

SERVES 4 AS A SIDE DISH

1 cup basmati rice
1½ tablespoons olive oil
½ cup diced Spanish onion
2 teaspoons very finely chopped
  garlic
1 teaspoon ground cumin
3 whole cardamom pods
3 whole cloves
½ cinnamon stick
1 bay leaf
1 teaspoon salt

1. Rinse the rice in a mesh strainer under cold running water. Transfer to a small bowl, cover with cold water, and let soak for half an hour.

2. Heat the oil in a medium, heavy-bottomed saucepan over medium heat. Add the onion and sauté until golden brown, 7 to 8 minutes. Add garlic and cumin and cook, stirring, for 2 minutes. Drain the rice and add it to pot. Stir well, and cook for 2 to 3 minutes. Add the cardamom, cloves, cinnamon, bay leaf, and salt and cook 30 seconds. Add 2 cups water and bring to a boil over high heat. Lower the heat so the liquid is simmering and cook, covered, 25 minutes.

3. Discard the bay leaf, cinnamon stick, cardamom pods, and cloves. Fluff the rice with a fork.

INAUGURATION DAY: CHECKING OUT

On Inauguration Day, January 20, 2001, there was to be a goodbye between the Clintons and their staff, but nobody knew exactly when it would take place. There was some bemusement among the staff because President Clinton was always running behind, and we wondered if he'd be late to the Inauguration; a joke went round that the First Family was going to miss the "check out" time at this most unique of hotels.

Finally, in the late morning, the staff was summoned to the State Dining Room, a place full of memories for all of us. There were more than one hundred of us there, all of the President's and First Lady's staffs, as well as butlers, ushers, florists, calligraphers, and right on down the line. We were all shoulder to shoulder in a ring around the perimeter of the room.

The President, Mrs. Clinton, and Chelsea arrived via the State corridor. This was to be sort of an inverted reception line, as the Clintons walked around the room, thanking each of us personally.

It was an emotional time for everybody. I think we all had the same thing going on in our

Over and out. The White House staff bids a fond, and tearful, farewell to the Clintons on Inauguration Day 2001. *(Courtesy William J. Clinton Presidential Library)*

minds: the realization that suddenly, after seven years together (eight for some of the others), this would be our last interaction with the Clintons.

Chelsea was the first to crack. She began to cry, and was followed closely by Mrs. Clinton. Even the President seemed to be tearing up, and was biting on his lip in that familiar way to keep himself in check.

It was a very revealing moment, a glimpse into the relationship between the First Family and their staff. Losing them was like losing a close friend or family member. We had spent almost all of our waking time taking care of these people, and it was about to come to a sudden and total end.

I'm not an emotional guy, but even I was fighting to keep my composure.

The Clintons arrived in front of me and we all looked at each other.

"Thank you, Walter," Mrs. Clinton said, hugging me.

"Thanks for giving me the chance to do this," I said.

Chelsea and I hugged as well, and the President and I shook hands. I wished them all the best of luck, and they continued on around the room.

By the end of this ordeal, you might have thought you were at a funeral rather than the State Dining Room because we were all wrecked, and many of the staff members were openly sobbing.

The Clintons had to leave for the Inauguration, so they made their way out of the House. From the windows, we watched as they got into their limousine and were shuttled away, for the last time.

I gave my crew five minutes, then took up my leadership role. "Okay, guys, let's get downstairs and get busy. This has been a nice chapter in the book but we have to get ready for the new chapter."

I wasn't just being a tough guy. There were speeches and a swearing-in happening on the Capitol steps down the street. And as soon as those events were over, a new First Family would be arriving in their own limousines, and we had to be ready to serve them.

★ ★ ★

MY
BUSH
YEARS

★ ★ ★

There's a New Sheriff in Town
Cooking for the Bushes

When George W. Bush was sworn into office on January 20, 2001, my working life was instantly and irrevocably altered, as was that of all White House employees.

It was almost surreal to be in the same place but have a completely different job. There's a famous phrase used by people who work for, or at, the White House: "I serve at the pleasure of the President." Well, that was certainly true of me and my coworkers, but I'd adjust the line a bit to truly describe what we did: We served to create pleasure for the President and the First Lady. Their happiness was our number one objective.

To do that now required that we throw out most of what we'd been doing for the past several years and essentially start from scratch.

MEET THE BUSHES

I'm not going to lie: When the Clintons left the White House, a piece of me went with them.

Hillary Clinton gave me the chance of a lifetime, and the work that my team and I did in conjunction with Ann Stock, Capricia Marshall, and the rest of the White House family was, in its own modest way, historic. We redefined the way the White House entertained, and put the focus squarely on American food, wine, and service. We made the "people's house" more accessible to the public than it had been in generations, and we brought a sense of contemporary style and sophistication to everything we did. We worked our butts off and challenged ourselves to continually set the bar higher and higher.

And just like that, it was all over.

I had an unavoidable sense of anticlimax on the afternoon of Inauguration Day. The Clintons, Capricia, and their staffs were all gone, and I was still there. If I hadn't fully appreciated the official chain of command before, I sure appreciated it now: Though I had worked arm-in-arm with them for seven years, I was not a member of Hillaryland (though I like to think they considered me an honorary one); I was an employee of the White House, a direct report to the Usher's Office, a chef for whoever occupied the Oval Office, his or her family, and his or her guests.

That's why although all my old friends and colleagues were all gone, I was still there, along with my assistant chefs, my steward, the ushers, butlers, florists, engineers, carpenters, and the rest of the House staff.

I hadn't met the Bushes yet, but I had met their new social secretary, Catherine Fenton, the soft-spoken and friendly woman who would be filling the position vacated by Capricia Marshall. Catherine had been deputy social secretary under both Nancy Reagan and Barbara Bush. In fact, it was President George H. W. Bush's former chief of staff, James Baker, who had initially phoned her up about this job.

Catherine and I hadn't gotten around to discussing any special events or functions, but the Bushes' disdain for the Washington social scene was so well documented in the media that I already knew that entertaining wouldn't be as much of a focus as it had been for the Clintons. (This reputation would endure throughout President Bush's first term. In 2005, the *New York Times* described the First Family's reputation as "shut-ins who had no interest in Washington social life beyond old friends from Texas and Yale," and that same year *Newsweek* magazine declared that "[i]n terms of social life, Bush's Washington is an oxymoron.")

My sense was that the scope of what we did was about to be drastically reduced, and I wondered how I'd perform when not asked to cook for a record-setting number of guests or to produce a dinner for world leaders in some far-off location.

Fortunately, I didn't have much time to dwell on these thoughts, because there were more immediate concerns before me.

Saying goodbye to one President and welcoming another was the first time that I had a job quit me. Usually when you change jobs, you leave one place of employment for another; you go to a new physical workplace every day, but your skills remain the same.

This was exactly the opposite. The physical surroundings and most of the people that I had worked with for the past seven years remained exactly the same, but the job was completely different. We suddenly served a new family, one that would bring with it an entirely unique set of expectations and desires. For seven years, we had geared everything we did—from what food was selected and served to how guests were greeted and hosted—to the Clintons' sensibility. As soon as the Clintons pulled away in their limousine, just about everything that I had spent the last seven years doing suddenly had no value to the new job at hand. I was reminded of a curious movie moment. In *Star Wars: The Empire Strikes Back*, Yoda uses a word that I'd never heard before. In trying to train Luke Skywalker, he tells the young Jedi that he must "unlearn" everything he knows. That was exactly what I had to do: unlearn the nuances, intuition, and imagination I had been honing to meet the very specific criteria of my previous "employers."

THE SCOUTING REPORT

Fortunately, we had a leg up on the task before us because, obviously, there was more than a little White House history with the Bushes. Many of the ushers and butlers had been there when President George H. W. Bush was in office, and had served our new President when he visited the White House during those years. John Moeller had been in the kitchen under my predecessor, Pierre Chambrin, and had actually cooked for George W. Bush many times. Additionally, Gary Walters had been in meetings with the Bush transition team in December 2000 and we had debriefed him on those meetings as they pertained to the kitchen.

From these myriad sources, we were able to piece together some conclusions about the new President: He didn't like soup or salad, and generally speaking did not care for food that is green, though he would occasionally eat broccoli. (I'm not being flip or irreverent; we were actually told that he does not like most green food.)

We were also told that President Bush did not like "wet fish," which he defined as fish or shellfish that has been poached, steamed, or boiled. Fried, grilled, or broiled were fine, as was fish that had been seared over high heat or stir-fried, but not "wet." Above all, President Bush,

I was told, loved beef tenderloin, and pretty much anything prepared in the Tex-Mex style; in fact, Mrs. Bush would soon comment to the *New York Times* that she was expecting Mexican food once a week. This was welcome news to me because it dovetailed nicely with one of Mrs. Clinton's favorite food "genres"—Southwestern—providing some comfort and continuity in my changing universe.

We also had useful intelligence about the First Family's snacking habits: President Bush loved a homemade version of Chex Mix, and we had secured the recipe from his Texas chef at the governor's mansion.

Mrs. Bush, we had learned, preferred McCann's Original Steel-Cut Irish Oatmeal to the Quaker oatmeal favored by Mrs. Clinton, and she also had a thing for Yucatan Sunshine habanera pepper sauce.

In contrast to Chelsea, who was barely into her teens when I arrived at the White House, the Bush's twin daughters, Jenna and Barbara Bush, were already enrolled in college, and only expected around during breaks and holidays. Accordingly, we didn't have, or solicit, nearly as much information about their preferences as those of their parents, figuring we would adapt to their wishes on the fly.

Based on all of the information we had gathered, as soon as the Clintons took off, we got rid of such Clinton basics as the oatmeal and the mountain of Dove Bars we kept in the freezer for Chelsea, and made room for Bush family staples.

Tex-Mex Chex

MAKES 8 CUPS

This is the snack mix President Bush brought with him from the Texas Governor's mansion. It's a Texas twist on an old American favorite, and we had to have it on hand at all times. In addition to eating it at the White House, the President never traveled without it.

1½ cups Corn Chex cereal

1½ cups Rice Chex cereal

1½ cups Wheat Chex cereal

½ cup pepitas (shelled pumpkin seeds)

½ cup shelled unsalted pistachios

1 cup small, thin, salted pretzel sticks

1½ tablespoons unsalted butter, melted and slightly cooled

½ tablespoon Yucatan Sunshine hot sauce or your favorite hot sauce

½ tablespoon Tabasco sauce

1 tablespoon Worcestershire sauce

¼ teaspoon ground cumin

¼ teaspoon dried oregano

¼ teaspoon garlic powder

Pinch of salt

1. Preheat the oven to 250°F.

2. In a large bowl, combine the cereals, pepitas, pistachios, and pretzel sticks.

3. In a small bowl, stir together the remaining ingredients until well incorporated. Pour this mixture over the cereal mixture and toss well to coat but gently so as not to break the cereal and pretzels.

4. Spread the mixture out on a baking sheet in a single layer and bake for 45 minutes, stirring gently every 15 minutes. Remove the baking sheet from the oven, let the mixture cool, and serve, or store in an airtight container at room temperature for up to 2 weeks.

The Bushes and the Clintons on Inauguration Day 2001. Back at the White House, we were busy preparing the kitchen for our new "guests." *(Courtesy William J. Clinton Presidential Library)*

INAUGURATION DAY: CHECKING IN

Based on the historic significance of the occasion, Inauguration Day is generally assumed to be a big event at the White House, but in fact it's a relatively quiet day. The swearing in takes place on the Capitol steps, and all of the big, celebratory balls are held at outside hotels.

Between the two stages of events the new First Family does visit the White House, "checking in" to their new residence, so to speak, and then returns that night after the festivities. On Inauguration Day 2001, the Bushes arrived at the White House around two o'clock. We had a buffet lunch ready for them and their guests, about thirty in all, at three o'clock, and we served a dinner for twenty in the residence that evening.

These events were my first opportunity to meet the Bushes, and they were very personable. Having been such a publicized hire by Mrs. Clinton, I felt sure that I would be replaced by the new administration, but Catherine Fenton had assured me otherwise, as had Gary Walters, and meeting the Bushes certainly gave me no indication that they planned to dismiss me; in fact, according to Gary, Laura Bush had asked, "Is he interested in staying on?"

This was also the first time I met the Bushes' twin daughters, who were nineteen years old at the time, and I was struck that they didn't look or seem at all identical. Barbara had dark brown hair verging on black, thin with a narrow face, while Jenna was more curvaceous, with blond hair and a broad face.

The most striking thing about the Bushes, from the new President to his wife and daughters to his extended family, and of course his parents, was that they seemed not at all awed by the moment, or by moving into the White House. They all seemed to know many of the ushers and butlers, where the closets and bathrooms where, and they were utterly at home.

A few family members who were staying in the residence, such as the President's brother, Governor Jeb Bush of Florida, called down from their guest quarters to order some food—a dynamic we were used to from all the holiday guests the Clintons entertained.

When all was said and done, we were busy from about two to six o'clock; then from six o'clock until eleven the House was more or less empty except for the staff. We stuck around in case they wanted something when they came back (they didn't).

At about eight o'clock, I got in my car and drove home to Great Falls. Having said goodbye to my de facto employers of the past seven years and greeted my new employers for the next four years, I was exhausted.

Catherine Fenton
Social Secretary, 2001 to 2005

I took an immediate liking to Catherine Fenton, who soon became known as Cathy to those who worked with her at the White House. She was a no-nonsense but friendly and thoroughly professional successor to Ann Stock and Capricia Marshall.

But Cathy was also a very different personality from her immediate predecessors: A somewhat preppy and demure young veteran (she was 46 at the time of her hire) of the Bush 41 and Reagan Administrations, for which she had served as deputy social secretary, Cathy had also served as social secretary to the Japanese ambassador to the United States from 1992 to 1995.

Married, with a young son, Cathy struck me as a recruit to Mrs. Bush's team very much in line with the type of people filling out the President's cabinet. Just as Vice President Richard Cheney had served for a number of Republican administrations and Secretary of Defense Donald Rumsfeld had come from the Ford era, over in the East Wing, Cathy was someone capable of engineering a return to the style of those bygone days as well—the more simple, traditional, intimate type of White House entertaining that the Bushes clearly desired.

She had the experience to function within the White House—she spoke the bureaucratic language of D.C. and knew whom to go to in order to get things done—but unlike her immediate predeccesors, Capricia Marshall and Ann Stock, she wasn't a member of the First Family's inner circle.

Filet of Beef with Three-Peppercorn Sauce

SERVES 4

To welcome President Bush to the White House, we made this dish using one of his favorite cuts of meat as part of the Inaugural Day buffet, served just hours after the ceremony.

1 center-cut beef tenderloin, 1½ to 2 pounds, trimmed and tied at 1-inch intervals with kitchen string
Salt and freshly ground black pepper
1 tablespoon olive oil
Three-Peppercorn Sauce (recipe follows)

1. Preheat the oven to 425°F.

2. Season the beef generously with salt and pepper.

3. Heat the oil in a large, heavy-bottomed sauté pan over high heat. Put the tenderloin in the pan and brown on all sides, 5 to 8 minutes total. Set aside the sauté pan; do not wash.

4. Set a rack in a roasting pan and transfer the tenderloin to the rack. Roast in the oven until an instant-read thermometer inserted in the center of the tenderloin reads 140°F for medium rare, 15 to 20 minutes, longer for more well done. Transfer the tenderloin to a cutting board and let rest for 7 minutes.

5. While the tenderloin is resting, return the sauté pan in which it was seared to the stovetop and heat over medium-high heat. Ladle in ½ cup of the sauce and cook, scraping the bottom of the pan to loosen any flavorful bits. Bring to a boil and let boil for 2 to 3 minutes. Strain the liquid through a fine-mesh strainer into the rest of the sauce.

6. To serve, snip off and discard the kitchen string and slice the tenderloin into ½-inch slices. Place 2 or 3 slices on each of four dinner plates. Spoon some sauce over each serving and pass any remaining sauce alongside.

Three-Peppercorn Sauce

MAKES ABOUT 1¼ CUPS

½ tablespoon olive oil
⅓ cup diced carrot
⅓ cup diced Spanish onion
2 tablespoons thinly sliced leek,
    white part only
2 tablespoons chopped shallot
½ tablespoon chopped garlic
1½ teaspoons crushed mixed pep-
    percorns (black, green, and pink)
2 sprigs fresh thyme
½ bay leaf
2 tablespoons Cognac
2 tablespoons red wine
1½ teaspoons balsamic vinegar
2 cups homemade or store-bought
    low-sodium beef or veal stock
Salt and freshly ground black pepper

1. Heat the oil in a small, heavy-bottomed saucepan over medium-high heat. Add the carrot, onion, leek, shallot, garlic, and peppercorns, and sauté until the vegetables are tender, 3 to 5 minutes. Stir in the thyme and bay leaf and cook for 30 seconds.

2. Add the Cognac and red wine. Bring to a boil and continue to boil until almost completely reduced, about 3 minutes.

3. Add the vinegar and stock, raise the heat to high, bring to a boil, then lower the heat and simmer until reduced by one third, about 30 minutes.

4. Strain the sauce through a fine-mesh strainer set over a bowl and discard the solids. Season to taste with salt and pepper and keep covered and warm.

A NEW WORLD ORDER

Gary Walters was openly delighted at what a Bush presidency would mean for the White House. The looseness and spontaneity of the Clinton Administration would be replaced by the Bush Administration's buttoned-up approach. State dinners would shrink back down to the "proper" size and return to the State Dining Room, and punctuality would replace President Clinton's frequent tardiness.

Every President selects his favorite butler, and that butler is designated "head butler," an unofficial title distinct from maitre d'. So although Buddy Carter and George Haney, who had been promoted when the former maitre d' retired late in the Clinton era, had been President and Mrs. Clinton's favorites, James Ramsey, whom President Bush knew and liked from the time his father was in the White House, quickly became head butler. In order to ensure that things ran smoothly, George Haney continued to serve as maitre d'.

One thing that I'm sure pleased Gary was that his cherished chain of command was back in full effect. It didn't take long for me to learn that the First Lady had no desire to speak to the kitchen staff unless she absolutely had to—for example, when tasting and approving dishes for a special function.

But there were pitfalls to this approach. One July, I found a Christmas reception menu in my in-box—a roster of canapés and carved items that would form the basis of all holiday functions. This struck me as odd, because I usually submitted menus, or menu options, to Mrs. Bush and her staff, and received feedback that would lead to a final menu. This was the first time I had ever received a menu in which I had no input.

Nonetheless, when December rolled along, my staff and I cooked as many of the mandated items as we could, storing them in our external refrigerators.

On the eve of the first reception, Gary Walters and I were summoned to see Mrs. Bush. We went to the West Sitting Hall, where she was waiting for us, a copy of the printed menu in hand.

"How did we come to this menu?" she asked.

"It came to me," I said. "I assumed it had been approved by you."

"Well, this is not my menu. I need to see some alternatives."

"Yes, ma'am."

Gary and I left and I went down to my office and assembled a list of about forty-five menu items from which Mrs. Bush could choose. I tried to put my best foot forward, offering some enticing possibilities, such as California rolls with marinated lobster and and barbecued duck with root vegetable cole slaw on jalapeño corn bread. In the end, the First Lady went with the simpler, more traditional fare, including caviar, smoked salmon, pasta primavera, honey baked ham, roast turkey with trimmings, and what appeared to be a favorite from back home, for which she provided the recipe via her staff—pickled shrimp cocktail.

Arriving back at my office at about seven o'clock, I got hold of the purchasing department, rattling off a list of ingredients I'd need first thing in the morning, because we were serving six hundred people the next afternoon.

Then I called all my assistant chefs, telling everybody to get there at six in the morning, whether or not they had late days or days off scheduled. I also pulled in a few extra SBA cooks to help get us caught up. We had our work cut out for us, but we were used to turning on a dime to pull off this kind of thing for the previous administration, if not for the same reasons.

Orange-Cranberry Salsa

MAKES ABOUT 2 CUPS

This salsa, a takeoff on the traditional orange-cranberry sauce, is enlivened with jalapeño, cumin, chipotle, and other Tex-Mex flavors. It became a mainstay of holiday receptions during the first Bush Administration. We used it to accompany a variety of roasts including turkey, pork, and beef. We also used it as a condiment for hors d'oeuvres.

12 ounces fresh or frozen whole cranberries
1½ cups orange juice
1 tablespoon diced seeded jalapeño
1 tablespoon honey
2 teaspoons grated orange zest
2 teaspoons ground cumin
2 teaspoons packed light brown sugar
½ tablespoon chopped garlic
½ teaspoon chipotle puree (see box, page 80)
¼ teaspoon ground cinnamon
2 medium Navel oranges, peeled, seeded, and cut into ½-inch chunks
⅓ cup chopped fresh cilantro leaves
Salt and freshly ground black pepper

1. In a small saucepan, combine the cranberries, orange juice, jalapeño, honey, orange zest, cumin, brown sugar, garlic, chipotle puree, and cinnamon. Bring to a boil over medium heat, then lower the heat and simmer, stirring occasionally, until the berries are soft, 10 to 12 minutes.

2. Transfer the mixture to the bowl of a food processor fitted with the steel blade and pulse until chunky. Transfer the mixture to a glass or stainless steel bowl and let cool to room temperature. (At this stage, the mixture can be refrigerated in an airtight container for up to 2 days.)

3. When ready to serve, fold in the oranges and cilantro and season to taste with salt and pepper.

COMPARE AND CONTRAST

For me, there was one key similarity between the Clinton White House and the Bush White House: All food cues came from the First Lady. But there were many differences between Laura Bush and Hillary Clinton, even in the very specific world of food.

Where Mrs. Clinton wanted to see the best of American food and wine, and entertaining, Mrs. Bush's mantra was that she wanted to serve food that was "generous, flavorful, and identifiable." She didn't want ingredients cut so finely that you couldn't discern one from another, or to see foods piled one on top of the other in architectural fashion.

She also steered clear of anything that might be perceived as highbrow. I once presented a menu for a special event that featured a twenty-five-year-old balsamic reduction. After reviewing it, she noted on the menu that was returned to me that we could use the reduction, but not the name, which she found pretentious.

Mrs. Bush's sensibility had been absorbed by Catherine Fenton. Cathy would periodically ask me if I could make dishes like tomato aspic and poached salmon, classics I probably hadn't cooked since culinary school—the kinds of things you see in gastronomic bibles like *Larousse Gastronomique*, but rarely in the modern world. But, as I have always done in my career, I was ready, willing, and able to do whatever it took to make my "customers" happy.

Having been a hotel chef most of my professional career, I had a certain kind of industry shorthand in my mind; I was quickly coming to think of what Mrs. Bush wanted as country club food—conservative, traditional American fare, executed with a minimum of style—versus the contemporary American restaurant-style food the Clintons favored.

As for what few interactions the First Lady and I did have, it was abundantly clear that these, too, would be a marked departure. In her book, *An Invitation to the White House*, Mrs. Clinton referred to me as her culinary "teacher." Mrs. Bush had no desire to be taught; her taste was defined and set, and that was how it was going to be.

This was as true of presentation as it was of food choice. Occasionally, Cathy would send cookbooks or magazines to my office with yellow Post-It notes on certain pages, indicating recipes she'd like me to prepare for the First Family; in these cases, I wasn't just to use the recipe, I was also supposed to mimic the presentation.

Because food wasn't much of a priority for the Bushes, whenever a dish met with Mrs. Bush's approval, the inclination among her staff was to have it served as often as possible. There's no better example of this than a fresh pea soup with mint we served one day; it was such a hit that it began showing up on every draft menu. Although I ultimately always followed orders, this was a rare time when I took exception to them, insisting that it was good to have a surefire hit in our pocket, but that if we called on it too often the First Family and their frequent guests would tire of it and we'd end up having to lose it.

As for our summertime events, Mrs. Bush wanted everything we did to have an unpretentious, down-home feeling. Our ambitious picnic menus that first year were replaced by menus featuring braised green beans, hominy casserole, and fried catfish, and the contemporary entertainment of the past seven years was replaced by traditional military bands.

It is likely clear that my personal leanings were much more in line with the Clintons, and I wasn't alone in my sentiment. There was a whispered sentiment around Washington that the Texas style the Bushes brought to the White House was a step backwards. However, I understood that Mrs. Bush was acting perfectly within her rights as First Lady of the United States. The House is a reflection of the family that occupies it. My sense was that Mrs. Bush felt that if what we were doing was good enough for her, it was good enough for the White House and, by definition, she was right.

Minted Pea Soup

SERVES 4

This recipe was so well received by Mrs. Bush that her social team would have happily served it at every function. Fresh peas make all the difference.

1½ cups shucked fresh peas (about
   1½ pounds in the pod)
1 tablespoon unsalted butter
⅓ cup thinly sliced leek, white part
   only
¼ cup diced Spanish onion
4 cups homemade or store-bought
   low-sodium chicken or vegetable
   stock
¼ cup chopped fresh mint leaves
   plus 4 sprigs for garnish
½ cup heavy cream
1 tablespoon freshly squeezed
   lemon juice

1. Bring a small saucepan of salted water to a boil and fill a large bowl halfway with ice water. Add the peas to the boiling water and blanch until tender, about 5 minutes. Drain the peas and transfer them to the ice water to stop the cooking and preserve their color. Drain again.

2. Melt the butter in heavy-bottomed soup pot over medium heat. Add the leek and onion and cook, stirring, until softened, 3 to 4 minutes. Add the stock, bring to a boil, then lower the heat and simmer for 4 minutes.

3. Set aside 2 tablespoons of the peas for garnish, and add the rest of the peas and the chopped mint to the pot. Simmer for 2 minutes.

4. Using a handheld immersion blender (or working in batches with a standing blender), puree the soup until very smooth. Strain the soup through a fine-mesh strainer set over a bowl.

5. Stir in the cream and the lemon juice, and season to taste with salt. Reheat gently just before serving. (If you prefer to serve the soup chilled, chill the soup by setting the bowl in a larger bowl filled halfway with ice water and stir to cool the soup as quickly as possible. Stir in the cream and lemon juice after the soup is chilled.)

6. To serve, ladle the soup into four bowls. Garnish with the reserved peas and the mint sprigs.

THE KITCHEN GOES TEX-MEX

In the White House, and in the media, there was quite a fuss made about the fact that Mrs. Bush wanted to eat Tex-Mex food as often as possible. This might sound like a big departure for me and my kitchen team, but we had done a lot of cooking in this style over the past seven years. Although journalists focused on the healthful, multicultural aspects of what we accomplished in the 1990s, in her family meals Mrs. Clinton also enjoyed Southwestern dishes, especially enchiladas. In fact, at one of her famous birthday parties, the entire menu was Southwestern.

Additionally, Leland Atkinson—one of my most dependable and regular SBA cooks, who had been indispensable in planning the G8 Summit menus in Colorado in 1997—had a wealth of experience with this kind of food, and I myself had brought a handful of Southwestern selections to the Greenbrier in my time there, in an effort to keep the venerable resort up to speed with the times. Put all that together, and you had a chef and a kitchen that were very comfortable cooking the food the Bushes wanted to eat.

And the early reception was positive. One night, after a Mexican-themed dinner, the President sent his favorite butler, James Ramsey, into the kitchen to pass along a message, which I took to be a tongue-in-cheek compliment: "The President said to tell the Mexican guy in the kitchen that dinner was really good." Similarly, in May of 2001, Mrs. Bush commented to a writer for the Scripps Howard news service that, "I remember the first week we had enchiladas one night and we were thrilled that the White House chef could make a great enchilada sauce."

Texas Green Chile and Hominy Casserole

This spicy dish became a popular family dinner side dish and buffet selection for the Bushes. The mixing of different peppers creates a complex heat and the bacon adds a nice, smoky undercurrent.

6 strips bacon
⅓ cup diced Spanish onion
1½ cups drained canned hominy
¼ cup hominy liquid from the can
¼ cup diced poblano peppers
1 tablespoon diced pickled jalapeño peppers
1 tablespoon pickled jalapeño liquid from the jar
½ cup shredded Cheddar cheese (about 2 ounces)

1. Preheat the oven to 325°F.

2. In a small, heavy-bottomed sauté pan, cook the bacon over medium heat until crisp. Drain on paper towels, then transfer to a cutting board, chop into small pieces, and set aside.

3. Spoon off 1 tablespoon of bacon fat from the sauté pan into a medium, heavy-bottomed saucepan set over medium heat. Add the onion to the bacon fat and sauté until tender, 4 to 5 minutes.

4. Add the hominy and hominy liquid, bring to a boil, then lower the heat and simmer for 2 minutes. Add the poblano and jalapeño peppers, the pepper liquid, and half of the chopped bacon and cook for 2 to 3 minutes.

5. Stir in two thirds of the shredded cheese. Cook, continuing to stir, until the cheese has melted, 3 to 5 minutes.

6. Pour the mixture into an ovenproof casserole. Top with the remaining bacon and cheese. Bake, uncovered, until bubbling, 15 to 20 minutes.

7. Remove the casserole from the oven, let rest for 10 minutes, then divide among plates or bowls and serve.

Chicken and Vegetables on Buttermilk Biscuits

SERVES 4

President and Mrs. Bush didn't eat only Tex-Mex food. Far from it, in fact. One of their favorite things was warm biscuits at any time of day. They also appreciated a rich, homemade chicken pot pie. This recipe combines the best of both dishes, with the pie filling served over warm biscuits.

The key to this dish is making the biscuits light and airy to balance the thick, flavorful chicken stew.

1 chicken, 2 to 2½ pounds, rinsed and patted dry with paper towels
½ cup dry white wine
½ cup chopped Spanish onion
½ cup diced celery
½ cup diced carrots
5 black peppercorns
2 sprigs fresh thyme
1 bay leaf
¼ cup pearl onions
2 tablespoons (¼ stick) unsalted butter
2 tablespoons all-purpose flour
¼ cup heavy cream
¼ cup diced peeled Idaho or russet potato
¼ cup diced cleaned button mushrooms
¼ cup fresh peas (about ¼ pound in the pod) or thawed frozen peas
3 tablespoons chopped fresh flat-leaf parsley leaves
1 teaspoon freshly squeezed lemon juice
Salt and freshly ground black pepper
Buttermilk Biscuits (recipe follows)

1. Put the chicken, wine, onion, ¼ cup of the celery, ¼ cup of the carrots, the peppercorns, thyme, and bay leaf into a large soup pot. Add enough cold water to just cover the chicken.

2. Set the pot over medium-high heat, bring to a boil, then lower the heat and simmer, uncovered, for 20 to 25 minutes.

3. Meanwhile, fill a medium saucepan halfway with water and bring to a boil over high heat. Fill a large bowl halfway with ice water. Add the pearl onions to the boiling water and blanch until tender, about 3 minutes. Drain, cool in the ice water to stop the cooking, and drain again. Peel each onion, gather the onions in a small bowl, and set aside.

4. Carefully remove the chicken from the pot, set it on a cutting board, and let cool slightly.

5. Remove the skin and bones from the chicken and return them to the pot with the cooking liquid. Simmer uncovered over medium heat until you have about 2 cups of liquid in the pot, 30 to 40 minutes. While the liquid is simmering, dice or shred the chicken meat according to your own personal taste. When the liquid is done, strain it through a fine-mesh strainer set over a medium, heavy-bottomed saucepan. Discard the solids. Bring the liquid to a simmer over medium heat.

6. Melt the butter in a separate small saucepan over medium heat. Add the flour and stir until a thick paste (called a roux) has formed, about 1 minute. Whisk the roux into the simmering liquid. Bring the mixture to a boil, lower the heat, and simmer until thickened, 10 to 15 minutes.

7. Stir in the cream and let simmer for 3 minutes. Add the remaining ¼ cup carrots, the potato, and the chicken meat, and simmer for 8 minutes.

8. Add the remaining ¼ cup celery, the mushrooms, and the pearl onions, and simmer for 4 to 5 minutes. Add the peas and 1 tablespoon of the parsley and cook for 2 minutes.

9. Remove the pot from the heat, stir in the lemon juice, and season to taste with salt and pepper. If the liquid is thicker than you like it, add a few drops of water to correct the consistency. Keep the stew covered and warm.

10. To serve, split two biscuits on each of four dinner plates. Ladle a heaping ½ cup of chicken stew over the biscuits on each plate. Sprinkle with the remaining parsley, and serve.

Buttermilk Biscuits

MAKES 8 BISCUITS

1½ cups cake flour, plus more for kneading
1 tablespoon sugar
2½ teaspoons baking powder
½ teaspoon baking soda
1 teaspoon salt
6 tablespoons solid vegetable shortening or chilled unsalted butter, crumbled into small pieces
1¼ cups buttermilk
1 large egg yolk
4 tablespoons (½ stick) unsalted butter, melted

1. Preheat the oven to 425°F.

2. In a large bowl, stir together the flour, sugar, baking powder, baking soda, and salt. Using your fingertips only, work the shortening into the flour mixture until the mixture becomes crumbly and pea-size lumps form.

3. Add 1 cup of the buttermilk and mix quickly by hand just until the dough comes together; don't overwork it or biscuits will be tough when baked.

4. Turn the mixture out onto a floured surface, and knead just enough to bring the dough together, 15 to 20 seconds.

5. Roll the dough out to a thickness of 1 inch, and cut 4 to 6 biscuits with a 2-inch cutter. Gently reform the remaining dough and cut 2 to 4 more biscuits to make a total of 8. Gently brush off any excess flour and place the biscuits on a nonstick baking sheet.

6. In a small bowl, whisk together the remaining ¼ cup buttermilk and the egg yolk. Brush the top of the biscuits with this wash.

7. Bake the biscuits until golden brown, about 15 minutes.

8. Remove the biscuits from the oven, brush with melted butter, and keep warm.

The Bushes with President Vicente Fox and his wife, Marta Sahagún de Fox, at the state dinner for Mexico. *(AP Worldwide)*

THE BUSHES' FIRST STATE DINNER

The Bushes decided to throw their first state dinner in September 2001. The guest of honor would be an old friend from the President's time as Governor of Texas, President Vicente Fox of Mexico and his new wife, Marta Sahagún de Fox.

The dinner was brought to my attention by Cathy Fenton, and she and I worked together to create a menu. I was pleasantly surprised to learn that we would maintain my tradition of making the dinner an amalgam of American food and food from the visiting dignitary's country.

To help me conceive the menu, I called a friend of mine from the Club des Chefs des Chefs who was President Fox's chef at the time of the dinner. A French chef married to a Mexican woman, he described a palate very similar to President Bush's: President Fox liked red meat, and didn't care for "wet fish," though he was fine with fried fish and shellfish.

In July, to hone a menu, we did a series of tastings for Mrs. Bush, who would invite some friends to dinner to sample the possibilities, often with the President in attendance as well. I'd send out the savory courses and Roland would send out desserts. At the end of the meal, Roland and I would come to the President's Dining Room and hear their feedback. For instance, I had made a blue cheese and bacon salad with a flauta (a fried filled-and-rolled corn tortilla) served alongside, and Mrs. Bush commented that the cheese was too strong, and wanted us to drop the flauta. She liked the crab stew I prepared "as is," and the President himself selected the bison which I found serendipitous because bison range from the Southwest into Mexico, the perfect metaphor for our evening. (Mrs. Clinton conducted similar tastings during the first six months I was at the White House, but became more and more comfortable working with written menus alone; Mrs. Bush continued to arrange these tasting parties before state and formal dinner throughout the four years I worked for her.)

The menu we agreed on featured such dishes as Maryland Crab and Chorizo Stew with Summer Vegetables and Pozole; Pepita-Crusted Bison with Poblano Mashed Potatoes and Fava-Chanterelle Ragout and Apple-Chipotle Sauce; and a Salad of Gold and Red Tomatoes.

MENU

MARYLAND CRAB AND CHORIZO POZOLE
SUMMER VEGETABLES
Mi Sueno Chardonnay "Carneros" 1999

PEPITA CRUSTED BISON
POBLANO WHIPPED POTATOES
FAVA BEAN AND CHANTERELLE RAGOÛT
APPLE CHIPOTLE SAUCE
Shafer Cabernet Sauvignon "Hillside Select" 1994

SALAD OF GOLD AND RED TOMATOES
MÂCHE AND MICRO GREENS
SHERRY DRESSING

MANGO AND COCONUT ICE CREAM DOME
PEACHES
RED CHILE PEPPER SAUCE   TEQUILA SABAYON
Schramsberg "Cremant" 1997

MENU

POZOLE DE CANGREJO DE MARYLAND Y CHORIZO
VERDURAS FRESCAS VERANIEGAS
Mi Sueno Chardonnay "Carneros" 1999

BISÓN CON EMPANIZADO DE PEPITAS
PURÉ DE PAPAS CON CHILE POBLANO
RAGÚ DE HABAS Y SETAS CHANTERELLE
SALSA DE MANZANA Y CHILE CHIPOTLE
Shafer Cabernet Sauvignon "Hillside Select" 1994

ENSALADA DE TOMATES ROJOS Y AMARILLOS
VERDURAS DE HOJITAS VERDES
ADEREZO DE JEREZ

HELADO DE MANGO Y COCO
MELOCOTONES
SALSA DE CHILE ROJO   TEQUILA SABAYÓN
Schramsberg "Cremant" 1997

The first bilingual state dinner menu, created in honor of President Vicente Fox of Mexico. (*Courtesy Walter Scheib 3rd*)

Mrs. Bush made a little news by suggesting that the menu for this event be printed in two languages (English and Spanish), the first time in White House history that this had happened. The bilingual menu proved a small challenge for White House calligrapher Rick Paulus, who had to have the menu translated, working with an ad hoc group of House staffers. As a matter of course, the calligrapher's office researched all unfamiliar words, and the pozole we were serving is both a noun and a verb. But once that issue was resolved, Rick rose to the occasion spectacularly, creating a folded menu with the image of an American flag crossed with a Mexican flag at the top. The menus were electronically printed, then Rick and his team hand-painted the appropriate colors onto each individual flag.

The dinner itself was a pleasure to cook. The guest list featured only about 130 people, who would all be served in the State Dining Room.

The commingling of cultures wasn't apparent only in the menu. One of the wines selected by assistant usher Dan Shanks was a California chardonnay with the Spanish name "Mi Sueño" (My Dream), and Chief Florist Nancy Clarke fashioned centerpieces of hydrangeas, white lilies, white roses, and limes, one of Mexico's essential crops.

It was a successful evening from start to finish. The State Dining Room was done up in a gold-and-white scheme, and Mrs. Bush selected the gold-rimmed Clinton china that Mrs. Clinton had commissioned for the White House in 2000.

The Bushes were clearly delighted to have old friends from their Texas days in the White House. When President Bush (who wore boots with his tux) toasted President Fox—with 7-Up, as he quit drinking in 1986—he said that the event was more than a state dinner. "It's like a family gathering." President Fox, who called his old friend "Jorge," dispensed with his prepared remarks to make some personal comments to the Bushes and the assembled guests.

Not only was the state dinner much smaller than those thrown by the Clintons, it was all but devoid of the Hollywood set that had become expected elements of state dinners. The only glimpse of the silver screen was Clint Eastwood, listed on the guest roster as The Honorable Clint Eastwood, no doubt because he was once mayor of Carmel, California. But he made quite an impression, especially as he was seated next to the First Lady herself.

The musical entertainment in the East Room after dinner was compliments of opera soprano Dawn Upshaw, and was followed by dancing in the Grand Foyer. After that, there were twenty minutes of fireworks engineered by the famous Zambelli company, which had created events for presidents dating back to John F. Kennedy and at locations as monumental as Mount Rushmore.

The next day, the reports were in. The evening was a rousing success, with positive notices from the *Washington Post*, Associated Press, *USA Today*, and others. The only negative notices involved a few noise complaints from the White House's neighbors, some of whom had been awakened by the fireworks display.

Calligraphy Office

To produce the vast number of invitations, menus, programs, and other artful documents called for in a given day, the White House has its own Calligraphy Office in the East Wing, next door to the Office of the Social Secretary. The Calligraphy Office, staffed by a chief calligrapher and two others, is an otherworldly place, where the employees work at easels. The room is cluttered with special equipment such as magnifying glasses and more writing implements than you'd probably see in the rest of the White House put together.

During the Clinton's second term, a new and very creative calligrapher by the name of Rick Paulus became Chief Calligrapher. Rick had a unique sense of style that elevated his department's work. Under his guidance, lunch menus became more causal in appearance, while dinner menus were more ornate. He also began adding hand-painted touches of color to certain pieces.

The calligraphers' talent wasn't only calligraphy. During the Bush years, they created many invitations in a homespun, traditional American style reminiscent of a county fair, to match the tone of the events thrown by the First Family.

★　★　★

Pepita-Crusted Bison with Poblano Mashed Potatoes and Fava-Chanterelle Ragout

SERVES 4

This dish was served at the first Bush state dinner, which was in honor of Mexican President Vicente Fox. The menu itself was printed in both Spanish and English to reflect the strong personal friendship between the two leaders. Likewise, the menu items included products and flavors common to both the United States and Mexico such as bison (also known as buffalo). I recommend making the potatoes first, since they can be kept warm in a double boiler for up to two hours, then making the fava-chanterelle ragout just before cooking the meat. You can also omit the potatoes, if you like, and serve just the meat and ragout.

2 tablespoons whole cumin seed
1 tablespoon whole coriander seed
½ teaspoon cracked peppercorns
¼ teaspoon ground cinnamon
¼ cup toasted pepitas (shelled pumpkin seeds), chopped
1 teaspoon grated lime zest
1 teaspoon grated orange zest
1 tablespoon packed light brown sugar
1 tablespoon olive oil
4 bison filet steaks (6 ounces each; see Sources, page 302)
Poblano Mashed Potatoes (recipe follows)
Fava-Chanterelle Ragout (recipe follows)

1. Preheat the oven to 350°F.

2. Toast the cumin and coriander in a small sauté pan over medium heat until the spices are fragrant, 2 to 3 minutes, shaking the pan to prevent scorching. Remove the pan from the heat and let the spices cool.

3. Transfer the cumin and coriander to a spice grinder or coffee grinder. (If using a coffee grinder, be sure to wipe out all traces of coffee before grinding spices; then wipe out all traces of the spices before using again for coffee.) Add the pepper and cinnamon and grind to a fine mixture. Transfer the mixture to a small bowl and add the pepitas, lime zest, orange zest, and brown sugar. Stir well.

4. Heat the oil in a large, heavy-bottomed sauté pan over high heat. Add the bison and sear on both sides, 2 to 3 minutes per side. Remove from the heat.

5. Firmly press the spice mixture onto one side of each steak. Put the steaks on a rack in a roasting pan, crusted side up, and roast until an instant-read thermometer inserted in the thickest part of a steak reads 140°F for medium rare, or a bit longer for more well done. Remove the pan from the oven and let the steaks rest for 3 minutes.

6. To serve, spoon some potatoes onto each of four dinner plates. Lean one piece of bison against the potatoes, and spoon some of the fava-chanterelle ragout over and around the meat.

Poblano Mashed Potatoes

SERVES 4 AS A SIDE DISH

1½ cups goat's milk or whole milk

1½ cups half-and-half

1 pound Yukon Gold potatoes, peeled and cut into 1-inch cubes

⅓ cup diced roasted poblano pepper (see box, page 80)

4 tablespoons (½ stick) unsalted butter

Salt and freshly ground black pepper

1. In a medium, heavy-bottomed saucepan, bring the milk, half-and-half, and potatoes to a boil over medium heat. Reduce the heat and simmer until the potatoes are soft to a knife tip, about 25 minutes. Drain the potatoes, reserving the cooking liquid.

2. Put the potatoes in a large bowl and mash them, leaving them slightly chunky.

3. Fold in the poblano and then fold in the reserved cooking liquid, ½ cup at a time, until you achieve the desired consistency, as smooth or stiff as you like. Fold in the butter until melted and incorporated and season with salt and pepper to taste.

4. The mashed potatoes can be kept warm in a covered double boiler or metal bowl set over simmering water for up to 2 hours.

Fava-Chanterelle Ragout

SERVES 4 AS A SIDE DISH

½ cup shelled fresh fava beans (from about 1 pound favas in their pods)

½ tablespoon olive oil

1 tablespoon chopped garlic

1 tablespoon chopped shallot

¼ cup apple cider

1 tablespoon apple cider vinegar

¼ teaspoon chipotle puree (see box, page 80; optional)

½ cup fresh chanterelle mushrooms, wiped clean and thickly sliced (about 4 ounces)

1 tablespoon unsalted butter

½ tablespoon chopped fresh chives

Salt and freshly ground black pepper

1. Fill a medium saucepan halfway with salted water and bring to a boil over high heat. Fill a large bowl halfway with ice water.

2. Add the fava beans to the boiling water and blanch until the skins are tender, about 3 minutes. Drain, cool in the ice water to stop the cooking, and drain again. Remove the outer skin from each fava bean and discard. Gather the beans in a small bowl and set aside.

3. Heat the oil in a large sauté pan over medium-high heat. Add the garlic and shallot and sauté until tender, 1 to 2 minutes. Add the cider, cider vinegar, and chipotle puree (if using). Bring to a boil over high heat, then lower the heat and simmer until the liquid has reduced by one third, 3 to 4 minutes. Add the chanterelles to the pan and cook until tender, 3 to 5 minutes. Add the fava beans and cook just until warmed through, 1 to 2 minutes.

4. Stir in the butter and chives and season to taste with salt and pepper. Keep stirring, gently, until the butter melts. Keep covered and warm until ready to serve.

What's For Lunch?
A Daily Guessing Game

A constant reminder that the White House, in addition to its symbolic significance, is also primarily a family home was the regular appearance of President Bush in the doorway of the kitchen asking, "What's for lunch?"

While I had limited interaction with President Clinton, President Bush and I had this exchange frequently when he was in residence. The answer to his question, though, was anything but simple—anticipating the President's wishes on any given day was one of the great challenges of my first year in his White House.

THE (FIRST) LADY LUNCHES

For all of the differences between them, Mrs. Bush seemed to quite enjoy the repertoire of lunch dishes we had created for Mrs. Clinton—the healthful salads, soups, wraps, and such met with her approval, and I used many of the same weekly menus for her lunches that I had for her predecessor. As with her affection for Southwestern food, this was a welcome area in which I could apply my work of the past seven years to the new First Family.

Like Mrs. Clinton, Mrs. Bush enjoyed a one-course lunch, relatively low in protein and fat, and liked to see a menu for the following week every Thursday.

Of course, there was tweaking to do. Mrs. Bush loved beets, so there was a premium placed on dishes featuring them, such as a beet and orange salad. She favored spicier food over mild food, so we livened up the dishes with chiles and hot sauces whenever it made sense. And, of

MENU FOR THE WEEK OF FEBRUARY 3 THRU FEBRUARY 9

	LUNCH	DINNER
Sunday, February 3 Dinner - 705	Camp David	Chili and Garnishes - 230 Guacamole and Salsa - 135 Tortilla Chips - 150 Apple Spice Cake - 190
Monday, February 4 Lunch - 500 Dinner - 690	Soft Pita Sandwich of Smoked Turkey and Grilled Vegetables - 210 Bibb Lettuce and Grapefruit Salad - 110 Caramel Custard - 180	Shrimp Pad Thai with Peanuts and Cilantro and Bean Sprouts - 200 Orange and Hearts of Palm Salad - 110 Pecan Pie with Vanilla Ice Cream - 380
Tuesday, February 5 Lunch - 510 Dinner - 532	Seared Snapper with Red Curried Vegetables - 285 Poached Pears with Honey-Vanilla Ice Cream - 225	Cheese Ravioli with Tomato Basil Sauce - 240 Caesar Salad - 120 Angel Food Cake with Fresh Fruit - 172
Wednesday, February 6 Lunch - 345 Dinner - 910	Chicken and Ginger Wontons in Golden Scallion Broth - 150 Lemon Tart - 195	Garlic and Rosemary Roasted Chicken - 230 Mashed Potatoes - 160 Peas and Carrots - 100 Sliced Tomato Salad - 110 Chocolate Cream Pie - 310
Thursday, February 7 Lunch - 590	Warm Scallop and Artichoke Salad - 220 Roasted Pepper Dressing - 80 Thin Apple Tarts with Cinnamon Ice Cream - 290	Tasting Menu for Governor's Dinner
Friday, February 8 Lunch - 605	Grilled Swordfish - 120 Cous-Cous Salad - 100 Spicy Shrimp Salsa - 100 Chocolate Profiteroles - 285	Travel
Saturday, February 8	Crawford	Crawford

A week of lunch and dinner menus for the Bushes, with calorie counts alongside. The lunches were the First Lady's lunches—the most enjoyable cooking we did on a regular basis. *(Courtesy Walter Scheib 3rd)*

course, she liked to be served Tex-Mex and Southwestern food as often as possible.

So I complemented the existing lunch rotation with dishes such as fresh tuna and olive salad; tortilla soup; and spinach and endive salad with calamari and a dressing made with black beans, ginger, and other Asian accents, doing some of my best, most compelling cooking of this period for a very private audience on the second floor of the White House.

Fresh Tuna and Olive Salad

SERVES 4

In her travels, Mrs. Bush would have the opportunity to dine in many restaurants. On occasion, when something struck her fancy, she would request that we get the recipe and add it to our repertoire. This recipe is based on one from Cipollina restaurant in Austin, Texas. It's delicious on its own, in a sandwich, or as the central component of a green leafy salad.

½ cup diced celery
½ cup diced Spanish onion
¼ cup diced carrot
½ bay leaf
½ cup dry white wine
2 lemon wedges
1 sprig fresh marjoram
1 sprig fresh thyme
1 pound skinless fresh tuna, trimmed
¼ cup diced red bell pepper
¼ cup sliced pitted dry-cured black olives
3 tablespoons olive oil
2 tablespoons chopped fresh flat-leaf parsley leaves
1½ tablespoons freshly squeezed lemon juice
1 teaspoon hot sauce
Salt and freshly ground black pepper

1. In a medium saucepan, combine ¼ cup of the celery, ¼ cup of the onion, the carrot, bay leaf, white wine, lemon wedges, marjoram, thyme, and 1½ cups water and bring to a boil. Lower the heat so the liquid is simmering, and simmer for 5 minutes.

2. Gently lower the tuna into the liquid and poach until just done, 12 to 15 minutes. Use tongs or a slotted spoon to remove the tuna from the poaching liquid and set it aside to cool. Once the tuna has cooled, break it up into large flakes.

3. Strain the cooking liquid through a fine-mesh strainer set over another pot. Discard the solids. Bring the strained liquid to a boil over high heat. Continue to boil until liquid is reduced to ¼ cup and almost syrupy, 10 to 15 minutes. Remove from the heat and let cool.

4. In a large bowl, combine the tuna, remaining ¼ cup celery, remaining ¼ cup onion, red pepper, olives, oil, parsley, lemon juice, hot sauce, and 2 tablespoons of the reduced cooking liquid. (Discard the remaining cooking liquid.) Mix gently but thoroughly, and season to taste with salt and pepper. Use as a sandwich filling or as a salad component.

Roasted Beet Salad

SERVES 4

Mrs. Bush enjoyed beets very much and would often have them when she dined privately. They didn't often make it to the public table because she didn't think everyone loved them as much as she did. Roasting the beets, as opposed to boiling them, intensifies their flavor and reduces nutrient loss.

1½ pounds beets, stems and leaves trimmed

⅓ cup halved, very thinly sliced red onion

¼ cup halved, pitted, very thinly sliced dry-cured black olives

3 tablespoons olive oil

2 tablespoons white vinegar

1 tablespoon freshly squeezed lemon juice

1 tablespoon chopped fresh cilantro leaves

1 teaspoon chopped garlic

1 tablespoon chopped fresh flat-leaf parsley leaves

1 tablespoon chopped fresh mint leaves

½ teaspoon dried oregano

¼ teaspoon harissa (see **Sources**, page 302)

¼ teaspoon ground cumin

Salt and freshly ground black pepper

2 cups loosely packed cleaned spinach leaves

⅓ cup diced or crumbled feta cheese

1. Preheat the oven to 350°F.

2. Wash the beets thoroughly under cold running water, and shake them dry. Put them on a rimmed baking sheet and roast in the oven, turning occasionally to ensure even cooking, until soft to a knife tip. Cooking time will vary depending on their size; for medium beets, it will be about 45 minutes.

3. While the beets are cooking, in a large bowl stir together the onion, olives, oil, vinegar, lemon juice, cilantro, garlic, parsley, mint, oregano, harissa, and cumin. Season to taste with salt and pepper and set aside at room temperature.

4. Remove the beets from the oven and let cool. Once cool enough to handle, but still warm, peel them and cut them into bite-size wedges.

5. Add the beets to the bowl and toss gently to coat with the dressing. Add spinach and toss again.

6. To serve, divide the salad among four salad plates and sprinkle each serving with feta cheese.

CUSTOMIZING THE PRESIDENTIAL MENU

President Bush's lunch habits were very different from those of his wife. While we knew that his tastes were more limited, we had no idea what a creature of habit he was. There was a handful of things that the President wanted for lunch, and he almost never deviated from that list.

There was a BLT, which I made for him using Nueske's bacon from Wisconsin, which for my money is the best brand on the market, thanks to its balance of applewood-smoked flavor and the pronounced flavor of the bacon itself. He liked his grilled cheese sandwiches made with Kraft Singles and white bread—and that was that. He also enjoyed peanut butter and honey sandwiches, and occasionally a burger, cooked between medium and medium rare, on a bun with lettuce and tomato on the side.

There was little challenge in preparing the President's lunch choices, and I found myself leaning more and more on the hotel credo of pleasing the customer above all else. In this particular place of employment, there was also some satisfaction in knowing that the leader of the free world was nourished and nurtured sufficiently by my sandwiches to get through the rest of his day.

President Bush likes things just so, and during his first few weeks in office, he would politely let me know exactly how he wanted me to tweak my lunch menu items when I saw him the next day. The key feedback was as follows:

- All sandwiches were to be served with Lay's potato chips;
- White bread was to be replaced with white toast for sandwiches;
- No grilled cheese sandwich was complete without a dish of French's yellow mustard on the side;
- My burgers were "just fine."

There was one more thing the President insisted on: He wanted his food to be prompt. President Bush does not like to be kept waiting, and is legendary for this. The word around the water cooler was that when he sat down for a meal, he wanted his food to hit the table at the same time his posterior hit the chair.

I'll never forget the time Gary Walters came running into the kitchen to tell me the President and some guests had already been seated. "Get the food out! Get the food out!" he repeated over and over.

"Don't you want it to be nice and hot?" I asked.

"No!" Gary exclaimed. "I want it on the table!"

He wasn't kidding.

Not only did the President like to start right away, but he liked to finish his meals quickly as well. I don't think more than twelve minutes ever went by between the time I sent lunch out with a butler and the time the plate came back to the kitchen clean. Even when he had company, he might linger a bit longer, but the food was always dispensed with efficiently.

President Bush's BLT

SERVES 4

This is the bacon, lettuce, and tomato sandwich I served to President Bush when he requested it for lunch. Its defining characteristics are a blend of mayonnaise and mustard and high-quality Nueske's bacon (see Sources, page 302). The method of cooking the bacon on a baking sheet in the oven, rather than in a pan on the stovetop, is used in most restaurants; it keeps the slices nice and flat.

12 slices bacon, preferably Nueske's
  (see Sources, page 302)
8 slices white bread
3 tablespoons homemade or best-
  quality store-bought mayonnaise
1 tablespoon Dijon mustard
4 leaves romaine or leaf lettuce,
  washed and dried
8 thin slices ripe tomato
3 cups potato chips, preferably Lay's
4 dill pickle spears

1. Preheat the oven to 350°F. Arrange the bacon slices on a rimmed baking sheet in a single layer and cook until crisp, 10 to 12 minutes. Remove the pan from the oven, and use tongs to transfer the bacon slices to paper towels to drain. Toast the bread slices in the oven until lightly golden brown. While the bread is toasting, stir the mayonnaise and mustard together in a small bowl.

2. Remove the toast from the oven and spread each slice with the mayonnaise-mustard mixture. Divide the bacon, lettuce, and tomato among four slices of the bread, then top with the remaining slices to make four sandwiches.

3. Cut the sandwiches in half diagonally and place each on its own plate. Add a generous clump of potato chips and one pickle spear to each plate and serve.

BANTERING WITH PRESIDENT BUSH

Though the Bushes weren't as adventurous eaters as the Clintons, making my job less interesting, there was one fascinating aspect to my life at the White House under the Bushes: While my personal interactions with President Clinton were rather limited, I had a frequent—often daily—exchange with President Bush.

When the President was in the White House, he usually took a midday run. After the run, he would appear in the kitchen, alone, in his shorts and sweat-soaked T-shirt, and say, "What's for lunch today?" On very rare occasions, he'd call me "Cookie" (the same nickname he used for my predecessor, Pierre Chambrin) or "Chef," or substitute my actual name, calling me "Walt."

For a few months, I entertained the idea that the President might join his wife for lunch. I always told him what she was having. I might say, "Well, Mr. President, Mrs. Bush is having Grilled Salmon with Endive and Watercress Salad." Usually that was the end of the discussion. The President would say, "Aw, I don't want that. Can I have a so-and-so instead?" So-and-so would be one of his go-to items, such as a peanut butter and honey sandwich.

On very rare occasions, usually when the First Lady was dining alone, the President would have what the First Lady was having—especially if it was a meat-based main course—and if she didn't have company, she'd wait for him to get back from his workout; usually on those occasions, he'd eat one of his preferred sandwiches while she had the lunch we had planned for her. He'd also join her if their daughters were in the House (typically, they'd eat what Mrs. Bush was having, perhaps with some chicken soup or something else comparably simple alongside), or if she was in the company of people he personally enjoyed.

On one memorable occasion, Mrs. Bush was hosting some guests who were members of the ladies-who-lunch set rather than the President's own personal friends, and we went into a routine that was funny enough to be movie dialogue. It went something like this:

"Hi, Cookie, what's for lunch today?"

"Well, Mr. President, the First Lady is having . . . ," I said, naming the lunch of the day.

The President replied, in a lowered voice: "She alone?"

"No, Mr. President, she has some friends with her."

At this point, the President of the United States tiptoed to the dining room door, making a joke of the situation, looked through the small window, and upon seeing with whom his wife was dining, turned away from the door and shuddered in mock terror.

"I'll have lunch in my study. Send up a sandwich in twenty minutes, please." He smiled, then took off.

Three-Bean Chili

SERVES 4

Mrs. Bush requested that when we cooked any beans for the Family that we not add any meat, because she thought meat makes it fattening. Though meatless, this chili is very satisfying, both in texture (thanks to a variety of beans) and in taste, with the expected mixture of chiles and spices.

⅓ cup dried black beans
⅓ cup dried pinto beans
⅓ cup dried red kidney beans
1 tablespoon olive oil
¾ cup chopped Spanish onion
1 tablespoon chopped seeded
   jalapeño pepper
1 tablespoon chopped garlic
2 teaspoons ground cumin
2 teaspoons chili powder
1 teaspoon ground coriander
1 teaspoon chipotle puree (see box,
   page 30)
¼ teaspoon red pepper flakes
4 cups homemade or store-bought
   low-sodium chicken or vegetable
   stock
1 cup diced plum tomatoes
¼ cup dark beer
1 tablespoon sherry vinegar
1 to 2 teaspoons masa harina
   (optional; see Sources, page 302)
Hot sauce
Salt and freshly ground black pepper
Chopped fresh cilantro (optional)
Sour cream (optional)
Grated Cheddar cheese (optional)

1. Put the beans in a colander and rinse under cold running water. Drain, transfer to a medium bowl, cover by 2 inches with cold water, and let soak overnight. Drain.

2. Heat the oil in a large, heavy-bottomed saucepan over medium heat. Add the onion, jalapeño, and garlic and cook until the onion and garlic are lightly browned, 4 to 5 minutes. Stir in the cumin, chili powder, coriander, chipotle puree, and pepper flakes, and cook for 30 seconds.

3. Add the beans, stock, tomatoes, beer, and vinegar. Bring to a boil over high heat, then lower the heat and simmer, uncovered, until the beans are tender, 30 to 40 minutes. For a thicker chili, more like a stew than a soup, dissolve the masa harina in a bit of water to form a thick liquid, and stir that into the chili along with the other ingredients in this step. Add a few dashes of hot sauce, to taste, then season with salt and pepper. If desired, garnish each serving with chopped cilantro, a dollop of sour cream, or a sprinkle of grated Cheddar cheese.

OUTFOXING THE PRESIDENT

After a month or so, I learned that the smart thing to do was to never assume that President Bush would join his wife for lunch. Accordingly, I would prepare two lunch menus, the First Lady's and the President's.

So when the President showed up at the door and asked "What's for lunch today?" I would tell him what the First Lady was having. When that didn't meet with his approval and he didn't immediately indicate what he would rather have, I'd say, "Well, Mr. President, today we also have a BLT."

Inevitably, this didn't work either, because the President would decide he was in the mood for a different dish from his personal play list. If we had a BLT, then he wanted a peanut butter and honey sandwich. If we had grilled cheese, then he wanted a burger.

We just couldn't win.

After a few weeks, I decided that there was one more step I could take to be prepared for the President on any given day. Because his personal menu was so confined, I had the ingredients for all options sent up from the downstairs kitchen every day. As the lunch hour approached, we had on hand the setup for a grilled cheese sandwich, ingredients for a peanut butter and honey sandwich, and the lettuce and tomato for a BLT, along with the requisite potato chips. If he asked for a BLT, I'd call down and have one of the cooks grill the bacon and get it up to me on the fly, and if he wanted a burger, I'd have it grilled down there and rushed up as well.

It wasn't the most efficient way to work, but it worked every time, and that's what was important.

WEEKEND LUNCHES

President Bush was much more predictable on the weekends. While he spent, on average, four out of every five weekends at Camp David or back in Crawford, Texas, early in his first term, he and Mrs. Bush eventually began to spend more and more weekend time at the White House.

On most Sundays, if the Bushes weren't at Camp David, in sharp contrast to his weekday modus operandi, the President wanted the same thing for lunch: A post-church meal of huevos rancheros. Maria Galvin, a domestic helper the Bushes brought with them from Texas to the White House, tipped me off to this fact, and told me just how the Bushes liked them prepared.

Another popular weekend snack for the President, according to Mrs. Bush herself, was deviled eggs. We often served them as a Saturday lunchtime indulgence, as well as at receptions and sometimes on the President's birthday.

Deviled Eggs

This is one of President Bush's all-time favorites. He had these at many receptions and picnics, and sometimes as a special request for weekend lunches.

12 eggs
¼ cup plus 2 tablespoons mayonnaise
1 tablespoon Dijon mustard
1 tablespoon white vinegar
1 tablespoon freshly squeezed
  lemon juice
1 teaspoon dry mustard
1 teaspoon Worcestershire sauce
¼ teaspoon hot sauce
Salt and freshly ground black pepper
Paprika
1 tablespoon chopped curly
  parsley

1. Carefully put the eggs in a medium saucepan and cover with cold water. Bring to a boil over high heat, then lower the heat and simmer for 10 minutes. Use a slotted spoon to transfer the eggs to a bowl and rinse until cold running water until chilled. Peel the eggs and halve them lengthwise.

2. Remove the yolks and put them in a small bowl with the mayonnaise, Dijon mustard, vinegar, lemon juice, dry mustard, Worcestershire, and hot sauce. Mash together with a fork until well incorporated and season to taste with salt and pepper.

3. Put the mixture into a pastry bag fitted with a medium star tip, and pipe into the egg white halves. The eggs can be arranged on a plate, covered loosely with plastic wrap, and refrigerated for up to 8 hours.

4. Sprinkle with the paprika and parsley and serve.

Huevos Rancheros with Fresh Tortillas and Red Beans

SERVES 4

President and Mrs. Bush frequently enjoyed this mainstay of Texas cooking after church on Sundays. Make the red beans first as they take about an hour to cook.

For the best results, use a tortilla press for this recipe (see Sources, page 302), or use quality store-bought corn tortillas (available at specialty markets and well-stocked supermarkets).

FOR THE BEANS
½ pound dried red kidney beans
1 tablespoon corn oil
½ cup diced Spanish onion
1 tablespoon chopped garlic
About 4 cups homemade or store-bought low-sodium chicken or beef stock
2 teaspoons chipotle puree (or less if less heat is desired; see box, page 80)
1 tablespoon ground cumin
½ tablespoon ground coriander
1 teaspoon dried oregano
1 bay leaf

FOR THE RANCHERO SAUCE
1 tablespoon corn oil
½ cup diced Spanish onion
1 tablespoon chopped garlic
¼ cup diced roasted poblano chiles (see box, page 51)
2 tablespoons diced roasted jalapeño pepper (see box, page 51)
1½ cups diced ripe plum tomatoes
1 cup homemade or store-bought low-sodium chicken stock
⅔ cup homemade or your favorite store-bought tomato sauce
1 tablespoon ground cumin
½ tablespoon ground coriander
Hot sauce

1. Make the red beans: Put the beans in a colander and rinse under cold running water. Drain, transfer to a medium bowl, cover by 2 inches with cold water, and let soak overnight. Drain.

2. Heat the oil in a medium, heavy-bottomed saucepan over medium heat. Add the onion and garlic and sauté until tender, about 3 minutes.

3. Add the beans, stock, chipotle puree, cumin, coriander, oregano, and bay leaf. Cover and simmer over low heat until beans are very tender, 45 minutes to 1 hour. If the beans start to become dry, add a little more stock; they should remain soupy throughout. Remove from heat; remove and discard the bay leaf.

4. Meanwhile, make the ranchero sauce: Heat the oil in medium, heavy-bottomed saucepan over medium heat. Add the onion and garlic and sauté until tender, about 3 minutes.

5. Add the chiles and sauté for 1 minute. Add the tomatoes and sauté for 3 minutes. Add the stock, tomato sauce, cumin, and coriander. Bring to a boil over high heat, then lower the heat and simmer, covered, for 30 minutes.

6. Season to taste with hot sauce, salt, and pepper. Remove from the heat and keep covered and warm. Just before serving, stir in the lime juice.

7. Make the tortillas: In a medium bowl combine the masa mix and water stir vigorously for 3 minutes.

8. Divide the dough into 8 to 10 equal-size balls and cover with a damp towel to prevent them from drying out.

9. One at a time, put one ball of dough in a tortilla press between two sheets of plastic wrap and press to flatten to about 6 inches in diameter and $\frac{1}{16}$ inch thick. Repeat until all dough balls are pressed.

Salt and freshly ground black pepper

2 tablespoons freshly squeezed lime
juice

FOR THE TORTILLAS

1 cup Maseca brand Corn Masa mix
(available at most grocery stores)

⅔ cup water, at room temperature

TO SERVE

8 eggs, scrambled, poached, or fried
in pairs

½ cup grated manchego or
Monterey Jack cheese

2 tablespoons chopped fresh
cilantro leaves

10. Heat a 12-inch ungreased cast-iron pan over medium-high heat. Remove a tortilla from the plastic wrap and place in the pan. Cook for 20 to 30 seconds on each side, cooking it through, but only until just warm. Repeat with remaining tortillas. As they are done, stack them on a plate and keep them covered and warm.

11. Preheat the broiler.

12. Put one tortilla on each of four flameproof plates, top with 3 tablespoons of ranchero sauce, then with a portion of 2 eggs. Top with some of the grated cheese. Flash under the broiler just to melt the cheese. Repeat with the remaining tortillas, sauce, eggs, and cheese.

13. Sprinkle some cilantro over each serving and serve, passing the extra tortillas and the beans alongside.

Take Me Out to the Ballgame
President Bush and America's Pastime

N o sooner was President Bush sworn into office than he began staging baseball-themed events—lunches and dinners at which he would talk baseball with players, historians, and commentators, or welcome Hall of Famers into the House.

President Bush also created a new White House tradition: Sunday afternoon tee ball games for Little Leaguers, for which a miniature stadium was constructed on the White House lawn, and hot dogs were cooked to the President's own exacting specifications.

BASEBALL WAS VERY, VERY GOOD TO HIM

President George W. Bush loved baseball from the time he was a little kid. In Midland, Texas, he grew up playing Little League ball. For a time, he thought he might become a professional player himself, but instead ended up the owner of the Texas Rangers, where he famously traded Sammy Sosa, who went on to set a few home run records, a fact the President joked about often during the 2000 campaign.

Baseball was in the President's blood: His grandfather, Connecticut Senator Prescott Bush, had played baseball at Yale, as had his father, President George H. W. Bush, who was actually captain of the university's team. His great-uncle, Herbert Walker, was one of the original owners of the New York Mets, and Bush himself was the first Little League graduate to become President of the United States.

President George W. Bush wasn't the first president to love baseball. There's evidence that a connection between the game and the Executive Branch goes all the way back to George Washington—our first president's diary reveals that he played an early version of the game, called rounders, with his men at Valley Forge.

But George W. Bush is certainly the most passionate baseball fan we've had in the Oval Office to date.

Baseball was so top-of-mind for him that he couldn't wait to host baseball-themed events once he moved into the White House; the first event took place on February 7, 2001, just nineteen days after he was sworn in.

The event was a dinner orchestrated by conservative columnist and well known baseball fanatic George Will. Among the guests were Will himself, Cal Ripken, New York Yankees manager Joe Torre, Chicago Cubs manager Don Baylor, Oakland A's general manager Billy Beane, and Atlanta Braves pitcher Tom Glavine.

As was becoming typical, I didn't learn of the dinner in a meeting or a phone call. It was posted on the Ushers Information Web page, which I checked several times each day, and that's the only way I knew about it. Working alone, I fashioned what I thought would be an appropriate menu—because it was a predominantly male gathering, and the subject of the evening was sports, I went for straightforward, hearty food—and sent it to the Usher's Office for approval.

The day of the dinner was one of the more dramatic ones in my time at the White House. That morning, a man waving a gun had appeared at the southwest gate and fired a few shots into the air before being shot in the leg by the Secret Service and taken to George Washington University Medical Center. Chillingly, the incident took place at about 11:30 a.m., on the same morning the President had hosted a tax-cut event nearby on the South Lawn.

But the President wasn't about to be denied his baseball, and despite the morning's drama, the dinner went forward as planned in the Old Family Dining Room.

At the end of the evening, the President gave the group a tour of the White House. The superstars in attendance also signed baseballs for the President, who had a collection of more than 250 autographed baseballs back home in Texas, and a few of them brought along baseballs for him to sign as well, a request he was only too happy to grant.

Pan-Seared Sea Bass with Saffron Risotto and Caponata Sauce

SERVES 4

This dish, which was served at President Bush's first baseball dinner, uses the flavors of Italian caponata, a sweet-and-tart eggplant salad, as the basis of the sauce, where it both flavors the creamy risotto and complements the crisp fish.

3 tablespoons olive oil
1 tablespoon freshly squeezed
    lemon juice
1 teaspoon chopped garlic
1 teaspoon dried oregano
4 skinless black sea bass fillets (4 to
    5 ounces each)
Salt and freshly ground black pepper
Saffron Risotto (recipe follows)
Caponata Sauce (recipe follows)

1. In a small bowl, stir together 2 tablespoons of the oil, the lemon juice, garlic, and oregano. Set aside.

2. Season the fish with salt and pepper. Heat the remaining 1 tablespoon oil in a large, heavy-bottomed sauté pan over medium-high heat. Add the fish and cook 3 to 4 minutes—until seared—per side. Remove the fish to a plate and brush with the lemon sauce.

3. To serve, spoon about ½ cup of risotto onto the center of each of four dinner plates. Place a fish fillet on top of risotto. Ladle the caponata sauce around fish and risotto and serve.

Caponata Sauce

MAKES ABOUT 1 ½ CUPS

1 tablespoon olive oil
¼ cup diced eggplant
¼ cup diced celery
¼ cup diced Spanish onion
½ tablespoon chopped garlic
¼ cup diced plum tomato
½ cup homemade or store-bought
    low-sodium chicken stock
2 tablespoons red wine vinegar
½ tablespoon capers
1½ tablespoons halved, pitted, thinly
    sliced dry-cured black olives
1 tablespoon thinly sliced fresh basil
    leaves
Salt and freshly ground black pepper

1. Heat the oil in a large, heavy-bottomed saucepan over medium heat. Add the eggplant, celery, onion, and garlic and sauté until ingredients are tender, 4 to 5 minutes.

2. Add the diced tomato and cook for 2 to 3 minutes. Add the stock and vinegar, bring to a simmer, and cook for 5 to 7 minutes.

3. Remove from the heat. Blend the contents of the pot with a handheld immersion blender or in a standing blender. Pulse a few seconds at a time, just until the sauce is chunky. If using a standing blender, return the sauce to the pot.

4. Stir in the capers, olives, and basil, bring to a simmer, and simmer for 1 to 2 minutes. Season to taste with salt and pepper. Keep covered and warm until ready to use.

Saffron Risotto

1½ tablespoons unsalted butter

¼ cup finely chopped leek, white part only

¼ cup diced Spanish onion

1 tablespoon very finely chopped shallot

1 tablespoon very finely chopped garlic

1 cup Arborio or other risotto rice

⅓ cup dry white wine

Pinch of saffron threads

5 to 6 cups homemade or store-bought low-sodium chicken stock, simmering in a pot on a back burner

¼ cup fresh goat cheese, at room temperature

Salt and freshly ground black pepper

1. Melt the butter in a medium, heavy-bottomed saucepan over medium heat. Add the leek, onion, shallot, and garlic and sauté until translucent and tender, 3 to 5 minutes. Add the rice and stir to coat with the butter. Add the wine and cook, stirring constantly, until absorbed by the rice, 3 to 4 minutes.

2. Add the saffron and 2 cups stock and cook, stirring constantly, until the stock is absorbed by the rice. Continue to add stock in ½-cup increments, cooking and stirring, and adding more only after the previous amount has been absorbed. Continue until you have used all of the stock, 25 to 30 minutes total cooking time, or until the rice grains are al dente and the risotto is still a bit soupy.

3. Fold in the goat cheese until it melts into the risotto. Season to taste with salt and pepper.

TO MAKE RISOTTO IN ADVANCE: Leave out the last addition or two of stock, transfer the rice to a baking sheet, and spread it out to cool. Transfer it to an airtight container, cover, and refrigerate for up to 2 hours. To proceed, transfer the reserved risotto to a clean, dry saucepan, gently warm it over medium heat, and stir in the final addition(s) of stock.

THE SHRIMP STRIKES OUT

On March 30, 2001, President Bush reinstituted a tradition that had last been carried out by Ronald Reagan when he invited a slew of Hall of Fame baseball players to the White House for a luncheon. Among the legends who attended were Johnny Bench, Jim Bunning, Bob Feller, Whitey Ford, Sandy Koufax, Nolan Ryan, and Edwin "Duke" Snider. Also on hand were Hall of Fame Chairman Jane Forbes Clark and President Dale Petroskey, Baseball Commissioner Bud Selig, and Billy Crystal, who was perhaps as well known a fan as the President himself.

In his opening remarks in the East Room, the President singled out a number of people, but none more humorously than Yogi Berra, who has uttered some of the most famous lines ever spoken by a baseball player. His seemingly nonsensical statements, such as "When you come to a fork in the road, take it," are legendary. President Bush joked that Yogi was an inspiration to him "for the enduring mark he left on the English language. Some in the press corps here even think he might be my speechwriter."

The President also hinted at an upcoming initiative: "I pointed out to . . . the First Lady that we've got a pretty good-sized backyard here. And maybe with the help of some groundskeepers, we can play ball on the South Lawn. She agreed, just so long as I wasn't one of the players." This announcement delighted the guests, who greeted it with applause. At the end of his remarks, the President said, "I hope you enjoy the lunch as much as I know I'm going to."

Well, he might have enjoyed the company, but there was a small disaster associated with the lunch itself. Once the guests had been escorted to the State Dining Room and seated, the first course, Crispy Shrimp with Roasted Artichokes and Wild Sorrel Soup, was served.

This dish was part of a menu that had been approved by the First Lady; she had selected it from a list of options I gave her to choose from—but, as I would soon learn from one of the butlers, when they began to serve the course, and set the President's serving before him, the President said something like, "What's this? Something that washed up on the shore?"

The butlers, thrown by the President's displeasure, immediately began to clear the plates, most of which had just been set down in front of the guests, or not set down yet at all. The diners were confused as to what was going on, but no explanation was offered.

As I saw the butlers scurrying back into the kitchen, it hit me: This was a presidential double-whammy, though not intended to be by me, and I'm sure not by Mrs. Bush. The fennel crust was green, as was the sorrel soup, and the shrimp, though sautéed, probably still qualified as wet to his eye—his two least favorite food characteristics.

My cooks and I went into overdrive, preparing the afternoon's main course, Veal Porterhouse with Garlic Polenta, Spring Vegetables and Wild Mushroom Sauce, as quickly as possible and sending it out with the butlers.

Thankfully, this time, the plates didn't come back until they were clean.

Crispy Shrimp with Roasted Artichokes and Wild Sorrel Soup

SERVES 4

We served this dish at the Baseball Hall of Fame lunch. It incorporates ingredients appropriate to the spring season, fennel pollen and sorrel, a slightly tart herb which can be found in specialty shops and farmers' markets. Fennel pollen can also be a little hard to find (check specialty shops or look online) and can be omitted, but it gives an intense anise flavor to the shrimp, which is pleasantly countered by the tang of the sorrel soup.

3 tablespoons olive oil
2 teaspoons freshly squeezed lemon juice
½ teaspoon grated lemon zest
1½ teaspoons fennel pollen (optional; see Sources, page 302)
1 teaspoon chopped garlic
Salt and freshly ground black pepper
1 pound jumbo shrimp, or the largest you can find, peeled and deveined
Roasted Artichokes with Fennel (recipe follows)
Wild Sorrel Soup (page 247)

1. Preheat the oven to 400°F.

2. In a small bowl, stir together 2 tablespoons of the oil, the lemon juice, lemon zest, fennel pollen (if using), and garlic until well incorporated. Season to taste with salt and pepper.

3. Heat the remaining tablespoon of oil in a heavy sauté pan over medium-high heat. Season the shrimp with salt and pepper and sear them for 30 to 45 seconds per side. Use tongs or a slotted spoon to remove them from the pan to a wire rack. Use a pastry brush to "paint" the shrimp with the marinade, then transfer them to a nonstick baking sheet. Roast in the oven just until firm, 6 to 8 minutes, depending on size. Remove the pan from the oven and set it aside.

4. To serve, put the artichoke and fennel in the center of four soup plates. Divide the shrimp evenly among the soup plates, arranging them on top of the vegetables. Ladle about ¾ cup of sorrel soup around the vegetables and shrimp and serve immediately.

Roasted Artichokes with Fennel

¼ cup olive oil

2 tablespoons chopped fresh basil
leaves

1 tablespoon balsamic vinegar

1 tablespoon freshly squeezed
lemon juice

1 tablespoon plus 1 teaspoon
chopped garlic

6 small or 3 large artichokes

½ cup thinly sliced fennel

Salt and freshly ground black pepper

1. Preheat the oven to 425°F.

2. In a large bowl, combine 3 tablespoons of the oil, the basil, vinegar, lemon juice, and 1 tablespoon of the garlic and stir together.

3. Cut off the top two thirds the artichokes with a heavy knife. Using a paring knife, trim the bitter, dark green exterior from the stem, leaving the stem intact. Pull off the tough, outer leaves, then use a paring knife to trim away the smaller leaves until you get to the yellow heart. Remove the hairy choke with a spoon and discard it. Cut the trimmed artichokes lengthwise into wedges (6 for the small or 12 for the large), slicing right down through the stem. Add the artichoke wedges to the dressing, toss gently to coat, and let stand for 5 minutes.

4. Drain the artichokes, discarding excess dressing, and arrange the wedges in a single layer on a baking sheet. Roast until golden brown and tender to a knife tip, 10 to 12 minutes.

5. While the artichokes are roasting, heat the remaining 1 tablespoon oil in a medium, heavy-bottomed sauté pan over medium heat. Add the remaining teaspoon of garlic and the fennel and sauté until the fennel is tender, 2 to 3 minutes.

6. When the artichokes are done, add them to the pan with the fennel and garlic and toss gently. Season to taste with salt and pepper. Keep covered and warm until ready to use.

Wild Sorrel Soup

½ cup loosely packed sorrel leaves, stemmed and washed

2 tablespoons (¼ stick) unsalted butter

½ cup plus 1 tablespoon heavy cream

1 tablespoon olive oil

½ tablespoon chopped garlic

⅓ cup thinly sliced leeks, white part only

½ cup peeled, diced Idaho or russet potato

3½ cups homemade or store-bought low-sodium chicken stock

Salt and freshly ground black pepper

1. Put the sorrel, butter, and 1 tablespoon of the cream in the bowl of a food processor fitted with the steel blade and blend to a green paste. Set aside.

2. Heat the oil in a heavy-bottomed soup pot set over medium heat. Add the garlic and leeks and sauté until tender, 3 to 5 minutes. Add the potato and cook, stirring periodically, until lightly golden, about 5 minutes.

3. Add the stock, bring to a boil over high heat, then lower the heat and simmer until the potato is tender to a knife tip, 15 to 20 minutes. Remove from the heat. Using a handheld immersion blender (or working in batches in a standing blender), puree until smooth.

4. Return to the heat, stir in the remaining ½ cup cream, and simmer for 5 minutes.

5. Just before serving, whisk in the sorrel paste, and season to taste with salt and pepper. Serve immediately to preserve the soup's green color.

Veal Porterhouse with Garlic Polenta, Spring Vegetables, and Wild Mushroom Sauce

SERVES 4

We served these steaks at a Baseball Hall of Fame lunch; veal porterhouse is a "masculine" cut and at the same time an appropriate portion size for a lunch. The cut is not typically available at most stores. If you cannot find it, special-order it from your butcher or use a similar-size veal chop instead. Be careful to not overcook this delicate meat. Fiddlehead ferns are young, coiled ferns available only in springtime; look for them at farmers' markets.

4 veal porterhouse steaks (12 ounces each; see Sources, page 302)
Salt and freshly ground black pepper
2 tablespoons vegetable oil
2 teaspoons chopped garlic
2 teaspoons chopped fresh basil leaves
1 teaspoons dried thyme

FOR THE VEGETABLES
4 baby turnips, peeled and halved
4 baby carrots, peeled
⅓ cup cleaned fiddlehead ferns or trimmed green beans
2 tablespoons (¼ stick) unsalted butter
2 teaspoons very finely chopped shallot
1 teaspoon chopped garlic
⅓ cup asparagus tips (about 8 tips)
4 yellow baby patty pan squash, halved through the stem
Salt and freshly ground black pepper
1 tablespoon fresh chervil leaves

Garlic Polenta (recipe follows)
Wild Mushroom Sauce (recipe follows)

1. Cook the veal steaks: Preheat the broiler or a charcoal grill, letting the coals burn until covered with white ash, or preheat a gas grill to high.

2. Season the veal with salt and pepper. In a small bowl, stir together the oil, garlic, basil, and thyme. Rub the mixture onto both sides of the veal and let stand for 10 minutes.

3. Broil or grill the veal until medium, 6 to 7 minutes per side. Remove to a plate and keep loosely covered and warm until ready to use.

4. Make the spring vegetables: Bring a large pot of salted water to a boil. Fill a large bowl halfway with ice water. Boil the turnips until soft to a knife tip, about 5 minutes. Use a slotted spoon to transfer them to the ice water. Boil the carrots until soft to a knife tip, about 5 minutes. Transfer them to the ice water with the turnips. Boil the ferns for 2 minutes. Transfer them to the ice water with the turnips and carrots. Drain the vegetables and set aside.

5. Melt the butter in a medium, heavy-bottomed sauté pan over medium heat. Add the shallot and garlic and sauté for 2 minutes. Add the asparagus, squash, carrots, turnips, and ferns and toss to coat with the butter. Cook until the vegetables are warmed through, 3 to 4 minutes. Season to taste with salt and pepper and scatter the chervil leaves over the top. Keep covered and warm.

6. To serve, spoon some polenta into the center of each of four dinner plates. Top with some mushroom sauce, then a veal steak. Arrange the vegetables around the polenta and serve.

Garlic Polenta

4 cups homemade or store-bought low-sodium chicken stock

1 teaspoon salt

1 cup finely ground yellow cornmeal

1 cup milk

½ cup grated Asiago cheese

3 tablespoons thinly sliced sun-dried tomatoes

2 tablespoons thinly sliced fresh basil leaves

½ tablespoon roasted garlic puree (see box, page 23)

2 teaspoons unsalted butter

1. In a medium, heavy-bottomed saucepan, heat the stock and salt over high heat. Slowly add the cornmeal, whisking constantly to prevent any lumps from forming. When the liquid comes to a boil, lower the heat so it's just simmering. Cook, whisking constantly, until mixture has thickened to a porridge-like consistency, 10 to 15 minutes.

2. Whisk in the milk, cheese, tomatoes, basil, garlic puree, and butter and cook, whisking, for 2 to 3 minutes. If the polenta is excessively thick, whisk in some more stock or milk to thin it slightly.

Wild Mushroom Sauce

MAKES ABOUT 1½ CUPS

2 teaspoons olive oil

⅓ cup (about 1 ounce) halved morel mushrooms, wiped clean

⅓ cup (about 1 ounce) oyster mushrooms, separated into individual caps, wiped clean, larger caps halved or quartered

⅓ cup (about 1 ounce) quartered cleaned cremini mushrooms

1 tablespoon chopped shallot

1 tablespoon chopped garlic

½ cup diced plum tomato

3 tablespoons homemade or your favorite store-bought tomato sauce

½ cup homemade or store-bought low-sodium beef stock

2 tablespoons red wine

1 tablespoon unsalted butter

1 tablespoon chopped fresh chives

Salt and freshly ground black pepper

1. Heat the oil in a medium, heavy-bottomed sauté pan over medium-high heat. Add the mushrooms and cook, stirring gently, until they begin to brown and give off their liquid, 3 to 4 minutes. Add the shallot and garlic and sauté for 2 minutes. Stir in the tomato and tomato sauce and cook for 2 minutes. Add the stock and red wine, bring to a boil, then lower the heat and simmer until the sauce has reduced by one third, about 10 minutes.

2. Just before serving, whisk in the butter and chives, and season to taste with salt and pepper.

PLAY BALL!

In the spring seasons of his presidency (1865 to 1869), President Andrew Johnson permitted his staff to play softball on the White Lot, located between the South Lawn and the Washington Monument, which was under construction during his first term. He had chairs set up alongside the first base line of the Lot so that others could watch the games.

I don't know whether or not it was inspired by that fabled tradition, but President Bush had his own ideas for how to bring baseball to the White House, by bringing the training-wheels version of baseball—tee ball—to the White House.

In May 2001, President Bush made good on the tee ball promise he had made at the Hall of Fame lunch. On a Sunday, May 6, he hosted his first tee ball event, for which two Washington Little League teams—the Red Sox and the Rockies—were invited, totaling about thirty kids in all, ranging in age from five to eight, and including both boys and girls.

The President and Mrs. Bush made quite an entrance, landing in *Marine One* right on the White House lawn, to the delight of the players and families who had already arrived.

I knew there was to be a game played that day, but—because this event was orchestrated by the press office rather than by Cathy Fenton—I had no idea what to expect. When I arrived on the South Lawn, I was pleasantly stunned to see that a pitch-perfect rendition of an all-American Little League ballpark had been created. There were bases, a pitcher's mound, a dugout, and bleachers—the White House carpenters had outdone themselves, and they had been aided by Little League International

Left: Gerald James Bowie Jr., of the Fort Lincoln Brewers Little League team, swings at the ball during a tee ball game on the South Lawn. *(AP Worldwide)*
Opposite: Baseball great Cal Ripken Jr. and President Bush greet a Little League player at the plate during a White House tee ball game. *(AP Worldwide)*

Corn and Green Bean Salad

SERVES 4

t the many tee ball games on the White House South Lawn, hot dogs and Cracker Jack were the major fare, but this simple, flavorful salad also made an occasional appearance at the post-game picnics.

¼ cup olive oil

3 tablespoons freshly squeezed lemon juice

1 tablespoon chopped garlic

2 teaspoons chopped fresh thyme leaves

2 teaspoons chopped fresh tarragon leaves

2 teaspoons chopped fresh basil leaves

2 teaspoons chopped fresh chives

2 teaspoons chopped fresh flat-leaf parsley leaves

½ teaspoon dry mustard

Salt and freshly ground black pepper

2 ounces green beans, trimmed

½ cup uncooked corn kernels (fresh or thawed and drained frozen)

¼ cup thinly sliced red onion

¼ cup diced red bell pepper

⅓ cup diced plum tomato

2 tablespoons diced scallions, white and green parts

1. In a small bowl, stir together the oil, lemon juice, garlic, thyme, tarragon, basil, chives, parsley, and mustard. Season to taste with salt and pepper.

2. Bring a small saucepan of salted water to a boil and fill a medium bowl halfway with ice water. Add the green beans to the boiling water and blanch until tender, about 90 seconds. Drain the beans and transfer them to the ice water to stop the cooking and preserve their color. Drain again. Cut in half lengthwise, then slice thinly lengthwise. You should have ¾ cup.

3. In a large bowl, combine the green beans, corn, onion, red pepper, tomato, and scallions. Drizzle the dressing over the vegetables and toss to combine. Serve at once.

Baseball and Softball, who worked with the House staff to make sure the field met league standards, and that all equipment used was regulation.

As if that weren't enough, one of the most famous mascots in the country, the San Diego Chicken, was there as well, mugging it up to the delight of the players' families, and of the First Family. But there were also touches that went well beyond what you'd see at a normal ballpark, most notably the announcer: parked at a commentator's desk was none other than Bob Costas, who narrated the game for the pleasure of the assembled guests, including the President and Mrs. Bush, his nephew George P. Bush, and Nomar Garciaparra, the Boston Red Sox's shortstop who was injured at the time.

Not that Costas had much to comment on. After the good-natured spirit of the afternoon, the game was more of an exhibition than a game. Everybody got a chance to hit, and there were no outs. It was the ultimate feel-good tee ball occasion: Everybody was a winner (they had been to the White House and met the President), and nobody was a loser (they didn't strike out or let their team down). Each child received an autographed ball, and the families got a tour of the White House.

For the game, I had planned a ballpark menu of grilled hot dogs and hamburgers, condiments, rolls, potato salad, and so on. In the lower left corner of our menu, where wines and other drinks were listed, were a few items that rarely appeared there: sodas, water, and sports drinks.

After the first tee ball game, Gary Walters informed me that the President didn't want the hot dogs to be grilled. "He says ballpark dogs are steamed, not grilled," was the reason shared with me. Subsequently, we steamed the hot dogs, in actual ballpark paper wrappers, in one of our ovens in the White House kitchen. One year, a butler was attending to the large wheeled multi-shelf rack filled with sheet pans that we used to hold the cooked hot dogs, when the Sterno we used to keep them warm lit one of the paper hot dog wrappers on fire. The next thing we knew, the entire rack, which held about 300 hot dogs, was engulfed in flames.

The Bushes planned to host such events every three to four weeks during the late spring and summer, and they did that first year. But they didn't host any tee ball events in 2002. There was a lot we didn't do in 2002. Because, shortly after our last tee ball game in the summer of 2001, everything changed at the White House, as it did everywhere else.

The Day the World Changed
September 11, 2001

T here are a few events in American history about which everybody can recall exactly where they were and what they were doing when it happened.

On the morning of September 11, 2001, I was working at the White House, overseeing the final preparations for the annual congressional picnic on the South Lawn. I came to work in one world that morning, and drove home in another.

Here, from the point of view of the White House Executive Chef, is what happened in and around the White House that day.

DARKNESS DAWNS

September 11, 2001, began with one of those perfect late-summer mornings when the heat of summer was alleviated by the light breeze of the coming fall, and the sky was a perfect, cloudless blue.

I was especially happy about the weather because that afternoon, my team was supposed to serve food at the annual congressional picnic. In the Bushes' preferred style, we had prepared enough mesquite-smoked peppered beef tenderloin with horseradish sauce; southern fried catfish with tartar and cocktail sauces; old-fashioned green beans; Texas green chile and hominy casserole; burgers, hot dogs; and salad to serve twelve hundred guests. (The scheduled musical entertainment was selected with the Bushes in mind, as well—the "Texas Swing" band Asleep at the Wheel.) As I parked my car in the staff lot that morning and walked to the guard booth, I remember thinking that, with weather like this, the event would go off without a hitch.

I made my usual morning rounds of the residence and staff kitchens, then just before nine o'clock, I dropped by the Usher's Office to see if there were any last-minute changes that I needed to know about.

The ushers kept a small television set in their office, and it was on, and on the screen there was an image of the Twin Towers in New York City. One of the towers was leeching smoke out of a huge hole that had been blown in its side and, before I could ask what was going on, a plane rocketed into the frame and slammed into the second tower.

It was such a powerful sight that I could scarcely process it in the moment.

Gary Walters turned to the only other usher in the room, Dennis Freemyer, and said, in a detached monotone, "Well, that's two."

I left the office with those words echoing in my mind. Gary said it with such finality, as though two were some kind of magic number. What was transpiring dawned on me. I thought, This is clearly intentional. It could be two. Or it could be ten.

I didn't really have time to dwell on what was happening; if I had, I might have realized that there was no way we'd still hold a picnic after what was clearly a terrorist attack.

I think that, like so many people, I was in a mild state of shock, not realizing the repercussions of what was playing out that morning. At that point in time, we didn't know how big the planes were that crashed into the towers, didn't know that other planes were headed for other targets, and didn't know that within a few minutes, the towers would collapse.

I headed down to the southeast gate to check on the Army guys who were delivering the mobile kitchens for the picnic that afternoon.

As I walked from the White House to the gate, I immediately noticed a change in the air. Word of the events in New York had spread around pretty quickly. Everybody—civilian employees and military personnel alike—knew that something was going on, but we had no idea what the full extent of it was.

As I got closer to the southeast gate, I noticed that many of the Emergency Response Team (ERT) members, dressed in black like SWAT officers, had taken up positions along the perimeter of the drive and they all had canvas sacks that housed their machine guns slung over their shoulders. This was the first time I had seen so many ERT members in one place, at the ready. It was disconcerting.

I got down to the southeast gate when all of a sudden there was the crackling of a transmission over the Uniformed Division's walkie-talkies. There were so many of these guys around, that collectively their radios became a sort of public address system. A lot of what was being transmitted was garbled, but the two words we could all pick up were "unidentified incoming."

When you work at the White House, you always know that there's a chance you might find yourself in the wrong place at the wrong time. If you spend enough time near the President, you run the risk of becoming "collateral damage" in somebody's efforts to get to him, and the same goes for spending time in the White House or any prominent D.C. building. Recent history offered sad examples of this truth: James Brady, the press secretary who was shot when John Hinckley tried to kill President Reagan; the two Capitol police who were shot and killed by an intruder in 1998; even the gunman who had fired shots back in February on the day of the President's first baseball dinner.

But to hear those words "unidentified incoming" was horrifying, and the picture-perfect weather made the moment surreal—how could things so terrible be happening in such beautiful, broad daylight?

At this point, everything started to happen very quickly. A team of Uniformed Division guys swung the big gates shut across the driveway, and started waving their hands at all the tourists and pedestrians along the walkway on East Executive Drive, essentially shooing them, telling them, "Get back, get back. Get away."

It didn't take a genius to realize what they were afraid of. With the image of the Twin Towers firmly in mind, and an unidentified plane moving in our direction, they clearly thought there was one headed right for us.

Like leaders in any field, chefs begin to feel a sense of responsibility for their cooks. At least that's the way it is for me. So I left the southeast gate and began running up the south drive back toward the House to tell the kitchen team we had to evacuate.

That's when I heard it: the high-pitched, whirring sound of an airplane accelerating. I've lived in Washington on and off all my life and had been working at the White House for seven years, and I was used to certain ambient sounds. I was positive that I had never heard anything like this before. I couldn't see the plane, but the revving of its engines was so loud that you could feel it bearing down on us.

I was about two thirds of the way up the drive when the acceleration intensified, and then I heard a loud thump, like a concussion, so powerful that it registered in my chest. I looked over my left shoulder, and saw a column of gray-beige smoke rising up in the distance, to the south of the city. (I would later learn that this wasn't really smoke; it was dust from a pulverized section of the Pentagon, which explained the color.) A few seconds later, dark gray smoke began billowing up under the khaki dust, and moments after that, the smoke turned an ominous, dark black.

On seeing this, the ERT guys began pulling the machine guns out of their sacks and moving out towards the perimeter that was being widened by the Uniformed Division.

For all of this attention being focused on the outside of the House, I was struck that there wasn't much of an exodus from the House. Then it hit me. The ERT, UD, and Secret Service teams were doing their jobs: protecting the House and the First Family. But, clearly, nobody was charged with getting the employees out. Was that possible? I thought. But any doubt that this was the case was immediately removed when I walked back into the White House. The scene inside was strangely calm as employees who had heard what was going on were telling others to leave. As these people made for the exits, more Secret Service and ERT guys were moving within the house, presumably headed for posts to which they were preassigned for a moment like this.

I ran downstairs to the residence kitchen. John Moeller was there, as was Cristeta Comerford. I started yelling to them, "Get out! Right now! Just turn off the ranges, and go out the north side." I said "north" because the plane that had crashed was to our south—not that it would make a bit of difference if a plane suddenly plowed into the building.

We got out of the building, and Cris turned to me and said, "What about the cafeteria?" She was referring to the staff cafeteria team. I didn't even say anything back; I just spun around and headed back into the House. I was about halfway down the spiral staircase that leads down to the cafeteria kitchen, when I was met by some cooks coming up toward me—Rachel Walker and Mary Beth Williams. They had heard what was going on and had just begun their evacuation.

We all headed back up the stairs and out of the building.

Standing in the driveway was a small elderly woman, a look of fright and confusion on her face. I think she may have been a volunteer attendant of the little mobile bookstand run by the White House Historical Society where they sold postcards and souvenir books, because I'd never seen her before. She was a fragile thing, and completely paralyzed by the moment. As staff and visitors rushed by her in every direction, she just stood there, too overwhelmed to even ask for help.

Going against the stream, I made my way over to her.

"Are you okay?" I asked.

She didn't speak, just looked up at me with desperate eyes.

"Come with me," I said.

Taking her gently by the shoulders, I faced her toward the north gate.

"Go that direction. Go there!" I said and she started making her way off the grounds.

Then I went back inside to see if anybody else needed any help getting out. I didn't see anyone lingering, so I finally left the White House and ran across Pennsylvania Avenue to Lafayette Park, where my kitchen staff was congregated, along with pastry chefs, florists, housekeeping staff, and so on. Everyone who had gone out the north side had basically found each other and clustered together; of the ninety or so staff members, there were thirty-five to forty of us there.

The area around the White House was beginning to fill up because personnel from other nearby buildings, such as the Old Executive Office Building, the Treasury, and Blair House, were also pouring out into the street.

By this time, there were also more security personnel trying to clear the area around the White House: Secret Service agents, Uniformed Division guards, and so on were trying to push people farther and farther away.

Just as I reached my colleagues, two more explosions went off in the distance. People were whipping out their wireless phones, PDAs, and such and reading the headlines over the Internet, and the word quickly began to spread that two car bombs had exploded at the State Department. Somebody hypothesized aloud that "they got us out of the buildings and now they're going to get us with car bombs."

Next thing we knew, there was another collective crackling over the walkie-talkies. Just like before, most of it was unintelligible, but three words were unmistakable: "Second unidentified incoming."

We all looked up to southeast of Lafayette Park. Off in the distance, about two or three miles out, was a four-engine jet coming right at the White House. I found this strange because no four-engine jets were permitted to fly in and out of National Airport, for security reasons. And I had never seen a plane coming from that direction in all my years in D.C.

As the plane got closer and closer, we were all frozen in our tracks, watching it with the same sense of wonder and fear I imagine would greet a spaceship. I think we all had the same thought at that moment: "Is this the one that's going to take us out?"

Even the Secret Service guys, the unflappable supermen who always seemed so invincible, looked helpless.

The plane continued its approach, coming in low over the city . . . and passed right over us. (I would later learn that the plane was the command and control jet from Andrews Air Force Base and that high above it, beyond where we could see, were two F-14 jets, which produce huge, sonic echoes, the source of the "explosions" that were taken for car bombs a few minutes earlier.)

Amidst all the people being directed away from the White House, a woman began crossing Pennsylvania Avenue toward the House. From her business attire, I surmised that she was a West Wing employee. There was a dazed look in her eyes, and she held her security pass aloft in her right hand, as though it were some sort of talisman that would grant her entry anywhere she wanted to go.

I wasn't the only one who noticed her. Directly in her path was a member of the Uniformed Division, shotgun in hand. As soon as he spotted her, he trained the gun on her and said, "Halt!"

She didn't seem to notice he had spoken. She just kept moving forward in a trancelike state, the pass held up in the air.

"I said 'Halt'," the guy repeated.

Still she kept moving toward him, and by this point was only about fifteen feet away.

He pumped the shotgun and retrained it on her. "Goddamn it, lady, I'm begging you. You've got to stop."

He seemed to have gotten through to her. She slowed down, almost to a standstill.

But almost wasn't good enough. "I'm telling you, if you keep going, I'm going to have to shoot you. It's my job."

Finally, she looked up at him.

"I'm not kidding you. When I tell you to stop, stop. I don't know who you are or what's going on. Nobody knows anything except there's explosions and fires, and you're not paying attention to an armed man."

I thought for certain I was about to witness a tragedy, but the woman finally stopped and disappeared back into the growing crowd.

COMING HOME

On top of the horror of that morning was the frustration of not being able to find out exactly what was going on. Every cell phone service provider was overwhelmed. The group with whom I was assembled in Lafayette Park were all trying to use their phones, but to no avail—the circuits were hopelessly busy. I myself couldn't reach my wife or my sons, whose school was near CIA headquarters in Langley, Virginia.

By this point, the scene was like something out of a movie. Traffic was at a dead stop; every single roadway was simply locked down. Drivers were honking to no avail, or simply abandoning their vehicles right in the middle of traffic. Pedestrians were flooding the sidewalks and flowing between the cars. I looked over to my side and saw that a prayer circle had formed spontaneously, with twenty or so people holding hands and crouching down low to the ground, their heads bowed.

With the scene around us seeming more and more like some apocalyptic spectacle, and unable to reach anybody, we figured it was a good idea to get away from the White House.

Our group began breaking up into smaller groups. Sticking with me was Mary Beth Williams, the wife of my Army pal Brian Williams, who was delivering the mobile kitchen trailer that morning, but whom we couldn't locate in all the chaos back at the House.

I said, "Stick with me. We're going to go up to the Washington Hilton." The Hilton is where my friend Gordon Marr was the executive chef. "We'll have a safe place to stay. We can get to a TV, and a land-line telephone, and we can try to find out what's going on here."

Miraculously, I managed to reach Gordon on his office phone and he told us to come over. We began the trek up Connecticut Avenue to the Hilton, which is about a mile and a half away, just north of Dupont Circle. The total pandemonium made it seem like New Year's Eve in the streets, except that it was ten o'clock in the morning.

Everyone was desperate for information. People who had internet connections on their wireless devices were holding court like town criers, delivering the latest updates to strangers who had gathered around them. Others crowded around parked cars with the news stations blaring on their sound systems, or in front of electronics shops, watching the images—mostly the endless loop of the Twin Towers collapsing—on television screens.

We wound our way up through this mess and up to the Washington Hilton, which had its own security measures in effect—the building was surrounded by uniformed personnel, and the food storage areas inside were being guarded as well.

Gordon was off figuring out what he needed to do to get through this day, but he had left word with the guards out front that Mary Beth and I were to be admitted to the hotel and shown to his office.

From Gordon's office, at around ten thirty, I called the White House and reached assistant usher Daniel Shanks, who hadn't left the grounds. I let him know where I was and how to reach me.

At about noon, Gary Walters called me and said, "Come on back."

I was surprised. "Come on back? To what? Why?"

"Just come on back. We're getting key staff back together again to try to find out what's going on."

I thought back to how all the security personnel were trying to expand the perimeter around the House. I could only imagine how wide the perimeter must be by now. I was perfectly willing to return, but had no idea how I'd get through the layers of security that must have been in place. "How am I going to get there?"

Gary instructed me to come across Thirteenth or Fourteenth Street, just east of the House. "Come down there, and there'll be a checkpoint," he said.

By this time, Mary had reached her husband Brian, who had managed, somehow, to get the truck off the White House grounds and back across the river to Fort Myers. She was going to find a way to get to him and then home.

So I did as instructed and headed back to the White House.

Normally, the first checkpoint one reaches en route to the House is at Pennsylvania Avenue, but there was a makeshift checkpoint set up at K Street, four or five blocks farther out. It was manned by the Metropolitan Police, who had parked their cars across the width of the street, blocking it.

I was wearing my chef's uniform, and I didn't know how I'd look to them, ridiculous or threatening. I kept thinking of that woman I had seen a few hours earlier, with the shotgun pointed at her. I put my hands up in the air, as though I were a convict surrendering to the authorities. In one of my hands, I held my White House pass, and I was walking very, very slowly because everywhere you looked was an officer with a shotgun, or a rifle. They all looked incredibly nervous, and as much as I was worried about an airplane crashing down out of the sky, I was just as concerned about the possibility of getting shot by an officer overwhelmed by the moment.

I explained who I was and they let me by. I began walking through the ghost town between K Street and the White House, my arms still held aloft, and I ran into a Uniformed Division sergeant who recognized me.

"What are you doing here?" he asked.

"Gary Walters told me to come back," I said.

He made a call on his walkie-talkie and confirmed this, then escorted me back to the House to be sure I wouldn't run into any trouble along the way.

I continued on through at least another four checkpoints that brought to mind a sense of being in a police state. There were armored carriers and uniformed army troops in the street by this time. I hadn't seen anything like it since the riots of the 1960s.

Arriving at the House, I couldn't believe my eyes. All the Uniformed Division guys, who usually just had a holstered pistol, were walking around with gigantic machine guns. I didn't know whether to feel safe because they were so well armed, or to be fearful that somebody might get shot accidentally.

When I finally got inside the White House, I breathed a huge sigh of relief. At last, I felt safe. I could hear F-14s flying overhead, and I knew that the entire building was surrounded by armed guards, and the White House felt like what it was supposed to feel like—the safest place in the world.

DOING MY PART

I got back to the kitchen. Although the assistant chefs had been instructed not to return to the House, ushers Buddy Carter and George Haney were there, as was Daniel Shanks.

Gary called down to the kitchen and asked if we could feed some of the Secret Service guys. I said this would be no problem, because we had all this food for the picnic that we were supposed to do that evening for more than a thousand people.

"What time do you want me to serve?" I asked him

"Four thirty."

I was the only cook on hand, but everyone pitched in. The butlers helped bring food from the mobile refrigerators parked out on the driveway, Dan Shanks dressed bowl after bowl of salad, and I did the cooking, grilling beef tenderloins, one after the other, and carving them as fast as I could.

Initially, Gary thought we'd serve about 150 people, then upped the estimate to four hundred. But the people kept coming. No sooner would we serve one group, than the ushers would escort another group in. We served them cafeteria style on paper plates, and off they went back to their posts, or to sit down somewhere and chow down before getting back to work.

Gary kept saying, "Can you serve more?" and I kept answering, "Just keep sending them through."

One of the most humbling moments in my career as a chef was when the military personnel thanked me for lunch that day. They were so appreciative, when in fact it was the least I could do.

I said, "Listen, you guys keep the guys on the outside that are supposed to be on the outside, and I'll feed you. You'll get all the food you want."

For the entire afternoon, we served everybody who was working: Secret Service, Metropolitan Police, and anybody else who needed sustenance. They'd been working since that morning and they were starving.

When all was said and done, we served between seven hundred and nine hundred people that day.

Before I left that afternoon, we packed up some of the remaining food to be sent over to the workers handling the rescue and recovery work at the Pentagon, and also packed up some of the hot dogs and burgers for delivery to Fort Myers.

OVER AND OUT

I finally left the White House around nine o'clock that night, driving through desolate streets and highways and arriving home around eleven.

When I got there, Jean asked me, "How are you?"

I said, "Well, I'm really tired, I've got to take a shower. I smell like steak." The smoke from all the grilling we had done had essentially smoked me.

"No, no, no," she said. "Not that."

"Oh, the other stuff," I said. It's odd, but, despite the events of the day—or perhaps because of them—I had been incredibly focused on my work. I had just put my head down and cooked for hours without looking up.

My sons had a typical boys' reaction to the events. Their first question was "Were there a lot of guns?"

"Yes," I told them. "More guns than I ever want to see again in my life."

CHIEF OF STAFF TO THE PRESIDENT

THE WHITE HOUSE

December 21, 2001

Mr. Walter Scheib
Executive Residence
The White House
Washington, D.C.

Dear Chef,

This letter is just to thank you for all that you do here at The White House. Just over one year ago, President George W. Bush asked me to be his Chief of Staff. The last eleven months have been filled with remarkable challenges and achievements, and for all of us serving on his team, it is an incredible honor.

As 2001 comes to an end, I hope you will take time to reflect on your contribution to the Administration and the country. In the wake of the tragic events of September 11th, you and your colleagues continue to show courage and resolve, dedication and compassion, grace under pressure, and above all, love of this great country and all that it represents.

On his second day in office, President Bush gave all of us a charge: "Let us begin the work we were hired to do and leave this a better place than we found it." You should be very proud of your service at The White House. America and the world are better for it.

President Bush and Vice President Cheney are grateful for your efforts; and, they know that the success of this Administration depends on the hard work of a competent and devoted team. Whether you came to The White House with this Administration or have been here through many, you are a valuable part of that team.

Kathi and I look forward to the year ahead, and we wish you and your family a wonderful holiday season. May God continue to bless America.

Sincerely,

Andrew H. Card, Jr.

I don't think much about what I experienced that day, but I do think of the passengers of United Airlines Flight 93. That plane, which is widely believed to have been bound for the Capitol Building or the White House, was brought down by a group of passengers who resolved to overtake the hijackers, and put the plane down in a field in Shanksville, Pennsylvania. When I do think of September 11, 2001, or on beautiful fall mornings when the sky is that same perfect blue, or on Thanksgiving Day, it is to those passengers that my thoughts go.

Chief of Staff Andrew Card sent very gracious notes of thanks to White House staff who offered special assistance on September 11, 2001. The personal nature of the note was underscored by the reference to his wife, Kathi. *(Courtesy Walter Scheib 3rd)*

The Long Goodbye
My Last Years in the White House

Everyone's world changed in the weeks, months, and years following September 11, 2001. Security was heightened, laws were changed, and we became a nation at war. The changes even affected how I did my job at the White House. For a long time after the attacks, to reflect the somber mood of the nation, we did virtually no social entertaining at the White House. In spring and summer 2002, we didn't even hold the tee ball games on the South Lawn. The prime focus of my job in those months was to feed the First Family, and to prepare working meals for the world leaders who visited the President in those dark days to offer support and to discuss the global war on terror.

Those days, and the changes they brought, were also the beginning of the end of my time at the White House, though it would be several years before I actually left. My departure from the White House in early 2005 transpired with head-spinning abruptness, but when I look back, I now realize that it was actually a long time coming.

BACK TO WORK

I get asked all the time about how the attacks of September 11, 2001, changed my view of working at the White House.

The truth of the matter was that my family and I—like all White House employees and their families—always knew that there was an inherent risk that came with working there. In my lifetime, a president has been shot and killed, and another was shot and survived. Shots have been fired at the White House itself. Someone even flew a small plane onto the White House lawn.

As a matter of practicality, we all kept this thought of possible harm at bay most of the time, in part because you needed to in order to perform your duties, but also because the risk was overshadowed by the grandeur and honor of going to work in the "people's house" every day. But the potential for something terrible to befall all of us was always there.

So on Wednesday, September 12, 2001, I got into my car early in the morning as I had for the past eight years and did what we all did: went back to the White House to serve the President and the First Family.

I got in early that day, around 5:30 a.m., and strangely, I felt safer in the House than I ever had. There were extra security checkpoints set up on the outskirts of the House perimeter, and you could hear F-16s flying overhead, which was reassuring.

I never considered not returning to work at the White House after the attacks, but I felt I owed my family a chance to weigh in on the decision. About a day or two later, I asked Jean if she had a problem with it.

"No. You're doing what you have to do. That's fine with me," was her response. Which didn't surprise me.

What did surprise me was the response I got from my sons, Walt and Jim, who said that they would be disappointed if I did anything else. I've always been proud of that reaction. Though just thirteen and ten at the time, I felt that they grasped the importance of not giving into the fear that could be brought on by the moment.

THANKS, BUT NO THANKS

With the best of intentions, somebody at the White House arranged for psychological counselors to speak with all House employees about a month after the attacks. We were summoned in small groups and met in a conference room, where we were encouraged to openly discuss our fears about coming to the White House.

I found this to be a waste of time, and I thought that many of my coworkers felt the same way. As I said, people who work at the White House are a unique breed, and I explained this to the counselor: "I think you're going to find that we are a different type of people, and that we are motivated by different things. I don't think anybody is scared."

In hindsight, I regret the force with which I made that point. Although I did and do believe we remained strong, I didn't realize at that moment how life-altering the experience had been—even to me. Years later, I realized that while I had performed my job just fine, I was angry in the months after the attacks—a bit short-tempered and edgy. I began to wonder how other people were affected. Private counseling had also been available, so I don't think I kept anyone from getting the help they needed, but I do wonder if I should have been more open to it at the time.

THE TIMES THEY ARE A-CHANGIN'

Our will was unbowed, but there were sweeping security changes that went into effect immediately after September 11. For my part, I worked with the Secret Service to strengthen the firewall around the kitchen, so that we'd be even more confident of the integrity of the products that arrived there.

While I was previously willing to sample unsolicited foods that were sent to me via FedEx or in the mail—from syrups to juices to smoked salmon—those items were now automatically discarded before I ever saw or heard of them. Moreover, owing both to the events of September 11 and to the anthrax mailings that October, I simply stopped receiving any mail at the White House. I began dealing with all purveyors by fax only, and dealt exclusively with people whom the Secret Service had personally visited and per-

As this sketch published in *US News and World Report* on June 2, 2003, shows, after 9/11 we had to be even more careful about the food allowed into the White House. *(Courtesy Richard Thompson)*

formed background checks on; our kitchen became closed to any new purveyors. If we weren't already in business with them, we weren't going to get into business with them. The same went for SBA cooks—if they weren't already cleared and possessing a sterling record, there was no admittance without a full background check, which was discouraged due to the cost and time involved.

By the time all new measures were implemented, our list of purveyors was whittled down from between thirty to forty to eight to ten. Those purveyors in turn helped us get items from third parties, who never knew they were providing food to the White House.

A LITTLE BIT PARANOID

I wasn't afraid but I did get even more careful. I began implementing some measures for my own personal peace of mind. It occurred to me that because I had been a fairly high-profile chef, somebody might get the idea to get to the First Family through me. Accordingly, on my way to and from the White House each day I began looking in my rearview mirror to gauge whether or not I was being followed. (I never was.)

I also sat my kids down one night: "Don't talk to anyone whom you don't know about what I do. If anybody asks what I do, just say I work for the Park Service." I thought about that, then added, "As a matter of fact, don't talk to anybody about it if you can avoid it at all."

I also stopped taking advantage of the little perks that come with being known to the people who guard the White House. In the months following September 11, there were bomb-sniffing dogs and other security measures on the roadways leading into the employee and visitor parking lots. One day, as I was driving in, one of the guards told another, "He's okay, he's the chef."

"Oh, no, no, no," I said. "Please, sweep my car, too." It was possible that someone might have visited my driveway during the night and I might be carrying some unknown cargo. "I don't want my family name to go down in history as the one who transported a bomb into the White House."

They understood. And they swept my car every day.

A NEW WHITE HOUSE FUNCTION

Mirroring the somber tone in the nation after September 11, there were no festive functions at the White House in the weeks and months that followed the attacks. In their place was a new, sometimes daily, event—the working meal with visiting heads of state and other dignitaries.

In September and October 2001, President Bush was visited by an endless parade of world leaders who came to commiserate with him, to talk about the sea change that was taking place in world politics, and to strategize for the budding war on terror.

In one week's time, from September 18 to September 24, we hosted many leaders in the White House: French President Jacques Chirac, Indonesian President Megawati Sukarnoputri, Japanese Prime Minister Junichiro Koizumi, British Prime Minister Tony Blair, and Canadian Prime Minister Jean Chrétien.

One thing didn't change after September 11: I still learned about the lunch events primarily via the Ushers Information Web page, although if a new one was scheduled on short notice (just a day or two), one of the ushers would call to give me a heads-up.

As was appropriate to the occasion, there was little emphasis on serving innovative food at these lunches. The meals took more of a comfort-food direction, and rather than two savory courses, we'd present one course, with a side dish. Some dishes we served during this time included Black Angus beef filet with gratin of silver corn and a warm bean salad; and rosemary and garlic-scented chicken breast with asparagus, chanterelles, and herb polenta.

There was never any official instruction conveyed to me or my cooks about the tone we were trying to set, or what kind of food we were to serve. I just depended on my tried-and-true sense of the temperature of the House I had refined over the past eight years, and knew what it needed in these days when it was far from healthy. In truth, I think we could have served the world leaders ham sandwiches and potato salad during this time, and they would've continued on with their work without a word.

UP CLOSE AND PERSONAL

The working lunches of fall 2001 were usually held in the Old Family Dining Room, which offered me and my assistant chefs an unusual peek at our visiting dignitaries. Our staging area was actually in the adjacent State Dining Room, which served as the receiving area for the lunches, set off only by a screened panel. We were able to see and hear the international power brokers on the other side, such as Italy's Prime Minister Silvio Berlusconi, Germany's Chancellor Gerhard Schröder, and Israel's Prime Minister Ariel Sharon.

From just the sound in the room, it was easy to tell whose company the President enjoyed and whose he didn't. If he were among close political friends, such as Tony Blair, the reception period would last for five to ten minutes, or longer, as the President made small talk with his

guests. If, however, the guest was someone with whom President Bush had a strained relationship, the greeting would be perfunctory—a quick handshake and a few photographs, and then
he'd say, with little fanfare or enthusiasm, "Okay, let's sit down and eat."

Veal Loin with Madeira Sauce and Potato-Leek Puree

SERVES 4

We served this lunch to Tony Blair, one of the few visiting dignitaries who always
remembered me, no doubt from all his visits to Camp David during the Clinton
years, where the staff was more visible than at the White House. He would invariably say hello or wave from across the room when he spotted me.

This classic dish, a riff on traditional meat-and-potatoes fare, is elegant enough to serve to a
visiting head of state, yet it is made from simple ingredients—not showy in any way. It offers a
good sense of the "comfort food" approach to even the most important meals that we adopted in
the wake of September 11.

¼ cup vegetable oil
1½ pounds boneless veal loin,
  trimmed of excess fat
1 tablespoon Dijon mustard
1 tablespoon chopped fresh thyme
  leaves
2 teaspoons chopped garlic
2 teaspoons chopped fresh flat-leaf
  parsley leaves
1 teaspoon chopped fresh rosemary
  leaves
1 tablespoon olive oil
Salt and freshly ground black pepper
Madeira Sauce (recipe follows)
Potato-Leek Puree (recipe follows)

1. Preheat the oven to 350°F.

2. Heat the vegetable oil in a large, heavy-bottomed sauté
pan over medium-high heat. Add the veal and sear on all sides
until lightly browned, 3 to 5 minutes total. Remove the veal to a
plate and let cool slightly.

3. In a small bowl stir together the mustard, thyme, garlic,
parsley, rosemary, and oil. Season with salt and pepper. Rub the
mixture over the veal. Set a rack in a roasting pan and set the
veal on the rack. Roast until an instant-read thermometer
inserted in the center of the veal reads 140°F for medium rare,
12 to15 minutes, or longer for more well done meat.

4. Transfer the veal to a cutting board and let rest 3 to 4 minutes before slicing.

5. To serve, slice the veal and divide the slices evenly among
four dinner plates. Spoon some Madeira sauce over and around
the veal and pass the potato-leek puree alongside.

Madeira Sauce

MAKES ABOUT ½ CUP

½ tablespoon olive oil
¼ cup (about 1 ounce) diced
  cleaned white mushrooms
1 tablespoon chopped shallot
1 teaspoon chopped garlic
¼ cup Madeira
1 tablespoon ruby or tawny Port
  wine
1 cup homemade or store-bought
  low-sodium veal or beef stock
¼ teaspoon white truffle oil (see
  Sources, page 302)
Salt and freshly ground black pepper

1. Heat the oil in small saucepan over medium heat. Add the mushrooms, shallot, and garlic and cook until the shallot and garlic are tender, 3 to 5 minutes. Add the Madeira and Port to the pan and scrape up any flavorful bits stuck to the bottom of the pot. Allow the liquid to reduce by half, 3 to 5 minutes.

2. Add the stock and bring to a boil over high heat. Lower the heat and simmer until the liquid has reduced to one half its original volume and is thick enough to coat the back of a wooden spoon, 5 to 6 minutes.

3. Strain the sauce through a fine-mesh strainer set over a bowl, pressing down on the solids with a wooden spoon or spatula to extract as much flavorful liquid as possible. Discard the solids. Stir the truffle oil into the sauce, season with salt and pepper, and keep covered and warm.

Potato-Leek Puree

SERVES 4 AS A SIDE DISH

1 pound Idaho or russet potatoes,
  peeled and cut into 1-inch pieces
¼ cup chopped bacon
½ cup thinly sliced leeks, white part
  only
1 tablespoon chopped garlic
About 1 cup half-and-half
4 tablespoons (½ stick) unsalted
  butter
Salt and freshly ground black pepper
¼ cup grated Asiago cheese (1
  ounce)
¼ cup sour cream
1 tablespoon chopped fresh chives

1. Boil the potatoes in a large pot of salted water until tender to a knife tip, about 20 minutes.

2. Meanwhile, cook the bacon in a small, heavy-bottomed sauté pan over medium heat. Once the bacon fat has been rendered, add the leeks and garlic and cook until tender, 5 to 7 minutes. Remove from heat and set aside.

3. Heat the half-and-half and butter in a small, heavy-bottomed saucepan over low heat until the butter melts, but do not let boil.

4. Drain the potatoes and transfer them to a large bowl. Mash the potatoes until very smooth. Beat in the half-and-half mixture and season with salt and pepper to taste. If not sufficiently smooth, beat in some more half-and-half.

5. Fold the bacon, leeks, and garlic into the potatoes, then fold in cheese, sour cream, and chives. Keep covered and warm in a double boiler until ready to serve.

Long Island Duck with Sherry Sauce and Kuri Squash

SERVES 4

When Canadian Prime Minster Jean Chrétien visited the White House on a chilly day in September 2001, we served him this dish. The Asian-leaning blend of spices that flavors the duck and perks up dulled senses is especially satisfying in cold weather. Kuri squash is a variety of pumpkin with a slightly sweet flavor and firm texture, and an ability to take on other flavors well. You can substitute butternut squash or pumpkin if you like.

4 skin-on duck breasts (about 6 ounces each; see Sources, page 302)
¼ cup soy sauce
¼ cup rice wine or dry sherry
1 tablespoon honey
1 tablespoon freshly squeezed lime juice
1 tablespoon hoisin sauce (see Sources, page 302)
1 teaspoon grated orange zest
1 teaspoon chili paste
1 teaspoon chopped garlic
1 teaspoon grated fresh ginger
¼ teaspoon ground star anise
Sautéed Kuri Squash (recipe follows)
Sherry Sauce (recipe follows)

1. Trim and discard any excess skin from duck. Using a sharp knife, score the center of the skin in a crosshatch pattern. Set the breasts aside in a glass baking dish or other shallow dish.

2. In a small bowl, stir together the soy sauce, rice wine, honey, lime juice, hoisin, orange zest, chili paste, garlic, ginger, and star anise. Pour this marinade over the duck, cover with plastic wrap, and refrigerate for 2 to 3 hours.

3. Preheat the oven to 350°F. Remove the duck from the marinade, brushing off any solids.

4. Heat a large heavy ovenproof sauté pan over medium-high heat. Put the duck in the pan skin side down to brown it, and continue to cook until the fat renders, 4 to 5 minutes, periodically pouring off the fat, leaving about 2 tablespoons of fat in the pan to prevent scorching. Turn the duck over and cook on the other side for 2 to 3 minutes, continuing to pour off any excess fat.

5. Turn the duck skin side down again and transfer the pan to the oven. Roast until an instant-read thermometer inserted into the center of a breast reads 150°F for medium rare, 12 to 15 minutes. Periodically drain off and discard the fat that gathers in the pan.

6. Transfer the duck breasts to a cutting board and let rest for 4 minutes. Slice each breast on a diagonal across the grain into ¼-inch-thick slides.

7. To serve, spoon some of the squash into the center of each of four dinner plates. Top with a duck breast and spoon some sauce over the duck and around the squash.

Sautéed Kuri Squash

SERVES 4 AS A SIDE DISH

2 cups peeled and cubed red kuri squash (from about 8 ounces unpeeled squash), in 1-inch cubes (butternut squash or pumpkin can be substituted)
1 tablespoon olive oil
1 tablespoon grated peeled fresh ginger
½ tablespoon chopped garlic
½ tablespoon ground coriander
1 teaspoon chili paste
¼ teaspoon ground cumin
¼ teaspoon turmeric
Pinch of dry mustard
2 tablespoons honey
¼ cup chopped scallions, white and light green parts only
1 tablespoon chopped fresh mint leaves
1 tablespoon chopped fresh cilantro leaves
Salt and freshly ground black pepper

1. Bring a large pot of salted water to a boil. Add the squash and cook until tender to a knife tip, 12 to 15 minutes. Drain and set aside.

2. Heat the oil in a large, heavy-bottomed sauté pan over medium heat. Add the ginger, garlic, coriander, chili paste, cumin, turmeric, and mustard and cook until the ginger and garlic are tender, 1 to 2 minutes. Stir in the honey and cook an additional 1 minute.

3. Add the squash to the pan and toss well to coat. Continue cooking until the squash is heated through, 3 to 5 minutes.

4. Add the scallions, mint, and cilantro. Season to taste with salt and pepper, stir, and cook for another 30 seconds. Keep covered and warm.

Sherry Sauce

MAKES 1 ¼ CUP

1 tablespoon olive oil
1 tablespoon chopped shallot
1 teaspoon chopped garlic
1 teaspoon grated fresh ginger
1 tablespoon honey
¼ teaspoon grated orange zest
Pinch of ground star anise
¼ cup dry sherry or rice wine
1 tablespoon soy sauce
1½ cups homemade or store-bought duck stock or low-sodium chicken stock
Salt and freshly ground black pepper

1. Heat the oil in a medium, heavy-bottomed saucepan over medium heat. Add the shallot, garlic, and ginger and sauté until tender, 1 to 2 minutes. Stir in the honey, orange zest, and star anise and cook for 30 seconds.

2. Add the sherry and soy sauce and scrape up any flavorful bits stuck to the bottom of the pot. Bring to a simmer and cook until reduced by half, 3 to 4 minutes.

3. Add the stock and bring to a boil over high heat. Lower the heat and simmer until reduced by one third, about 8 minutes.

4. Strain the sauce though a fine-mesh strainer set over a bowl and season to taste with salt and pepper. Discard the solids. Keep covered and warm until ready to serve.

Pomegranate-Glazed Lamb with Sautéed Eggplant and Roasted Peppers

SERVES 4

In the midst of the working lunches in fall 2001, on November 19, President Bush hosted an Iftaar dinner, at which the fast of the Muslim holiday of Ramadan is broken. Present at this dinner held in the State Dining Room, were a number of Islamic ambassadors to the United States, as well as Secretary of State Colin Powell and other members of the administration. This lamb dish was the main course that night, with a spice rub and pomegranate glaze that gave it a Middle Eastern flavor. For this event, we used halal meat, meaning it had been killed, cleaned, and prepared by methods approved by Islamic law. Halal meat tastes more or less the same as non-halal meat, although it may be a bit saltier, so consider that when doing the final seasoning.

1 tablespoon plus ½ teaspoon grated garlic
1 tablespoon grated peeled fresh ginger
2 tablespoons grated Spanish onion
½ tablespoon ground cumin
1 teaspoon paprika
¾ teaspoon ground cinnamon
1 teaspoon harissa (see Sources, page 302)
1 teaspoon freshly ground black pepper
1 teaspoon ground coriander
Two 8-rib lamb racks, chine bone and fat removed (14 to 16 ounces each)
1 cup pomegranate juice
2 tablespoons honey
1 tablespoon freshly squeezed lime juice
½ cup vegetable oil
Sautéed Eggplant and Roasted Peppers (recipe follows)
Orange-Pomegranate Sauce (recipe follows)

1. In a small bowl, combine 1 tablespoon of the garlic, the ginger, onion, cumin, paprika, cinnamon, harissa, pepper, and coriander and stir until well incorporated. Rub onto the meat side of the lamb. Place the lamb on a plate, cover loosely with foil, and refrigerate for 2 hours.

2. In a small saucepan, combine the pomegranate juice, honey, lime juice, and the remaining ½ teaspoon garlic and bring to a simmer over medium heat. Cook, stirring occasionally, until the liquid reaches a syrup consistency, 10 to 12 minutes. Remove from heat and set aside.

3. Preheat the oven to 375°F.

4. Heat the oil in a large sauté pan over high heat. Add the lamb and sear until browned, 3 to 5 minutes per side.

5. Set a rack in a roasting pan, set the lamb on the rack, and use a pastry brush to "paint" the lamb with the glaze. Roast the lamb until an instant-read thermometer inserted into the thickest part reads 140°F for medium, 20 to 25 minutes. Remove from the oven, paint the lamb with the glaze again, and let rest for 4 minutes.

6. To serve, divide the eggplant and roasted peppers among four dinner plates. Slice the lamb into individual chops, and arrange four chops over the vegetables on each plate. Spoon the sauce over and around the lamb.

Sautéed Eggplant and Roasted Peppers

MAKES ABOUT 1¼ CUPS

1 tablespoon olive oil
¼ cup diced Spanish onion, in ½-inch pieces
1 cup peeled, diced eggplant, in 1-inch cubes
¼ cup diced roasted red bell pepper (see box, page 51), in ½-inch pieces
¼ cup diced roasted yellow bell pepper (see box, page 51), in ½-inch pieces
2 tablespoons red wine vinegar
2 tablespoons chopped fresh basil leaves
¼ cup diced plum tomato
1 tablespoon chopped garlic
1 tablespoon chopped fresh flat-leaf parsley leaves
1 teaspoon fresh thyme leaves

Heat the oil in a large sauté pan over medium heat. Add the onion and sauté until lightly browned, 5 to 7 minutes. Add eggplant and cook, stirring, for 5 minutes. Add the red and yellow peppers, vinegar, basil, tomato, garlic, parsley, and thyme and cook 5 minutes more. Keep covered and warm until ready to use.

Orange-Pomegranate Sauce

MAKES ABOUT 1¼ CUPS

1 cup homemade or store-bought low-sodium beef stock
1 cup pomegranate juice
½ cup orange juice
½ cup red wine
1 tablespoon red wine vinegar
1 teaspoon grated fresh ginger
1 teaspoon grated garlic
½ teaspoon ground cumin
$\frac{1}{16}$ teaspoon harissa
1 tablespoon thinly sliced fresh mint leaves

In a medium, heavy-bottomed saucepan, combine the stock, pomegranate juice, orange juice, wine, vinegar, ginger, garlic, cumin, and harissa and bring to a boil over high heat. Lower the heat and simmer until the liquid has reduced by two thirds, 10 to 12 minutes. Strain the sauce through a fine-mesh strainer set over a bowl and stir in the mint. Keep covered and warm.

Salmon over Roasted Seckel Pears with Acorn Squash Sauce

SERVES 4

I created this dish for a dinner honoring Israeli Prime Minster Ariel Sharon. The sweet, caramelized, roasted pears offer a counterpoint to the rich, fatty salmon (a similar contrast is offered by the squash sauce), while the vegetable-based sauce is much lighter than traditional fish sauces. Be sure not to overcook the salmon as it will lose its silky texture and become dry and tough.

1 tablespoon olive oil
4 boneless, skinless salmon fillets (5 ounces each)
Salt and freshly ground black pepper
Roasted Seckel Pears (recipe follows)
Acorn Squash Sauce (recipe follows)

Heat the oil in a large sauté pan over medium heat. Season the salmon with salt and pepper and cook until just warmed through and opaque in the center, about 4 minutes per side.

To serve, divide the pears among four dinner plates. Put one salmon fillet over the pears on each plate. Spoon the sauce over and around the salmon and the pears.

Roasted Seckel Pears

SERVES 4

2 tablespoons balsamic vinegar
2 tablespoons (¼ stick) unsalted butter, melted
1 tablespoon freshly squeezed lemon juice
½ teaspoon grated lemon zest
1 tablespoon sugar
2 teaspoons grated garlic
1 teaspoon grated peeled fresh ginger
¼ teaspoon freshly ground black pepper
1½ cups peeled and thinly sliced Seckel or other ripe pears (from about 2 pears)

Preheat the oven to 350°F. In a medium bowl, combine the vinegar, butter, lemon juice and zest, sugar, garlic, ginger, and black pepper and stir together well. Add the pears and gently toss to coat them. Arrange the pears on a nonstick baking sheet in a single layer without crowding and roast until cooked through, 10 to 12 minutes.

Acorn Squash Sauce

SERVES 4

½ medium acorn squash
2 tablespoons olive oil
Salt and freshly ground black pepper
¼ cup thinly sliced leek, white part
   only
2 teaspoons chopped garlic
¼ cup diced pear
1½ cups homemade or store-bought
   low-sodium chicken stock
2 tablespoons orange juice
¼ teaspoon curry powder
1 tablespoon crème fraîche

1. Preheat the oven to 375°F.

2. Put the squash, skin side down, on a baking sheet. Rub 1 tablespoon of the oil over the flesh, season with salt and pepper, and roast in the oven until tender to a knife tip, about 30 minutes. Remove the squash from the oven and let cool slightly. When cool enough to handle, use a spoon to transfer the flesh to a bowl and mash it with a potato masher or the back of the spoon.

3. Heat the remaining tablespoon oil in a medium, heavy-bottomed saucepan over medium heat. Add the leek and garlic and sauté for 2 to 3 minutes until soft. Add the pear and cook, stirring gently, for 3 minutes. Add the stock, squash, orange juice, and curry powder. Bring to a simmer and cook, stirring occasionally, for 10 minutes.

4. Transfer the sauce to a standing blender and puree it, in batches if necessary. Strain through a fine-mesh strainer set over a bowl. Stir in the crème fraîche and season to taste with salt and pepper. Keep covered and warm until ready to use.

AS TIME GOES BY

In the years after 2001, life in the White House mirrored life in much of the country. It slowly but surely returned to normal, or at least to what Vice President Dick Cheney called "the new normalcy."

Of course, we never forgot that the United States was at war, with terrorism in general, and on the ground in Afghanistan and Iraq, but the Bush Administration also let vestiges of everyday pleasures back into the White House; for example, tee ball games, which had been called off in 2002, were back on the South Lawn in the spring and summer of 2003 and 2004—a welcome bit of innocence that did us all a world of good.

And yet, as the normal course of White House dining and entertaining resumed during those years, I had an increasingly nagging sensation that I just couldn't shake: My work had ceased being fun a long time prior. There were very few state dinners, almost no large social occasions, and menus were largely culled from a go-to roster of favorite dishes that continued from year to year.

Not that I was there to be entertained, but I've long believed that if you aren't happy in your work then complacency can't be far behind. To be honest, I hadn't felt truly tested in about four years. Once I had figured out how to cook to suit the Bushes' taste, a puzzle I had solved within a few months of their arrival, everything was fairly routine, in every since of the word—we had a routine, our menus were routine, and executing them was routine.

The one exception to this dynamic, and I was grateful for it every day, was that Mrs. Bush still enjoyed the same type of lunches we had prepared for her all along. While these weren't necessarily new dishes—indeed many of them, or versions of many of them, dated back to the Clinton years—they were a welcome outlet for me and my team to express ourselves in the kitchen.

As time marched forward, and September 11 receded further and further into the past, I began to realize that it wasn't really the terrorist attacks that marked the change; it was the departure of the Clintons, in particular Mrs. Clinton and her ambition to make the House a showcase for American food, wine, and entertaining.

Under the Bushes, we weren't trying to do very much at the White House that was new. I found myself thinking with profound nostalgia of Mrs. Clinton and her passion for inclusion, her interest in learning about and trying new foods, and her desire to show off her nation's best to visitors foreign and domestic.

These days, we weren't trying to make events ever more inclusive, and we sure weren't pushing the envelope when it came to the food itself. We were cooking and serving predictable fare to relatively small numbers of people. Except for the fact that I was working in the White House, I was basically living a life that was one part private chef and one part chef of a midsize suburban restaurant.

There were even times when my team and I did less than that. In June 2004, for example, at the congressional picnic, we served food from KC Masterpiece, a foodservice company that produces bottled sauces and heat-and-eat dishes. I had no say whatsoever in the menu, which was essentially dictated to me by representatives of KC Masterpiece, whose founder, Dr. Rich Davis, was at the White House on the day of the event. That year, my chefs and I were reduced to oven technicians, heating and setting out a menu of ready-made spare ribs, smoked turkey breast, dirty rice, and other prepackaged foods that were commercial quality at best. Even Roland's creativity was muzzled; instead of his usual beautiful desserts he served pound cake, strawberries, whipped cream, chocolate chip cookies, and vanilla ice cream—things that any pastry chef (or home cook, for that matter) could have pulled off.

Incidents like this made it hard to work up any real enthusiasm for my job.

I had the sense that I wasn't alone. I have no way of knowing if I was right or wrong, but I remember looking around the room in one of Gary's Monday morning staff meetings late that summer and thinking how utterly bored and detached everyone seemed, just going through the motions, with none of the old vim and vigor.

HANGING IN THERE

Despite these incidents and observations, I had my reasons for staying. After September 11, 2001, it was a point of pride: I'd be damned if I was going to leave at a time that even suggested it was done out of apprehension.

That motivation sustained me for about a year. After that, I kept telling myself that it was an honor to serve the First Family, and it was. But there continued to be an unavoidable sense of anticlimax about the work I was doing for the current occupants of the White House, and that feeling grew every year. If anything, the food we were asked to cook in 2004 was becoming even more ordinary than it was when Mr. Bush first became President, and by the time the fall of 2004 rolled along, the White House kitchen had become a more mundane place than I ever imagined it could be. I still felt that swelling of pride and awe when I parked my car and made the walk up to the House each morning, but once I got there, it was a struggle to keep positive.

In the fall of 2004, running out of reasons to stay, I pulled another one out of my toque: I was hoping that the holiday season might finally perk things up. President Bush had just won reelection and had plenty to be happy about.

But the 2004 holiday season proved to be the worst time for me, personally, in the White House—the days when I realized my time, one way or another, would be coming to an end sooner rather than later.

FIRST IMPRESSIONS

In my career, I'd never felt the ground moving under my feet, never had that sinking feeling that I wasn't long for this world, never had a new executive cast an ominous shadow across my desk. But that all changed in December 2004.

After that year's presidential election, a rumor rippled through the White House's residence staff that we would all be asked to resign, then rehired on a case-by-case basis—if we were lucky.

Gary Walters had been around the House long enough (eighteen years at that point) to have seen it all, so one day I pulled him aside and asked him if the anxiety among the ranks was well-founded. "Absolutely," he told me, then went on to explain that it wasn't just the political team in the West Wing that changed after a reelection; often it was the First Lady's staff as well. (I guess I knew this in the back of my mind, but it was such a nonissue when President Clinton was reelected, that I had forgotten about the possibility.)

We were never summarily asked to resign, but in the weeks after the election, Mrs. Bush made it clear that she was going to put a more personal stamp on the White House. Though the formal transition wouldn't occur until the New Year, there was substantial buzz in the house, much of it generated by "water-cooler" talk like you'd encounter in any work environment, that she was going to bring in a new chief of staff and a new press secretary. In my own department, we had recently witnessed the hiring of a new pastry chef, Thaddeus DuBois, when Roland Mesnier retired.

Most relevant to my life was Cathy Fenton's announcement in the summer of 2004 that she would retire after President Bush's second inauguration, assuming he won the upcoming election. On the heels of that news, Mrs. Bush, hired a new social secretary named Lea Berman.

Lea Berman was well known before she took on the role of Mrs. Bush's social secretary. She had most recently held that job for Lynne Cheney, wife of Vice President Dick Cheney, and was herself a Washington socialite. Married to former sugar lobbyist and Republican fundraiser (and contributor) Wayne Berman, Lea had also worked for the Bush-Cheney campaign. We all knew a lot about her, because she and her husband were often mentioned in the papers, and almost inevitably the mentions included a reference to their 13,000-square-foot Embassy Row mansion.

Lea, whose aggressive style and penchant for flashy suits instantly differentiated her from the more prim, proper Cathy Fenton, set up meetings with key personnel from all departments. I had a private meeting with her in the Map Room, which was often used as a conference room for sensitive conversations (in fact, it was the site of my very first meeting with Ann Stock and Gary Walters), followed a few days later by a meeting in which I was joined by Gary Walters, John Moeller, and Cris Comerford.

The interviews were complex. In many ways, it seemed to me that Lea was using us to get her bearings, asking about how we interacted with Cathy Fenton, the First Lady, and so on.

But Lea also let us know about her vision for the White House. One of the things I'll never forget was when she looked me in the eye and said, "We need to stop serving this country club food."

Cris, John, and I exchanged a subtle glance at one another. I think we all had the same

A rare and welcome moment of fun in late 2001 as Chef Emeril Lagasse pays a visit to the kitchen. *(Courtesy Walter Scheib 3rd)*

thought: that what Lea called "country club food" was exactly the type of cuisine that Mrs. Bush had been requesting, and the style she had been honing, through her direction and feedback to us, for four years.

I pointed out to Lea that we didn't do anything that we weren't asked to do either by Mrs. Bush or her representatives.

"I don't know if that's true," Lea replied, and we moved on.

To this day, I'm not sure if she was doubting what I was reporting to her, or questioning the accuracy of the wishes being conveyed to me by the people I was referring to.

For my part, I began to wonder how many of Lea's mandates came from the First Lady and how many were dictated by her own personal taste. In one of those early meetings, she referred to a meal her husband had recently enjoyed at one of Marco Pierre White's Michelin-starred restaurants in England. I instantly thought that if she tried to bring hypercreative food to the White House, we'd all be out on the street before you could say *merci, non*.

Things were about to get very interesting.

WHEN WORLDS COLLIDE

Cathy Fenton had had a long and, as I understood it, distinguished career as a government employee, having worked for the Reagan and George H. W. Bush Administrations before assuming her current role. It would have been nice, I think, for someone with that history of service to finish out her career on a high note.

But that wouldn't come to pass because, with Cathy still in her office, Lea started work in December 2004, acting as de facto social secretary, essentially pushing Cathy to the sidelines.

As a pragmatist, I've never believed in making big changes during your busiest times, which in the White House is during the holidays. But that's just what happened. Not only was Lea taking over for Cathy, but all of a sudden, everything we did was being second-guessed.

For example, there was a character who joined the cast that holiday season, one who had shown up every autumn since 2001: Kenneth Blasingame, Mrs. Bush's interior decorator from Texas and president of Blasingame Design, who put the Bush stamp on the House for the season each year with stylistic touches that were in sync with Mrs. Bush's sensibility.

Mr. Blasingame had clearly absorbed Mrs. Bush's predilection toward things that were "generous, flavorful, and identifiable." One of the ways he brought this ideal to life was with big platters. He wanted there to be platters everywhere during receptions, all of them overflowing with food. So, for instance, on the day of a reception, he'd show up in my kitchen with three-and-a-half-foot silver platters and instruct me to load them up with honey-baked ham, sliced turkey, and so on—putting several pounds out at once rather than smaller amounts that would be replenished. This was another of an ever-growing list of cases where menus were being driven by somebody other than the food expert on the staff and, predictably, it resulted in some imperfections.

One day, somebody on the staff relayed to me that a reception guest complained that the sliced turkey on one of the platters was dry.

"Of course it is," I said. "It's been sitting out there for three hours."

Despite this dynamic, I got along just fine with Ken, and he and Cathy Fenton peacefully coexisted for three years. But such was not the case between him and Lea Berman, and my team was often caught in the crossfire.

One day, early in Lea's unofficial tenure, I had just set down a platter of hors d'oeuvres for a reception when she appeared at my side and asked, "What's up with the giant platters?"

My answer to this question was the same answer I had to all of her questions, from why we served "country club" food to why we had gigantic platters all over the place: "That's the way we were told to do it."

She indicated that this was something she'd need to take up with Ken, and left.

A few days later, during the height of the holidays, Ken shared with me that he had decided that this year there were to be long-stemmed white tulips everywhere. I remember setting out a platter of food when he walked over and told me to garnish it with a tulip "for flair."

I'd put small centerpiece arrangements in the center of platters, but I'd never put flowers on my food before. Nonetheless, I did as directed. A few minutes later, Lea happened on the scene and asked me what was going on with the tulips. I explained Ken's directive, then Lea considered it and decided it was a great idea, instructing me to add more tulips.

I complied, arranging close to ten of them over and around the food on each platter on the buffet.

Ten minutes after that, Ken reappeared and had me lose all but one tulip.

Before he departed the scene, Lea returned, took one look at the platter, and asked where the other flowers had gone.

I couldn't take it anymore. "Ken Blasingame, Lea Berman," I said, making a faux introduction. "Lea Berman, Ken Blasingame."

They both looked at me disdainfully, clearly not appreciating my little joke.

"Sorry, guys," I said, "but you need to get together on this." I gestured toward a cluster of my cooks who had been watching the farce play out for the past half an hour, and said, "You're scaring the kids."

They ended up compromising, leaving a few tulips on the platter and calling it a day.

But the incident stayed with me, and I think it stayed with Lea as well, an early indication to us both that this was an ill-fated relationship.

A PICTURE IS WORTH . . . NOTHING!

Lea and I had different ideas about food. One day, a week or two after the flower incident, she showed up in my kitchen with a cookbook tucked under her arm. "Your vegetables for meals are always overcooked," she told me matter-of-factly.

I was incredulous. You might take exception to my palate, or my presentation style. But I was

fairly certain I wouldn't have made it this far in my career if I didn't know how to cook vegetables.

Lea opened the book to a picture of cooked vegetables, all glistening and firm.

"Can you make this?" she asked.

"Which? The book or the dish?"

"What do you mean?"

"I can cook that dish, and I can write that book if you like."

It probably wasn't the smartest thing to say, but her comments were so out of left field that I was dumbfounded. We had been cooking for two first families for more than a decade and never heard a peep of criticism, and now this?

All season long, Lea brought books and

Setting up a food shot for Mrs. Clinton's book *Invitation to the White House*, with *Gourmet* magazine photographer Romulo Yanes. To ensure that the food looked inviting but real, we shot all the food without the styling tricks I described to Lea Berman. *(Courtesy Walter Scheib 3rd)*

magazines to my office, with tabs sticking out to mark the recipes she wanted me to make. Lea also made clear that she didn't just want me to follow the cooking instructions step by step; she also wanted me to duplicate the presentations depicted in the photos. The growing stacks of tabbed cookbooks in my office became a constant source of irritation and insult, an omnipresent reminder that my input had outlived its welcome.

After weeks of this, Lea walked into my office with yet another cookbook under her arm. Unlike many of her books, which in my opinion were fairly lowbrow, this time she had one of Martha Stewart's in tow. She opened it to a flagged page, on which was depicted a picture of a platter of sliced vegetables, with a half-peeled peapod and some pea blossoms scattered artistically over its surface and told me she wanted me to duplicate it for a large private party.

I could certainly make the recipe, but there was no way I'd be able to plate more than one hundred dishes exactly like that. Nonetheless, I told her I'd do my best to meet her wishes. Despite my growing frustration, I never stopped trying to meet any task set before me, to make the food as delicious as possible, even if it wasn't my recipe or my natural presentation style.

I had come to the conclusion that Lea just didn't realize what went into these shots. Cookbook photographs aren't snapped spontaneously. They are usually carefully crafted. Not only are the dishes fussed over by stylists, food is often propped up and placed just so with hidden toothpicks and other paraphernalia; vegetables are often undercooked to ensure they'll hold firm over the time it takes to light and shoot multiple takes; and sometimes the food is inedible, because crucial ingredients like flavorings or spices are left out if they will mar the visual impression in some way or because the food may be repeatedly painted with oil or other liquids to make the food shine.

I couldn't keep silent.

"You know, Lea," I said. "I think it might be helpful if we went to a photo shoot together sometime so you can see what really goes on."

Lea reacted curtly, insisting that I make the dish anyway.

Of course, I have no way of knowing for sure, but I think it was right then and there that she stopped paying attention to me altogether.

HOME FOR THE HOLIDAYS

Things were tense for me at work, so I was only too happy when the last of the holiday receptions came and went. When the First Family decamped for Crawford, I headed home and decompressed until the New Year.

To Walter Scheib and Family
With best wishes,

My family and the Bushes at the staff Christmas party in December. No matter how I was feeling about my work, the holidays always brought a sense of optimism. *(Courtesy Walter Scheib 3rd)*

I had a lot of time to reflect during that time off. Did I think about quitting? You bet I did. There were plenty of arguments for my doing just that.

But there were also, even after the unpleasantness of that December, reasons to stay. It was still a privilege to call the White House my place of employment, and there was the kitchen— which I have to admit I thought of as my own, having spent so much time transforming it when I first got to the House eleven years earlier.

Eleven years! That was another factor in my perpetual professional masochism—the White House had become my home away from home for more than a decade. It might have become a dysfunctional home, but I simply didn't know any other working home at this point. I thought of Rod Stoner's old line about nobody ever leaving the Greenbrier for someplace better. I never agreed with that, but I had developed that bias about the White House—I mean, what could be a better place to work than that? Jean, the boys, and I also had a nice life in Great Falls, Virginia. If there was an upside to the Bushes' lackluster social calendar and frequent trips to Crawford, it was that I wasn't putting in especially long hours, leaving me time to attend my kids' hockey games and spend time with Jean.

I guess you could say I was in denial, constantly looking for excuses to stay in an unhealthy relationship, when the best thing for me would have been to get out while the getting was good.

BACK TO WORK

Having decided to stay on, I returned to the White House in early January determined to put my best foot forward. Okay, I thought, it's no longer an adventure, but if it's going to be my job, I'll do the best job I can and see if that becomes satisfying.

There was plenty going on that January, a strong contrast to the normally quiet post-holiday lull. One of the first orders of business was the President's inauguration, scheduled for January 20, 2005. As we had four years ago, we planned a buffet lunch for the First Family's return to the White House from the steps of the Capitol.

On January 3, I submitted a very conservative menu to the social office that included sliced mozzarella and basil, corn and black bean salad, the ubiquitous beef tenderloin, and hummus, something we'd been serving, to good response and with great frequency to Mrs. Bush over the past four years; grilled vegetables and hummus was even one of the dishes in regular rotation on the First Lady's lunch menu.

When the menu came back to me, Lea had scribbled "yuk [sic] on hummus" next to the list. Also, affixed to the draft menu when it arrived back in my in box was a note, on which Lea had written "Need my cookbooks back."

I was only too happy to comply.

That same week, on January 6, there was an event scheduled, listed on the Ushers Information Web page simply as "Lunch for Portrait Artist." I submitted a menu for that event, and this time Lea changed every course. I offered a choice of two soups—kuri squash with ginger or chicken consommé with herbed quenelles—which she crossed out and replaced with sweet potato soup with rum crème. On a main course of Dover Sole with northern shrimp, she crossed out the shrimp, leaving just a piece of fish. And next to a salad featuring warm goat's cheese galette, she wrote "no galette, just use the cheese."

When the menu was returned to me, it also had a note from her to me written on it that read: "From Mrs. Bush, I have the recipes in my office for soup and dessert if you want to get them, Lea."

It turned out that the soup Lea wanted me to prepare was from *Martha Stewart Living* magazine, the same place from which she had selected two desserts for our newly hired pastry chef to choose from—triple citrus coffee cake or berry tartlets. The tartlets instantly reminded me of my conversation with Lea about food styling because they were topped with little clusters of cassis berries attached by the stick-like stem, something no pastry chef would feature on a real-world plate.

So, with all the continual requests to make dishes that were not my own and that I thought were contrary to what I believed Mrs. Bush wanted, it wasn't great to be back to work. I continued to do what was asked of me and tried to find ways to stay motivated and keep a smile on my face.

One of the things that kept me focused during this period was the unusual number of special functions that were calendared for January. We orchestrated goodbye dinners for outgoing Chief of Staff Andi Ball and for Cathy Fenton, and, on January 6, in addition to the portrait artist lunch, we cooked a sixtieth anniversary dinner for President George H. W. Bush and Barbara Bush that was held in the White House and attended by many Bush family members including the President's brother, Florida Governor Jeb Bush. I was delighted on that occasion when one of the butlers came into the kitchen and told me that Barbara Bush had asked him to convey her thanks for our efforts and tell me how pleasurable the meal was. For a fleeting moment, it almost felt like old times again.

Cream of Celery Root Soup

This soup is rich and satisfying enough for a cold winter's day, but still elegant enough for the sixtieth wedding anniversary of the President's parents, for which it was served. The same basic recipe can be used for a variety of winter or root vegetables, substituting parsnip or butternut squash for the celery root.

2 tablespoons (¼ stick) unsalted butter
1½ cups (about 5 ounces) peeled, diced celery root (celeriac)
½ cup peeled, diced Idaho or russet potato
¼ cup diced leek, white part only
About 4 cups homemade or store-bought low-sodium chicken stock
½ teaspoon dried thyme
½ cup heavy cream
Salt and freshly ground black pepper
croutons, homemade or store-bought, optional
1 tablespoon chopped fresh chives

1. Melt the butter in a large, heavy-bottomed saucepan over medium heat. Add the celery root, potato, and leek and cook just until the celery root is tender to a knife tip, 6 to 8 minutes. Add 4 cups of the stock and the thyme. Cook until the celery root and potato are very tender, 20 to 25 minutes.

2. Puree with a handheld immersion blender, or in batches in a standing blender, until very smooth. (If using a standing blender, returned the pureed mixture to the pot.) Add the cream, bring to a simmer, and cook 5 minutes. Strain through a fine-mesh strainer set over another saucepan. If the soup seems excessively thick, stir in a bit more stock. Season to taste with salt and pepper and keep warm.

3. To serve, divide the soup among four bowls. Garnish with the chives and thyme croutons.

Mâche, Frisée, and Peppercress Salad with Roquefort Cheese and Walnut Dressing

SERVES 4 AS A SIDE DISH

This salad of winter lettuces, which we served at the Southworth-Johnson marriage celebration dinner, is brought to life by the warm sharpness of the Roquefort tartine and the rich nuttiness of the walnut oil in the dressing, a much creamier dressing than we usually served at the White House. The goat's milk adds a nice, full-bodied tanginess, but can be replaced by buttermilk or half-and-half. Peppercress is the ideal, tender green to use here, but other peppery greens such as arugula or watercress can be substituted.

6 small heads mâche, washed and trimmed

¼ cup julienned Belgian endive

¼ cup torn frisée, white part only

¼ cup peppercress, watercress, or arugula torn into bite-size pieces

4 slices Roquefort cheese (1 ounce each)

4 ½-inch-thick baguette slices baguette

1½ tablespoons chopped toasted walnuts

Roquefort Cheese and Walnut Dressing (recipe follows)

Salt and freshly ground black pepper

1. Preheat the oven to 350°F.

2. Put the mâche, endive, frisée, and peppercress in a large bowl.

3. Make the Roquefort tartines: Put one slice of cheese on each baguette slice and sprinkle with the chopped walnuts. Arrange the bread on a baking sheet and bake until the cheese is soft and melted, 2 to 3 minutes.

4. Meanwhile, drizzle the dressing over lettuces and toss well. Season to taste with salt and pepper.

5. To serve, put one tartine on each of four salad plates and top with some salad.

Roquefort Cheese and Walnut Dressing

MAKES ABOUT ½ CUP

2 tablespoons freshly squeezed lemon juice

2 tablespoons crumbled Roquefort cheese

1 tablespoon crème fraîche

In the container of a standing blender, combine the lemon juice, Roquefort, crème fraîche, goat's milk, vinegar, and walnut oil and blend until creamy. Transfer to a small bowl and fold in 1 tablespoon of the walnuts. Season the dressing to taste with salt and pepper.

1 tablespoon goat's milk, buttermilk, or half-and-half
1 tablespoon apple cider vinegar
2 teaspoons walnut oil
1 tablespoon chopped toasted walnuts
Salt and freshly ground black pepper

Tomato and Corn Custard

SERVES 4 AS A SIDE DISH

One of the dishes the Bushes enjoyed at many of their private dinners was corn custard, usually baked in a large casserole. For the Johnson-Southworth dinner, we added a touch of tomato to bring complexity and color to the plate, and baked them individually for each guest. Cooking the custards at a low temperature for a long time gives them a velvety texture and prevents curdling. Serve these alongside grilled and roasted meats.

¾ cup heavy cream
¾ cup uncooked fresh corn kernels
1 teaspoon chopped garlic
2 large eggs plus 3 large egg yolks
¼ cup homemade or your favorite store-bought tomato sauce
Pinch of freshly grated nutmeg
1½ tablespoons unsalted butter, melted

1. Preheat the oven to 250°F.

2. Puree the cream and corn in a standing blender until smooth. Pour the corn mixture into a large bowl. Stir in the garlic, eggs, egg yolks, tomato sauce, and nutmeg.

3. Use a pastry brush to brush the melted butter into four 5-ounce ramekins or soufflé cups.

4. Fill ramekins to ¼ inch from the top with the corn mixture and place the ramekins in a roasting pan with sides at least as high as the ramekins. Pour hot water into the roasting pan to 1 inch from the tops of the ramekins, being careful not to get any water into the ramekins. Carefully transfer to the oven and bake in the oven until the custards are just set (a toothpick inserted to the center will come out clean), 20 to 25 minutes.

5. Remove the pan from the oven and let the custards cool in the pan for 15 minutes. Carefully remove them from the pan and invert one custard onto each of four salad plates. Serve.

THE BENEFITS OF DISTANCE

Toward the end of January there was another large and very personal dinner scheduled at the White House, a wedding celebration for Coddy Johnson, a former associate political director of the White House who had worked on the Bush-Cheney reelection campaign in 2004, and Carrie Southworth, a model and actress.

Johnson was the son of Collister Johnson Jr., who had been a roommate of the President's at Yale. When the Johnsons invited the Bushes to the wedding, the First Family declined because of all the security issues it would create. Instead, they invited the two families and about one hundred guests to join them for a celebration dinner at the White House.

The dinner was held in the State Dining Room, and we served a menu of wild mushroom soup (based on a recipe Lea forwarded to me); rack of lamb with several accompaniments including one of the Bushes' favorites, tomato and corn custard; and mâche, frisée, and peppercress salad with roquefort cheese and walnut dressing.

An unfailingly happy affair, the dinner was yet another reminder that the White House was as much a private home as it was public property. But there was one unhappy footnote for me: At Lea Berman's request, the dinner was served from platters, a return to the formal, less personal French-style service that we did away with more than a decade ago. Was this a sign of things to come? I could only assume that it was.

That smile I was trying so hard to keep on my face was becoming less and less convincing—both to me and, I'm sure, to anyone who saw it.

The dinner was also occasion for me to reflect on the benefits of not having the same kind of access to the First Family as I did under the Clintons. Because, as tense as things were between Lea Berman and me, the relationship with Mrs. Bush never corroded.

After dinner that night, I was in the Old Family Dining Room on the State Floor, along with a few of my chefs and Gary Walters. As Mrs. Bush got into the elevator with the President to head upstairs, she paused and called out to us just before the doors slid closed between us, "Guys, that was just about perfect."

Ironically, that compliment is the last exchange I recall between the First Lady and me.

END OF AN ERA

About two weeks later, on Wednesday, February 2, 2005, Gary Walters called me in the kitchen and asked me to come see him in his private office, one floor above the Usher's Office.

I knew this couldn't be good.

I got to his office and he and Dennis Freemyer were there. "Have a seat," Gary said.

I did.

"Listen," he continued, delivering some unsurprising news. "The First Lady has decided that's she going to go a different direction."

I had been prepared for this on some level for a few months, so I was able to make a joke of it: "Actually she's decided I'm going to go a different direction; she's staying right where she is."

Gary seemed disarmed. "You're taking this very well," he said.

"I don't have a choice, do I?"

We discussed what kind of severance package I might receive, how I'd need to remove my books from the office, and other logistics.

"Am I going to be escorted out right now?" I asked.

"Oh, no," Gary said, sounding genuinely surprised that I'd even suggest such a thing. "You can stay on until we find a replacement."

That ended up not being the case. Once my departure left the purview of the Usher's Office and fell into the hands of the bureaucratic machine, things got messy and even a little contentious. That Friday, Mrs. Bush's press secretary, Gordon Johndroe, told the media that I was "already gone," a comment he ended up correcting by the same evening. But I was so rankled by it that on the very same afternoon, when I was asked by Marian Burros from the *New York Times* why I was resigning, I told her the truth: that I had been fired.

This was a big violation of an unspoken rule in the White House, which was subtly reinforced by Gary when he promised me a letter of recommendation from Mrs. Bush in exchange for a letter of resignation from me. Every high-profile person who had left the Administration publicly said they had resigned. My candid response, which was prominently featured in that Saturday's *New York Times*, brought my tenure to a speedy end. Gary phoned me at home that afternoon and said he had been instructed to tell me not to return to work.

And just like that, I was no longer the chef of the White House. I was once again Walter Scheib 3rd, private citizen.

Scallop and Corn Chowder

Bay scallops are delicate and sweet and are the perfect complement to fresh corn, making this a perfect, easy-to-make summer soup.

This is one of about two or three dozen scallop dishes I served to the Bushes during the four years I cooked for them. Interestingly, nearly a year after I left the White House, a member of Mrs. Bush's staff complained to the media—anonymously—that I frequently served scallops even though the First Family hated them. The funny thing is that I never served anything at private family meals or state dinners unless Mrs. Bush or a member of her social team approved it in advance. When this story surfaced, I pulled out my files and discovered several approved menus featuring scallops, as well as a draft of a state dinner menu (in honor of the President of the Philippines) on which scallops were selected from a list of options for one course. State dinner menus were always approved by the First Lady herself. The bottom line was that if the First Family didn't like scallops, and said so, they never would have seen another one again.

So, there is no "scallop scandal." As far as I knew, they liked this soup and so will you.

¼ cup diced bacon
⅓ cup diced Spanish onion
¼ cup diced celery
¼ cup diced Idaho or russet potato
1 tablespoon very finely chopped garlic
1 cup fresh corn kernels
1 tablespoon chopped fresh tarragon leaves
½ tablespoon chopped fresh thyme leaves
3 cups homemade or store-bought low-sodium chicken stock
2 cups heavy cream
Salt and freshly ground black pepper
1 teaspoon olive oil
6 ounces fresh bay scallops

1. Cook the bacon in a heavy-bottomed soup pot over medium-high heat until it renders enough fat to coat the bottom of the pot, but don't let it brown, 3 to 5 minutes. Add the onion, celery, potato, and garlic and cook, stirring occasionally, until the vegetables are tender, 4 to 5 minutes. Add the corn, tarragon, and thyme and cook, stirring occasionally, for 3 to 4 minutes. Ladle out about one third of the mixture and set aside in a small bowl.

2. Add the stock to the pot, bring to a simmer, then lower the heat and let simmer until the potato begins to break apart, 12 to 15 minutes. Using a handheld immersion blender (or working in batches with a standing blender), puree the mixture until uniformly thick and smooth. If using a standing blender, return the purred mixture to the pot. Stir in the cream and season to taste with salt and pepper. Raise the heat to high and bring the soup to a boil. As soon as it boils, turn off the heat and cover the soup to keep it hot.

3. Heat the oil in a 12-inch sauté pan over high heat. Add the scallops to the pan and cook, shaking the pan to lightly caramelize them all over, until warmed through, 2 to 3 minutes. Add the reserved vegetable mixture to the pan and cook for 1 minute to reheat.

4. Divide scallop-vegetable mixture among four soup bowls and ladle the soup over the mixture in each bowl. Serve hot.

THE VIEW FROM HERE

How do you move on from a job like White House Executive Chef, or any White House job?

For me the answer to that question had come years earlier, in a piece of wisdom conveyed to me by Mrs. Clinton's first social secretary, Ann Stock: "Don't fall into the trap of estimating your personal value by how close you stand to the First Family."

I thought of those words often in my first days after that unfortunate ending to my White House career. No, I wouldn't be going back to work at the White House, but that didn't diminish what I had accomplished there: Working with a team of people I came to admire and respect, we had updated the White House kitchen, modernized the menu, taught the world a little something about contemporary American flavors, and pulled off thousands of lunches and dinners, and scores of picnics and state dinners, that most experts probably would have thought were impossible before we took them on. I like to think that we redefined what the White House kitchen was capable of, and that in my own way, I left a bit of a legacy behind.

I'll probably never fully understand exactly what happened between the Bushes and me. There were too many layers of people between us, too little direct communication. And that's okay. I've made my peace with it.

I still live in the same home in Virginia that I did while I was the chef of the White House. My kids go to school in D.C., and I often drive past the House. I can't park in the employee lot, or walk through the gate with a wave to the Uniformed Division guys, and into what I'll always think of as my kitchen. But a treasure trove of memories stay with me to this day, like standing with Jean in the Blue Room and watching the fireworks on the Millennial New Year's Eve, serving all those workers during the sad chaos of September 11, the adrenaline-rush of riding in the President's motorcade along the East River of Manhattan, and the tingle of excitement I felt whenever my kitchen phone rang and I saw that little asterisk telling me that Mrs. Clinton was on the other end of the line.

Most chefs never get to know moments like those. I got to know them for eleven years.

That's how you move on from being the chef of the White House.

You know that you did it, and did it to the best of your ability.

And then you start looking for the next adventure . . .

Cristeta Comerford
White House Executive Chef, 2005–

I n mid-1995 Keith Luce, the assistant chef whom I had brought with me from the Greenbrier, decided that it was time for him to move on and start his own restaurant, which he did. This gave me the opportunity to hire a new assistant chef and I interviewed six or seven candidates.

Among them was Cristeta Comerford, who had been an SBA team member for several months. A soft-spoken, shy woman of Filipino descent, Cris didn't say much at first, but I had developed a sixth sense for detecting whether or not someone respected the idea of working for the White House—people who could resist the temptation to try to get too close to the First Family, and were capable of keeping the things they saw and heard there to themselves.

As Cris began to work, her tremendous ability became readily apparent. She wasn't a show-boat, but was highly organized (her station was a model of efficiency), and she had a great eye and palate. Even the most simple salads were beautiful when she made them, and the vinaigrettes were balanced and seasoned superlatively.

Cris's enthusiasm for the White House and professionalism on the job moved her right to the top of my SBA list. After she had been with us for just a few months, I began to enlist her as much as possible. In time, I began to entrust her with more and more. Instead of considering

Christa Comerford, left, in the upstairs kitchen Mrs. Clinton had remodeled as a home kitchen in her days as one of my assistant chefs. *(Courtesy William J. Clinton Presidential Library)*

her just a line cook who executed dishes during service, I began asking her to do everything from butchering to baking, and she did it all with a master's touch and admirable humility.

Cris worked well with the kitchen team, no matter what the occasion or combination of people in the kitchen, and she was also very good at coordinating our efforts with those of the butlers.

Taking all of this into account, I told the Usher's Office that I wanted to hire her to replace Keith. The suggestion was met with some resistance as ushers also suggested other candidates to me, all but one of them men, which I find hard to believe was a coincidence.

I insisted, and I got my wish: Cris was hired as one of my two assistant chefs.

It wasn't easy for Cris. The White House staff (as I knew all too well from my personal experience) didn't warm up to new hires right away, plus she had to contend with some sexism. One butler asked me who the new "little girl" in the kitchen was. I replied that "this 'little girl' is going to be the engine that is going to help us do what we need to do over the next couple of years."

I'm not just being humble when I say that, in many ways, Cris is a better cuisinier than I am. Early in my career, I was quickly promoted out of cooking positions and into management roles so I did not have the chance to hone my cooking ability as finely as she did hers. If I hadn't hired her, a lot of our successes would have been much harder to come by because she had the tremendous ability to hear what I requested, understand its essence, and make it real.

Simply put, Cris was the best cook that I ever worked with, and I was thrilled for her when, in August 2005, six months after my departure, Mrs. Bush selected her to be my successor as White House Executive Chef, the first woman ever to hold that position.

Recipe List

Here's a list of the recipes in this book, organized by category.

Salads and Salad Dressings

Pasta and Grains

Fish

Poultry

Meat

Side Dishes

Sauces

Miscellaneous

Sources

We frequently used exotic and hard-to-procure ingredients at the White House, but the recipes in this book have been selected with an eye toward accessibility. However, if you can't find certain ingredients called for by some of the recipes locally, such as some of the more ambitious state dinner dishes, these companies will ship them to you.

Artisanal Premium Cheese

American and international cheeses.
877-797-1200 (toll free)
www.artisanalcheese.com

D'Artagnan

Duck and duck products, game birds, poultry, smoked, cured, and specialty meats, truffle oil, veal demi-glace.
800-327-8246, ext. 0 (toll free)
www.dartagnan.com

Jamison Farm

Lamb and lamb products.
800-237-5262 (toll free)
www.jamisonfarm.com

Kalustyan's

Beans, chili and curry pastes, coconut milk, dried and canned chiles and chili powders, fish sauce, harissa, hoisin sauce, honeys, kaffir lime leaves, masa harina, oils, salts, spices (including fennel pollen), tahini, tamarind puree, and vinegars; kitchen equipment and tools.
800-352-3451 (toll free)
www.kalustyans.com

Browne Trading Company

Fish, shellfish, smoked fish, and caviar.
800-944-7848 (toll free)
www.browne-trading.com

Nueske's

In my opinion, the best bacon you can buy.
800-382-2266 (toll free)
www.nueskemeats.com

Niman Ranch

Beef, lamb, and pork.
866-808-0340
www.nimanranch.com

Williams-Sonoma

Kitchen equipment and tools, and specialty items.
877-812-6235 (toll free)
www.williams-sonoma.com

References

Books

Clinton, Hillary Rodham. *An Invitation to the White House*. Simon and Schuster, 2000.

Doherty, Robert H. (Coordinating Editor). *The First Ladies Cook Book*. Parents Magazine Enterprises, 1982.

Haller, Henry with Aronson, Virginia. *The White House Family Cookbook*. Random House, 1987.

Articles

Bruni, Frank. "Children Step Up to Plate at White House." *New York Times*, May 7, 2001.

Bruni, Frank. "No. 1 Fan Plays Host to Legends of Baseball." *New York Times*, March 31, 2001.

Bumiller, Elisabeth. "In the East Wing, a New Order and a Busier Schedule." *New York Times*, February 14, 2005.

Bumiller, Elisabeth. "Where Heads of State Lay Their Heads." *New York Times*, October 21, 1995.

Burros, Marian. "High Calories (and Chef!) Out at White House." *New York Times*, March 5, 1994.

Burros, Marian. "Making the White House a Home." *New York Times*, February 23, 2001.

Burros, Marian. "The New Presidency: Social Scene: A Highly Sensitive Post is Filled by the Clintons." *New York Times*, January 12, 1993.

Burros, Marian. "State Dinner Showcases Tradition Even as New Cuisine Breaks with It." *New York Times*, June 14, 1994.

Burros, Marian. "White House Chef is Leaving, an Idea that Wasn't His." *New York Times*, February 5, 2005.

Cooper, Christopher. "Laura Bush Takes a Larger Role." *Wall Street Journal*, December 30, 2005.

Copp, Tara. "Lady of the Nation's House." Scripps Howard News Service, April 20, 2001.

Darman, Jonathan and Bailey, Holly. "Jesus and Jack Daniels." *Newsweek*, January 24, 2005.

Dowd, Maureen. "Up Close and Personal." *New York Times*, January 2, 1994.

Editorial Desk. "Bill Clinton's Arteries—And Ours." *New York Times*, April 8, 1994.

Gerhart, Ann. "White House Chef Is Out in East Wing Social Shuffle." *Washington Post,* February 4, 2005.

Harris, John F. "The Roosevelts, Kennedys, and Now the Bushes." *Washington Post*, January 17, 2005.

Keen, Judy. "Foxes Taste the Glam Side of the White House." *USA Today*, September 5, 2001.

Molotsky, Irvin. "Laura Bush Designates Keepers of Her Calendar." *New York Times*, January 9, 2001.

Newton, Ken. "Couple Go to White House Dinner." *St. Joseph News-Press*, February 1, 2005.

O'Neill, Molly. "At Last, a Chef Who Sees the Light." *New York Times*, April 10, 1994.

O'Neill, Molly. "At White House, a Taste of Virtue." *New York Times*, April 6, 1994.

Radcliffe, Donnie, and Roberts, Roxanne. "Basking in the Rising Sun." *Washington Post*, June 14, 1994.

Roberts, Roxanne, and Boustany, Nora. "Haute Boy! A Classy Bash." *Washington Post,* February 2, 1996.

Roberts, Roxanne. "An Inviting Presence." *Washington Post*, March 1, 2005.

Roberts, Roxanne, and Gerhart, Ann. "The State Dinner that Ended with a Bang." *Washington Post,* September 6, 2001.

Vigoda, Arlene. "Toques Off." *USA Today*, March 28, 1994.

Walden, Grace Ann. "White House Picks One of Napa Valley's Best to Run Its Dining Room." *Wine Spectator*, March 31, 1995.

—— (uncredited). "Bushes Bring Capital's Elite to Fiesta for Foxes." Associated Press, September 6, 2001.

—— (uncredited). "Executive Batting Order." *USA Today,* February 28, 2001.

——- (uncredited). "A New Chef is Chosen for the White House." *New York Times*, March 27, 1994.

Note: The *Washington Post* was also consulted for state dinner guest lists.

Web Sites

www.cnn.com (CNN)

www.littleleague.org (Little League International Baseball and Softball)

www.nps.gov (National Park Service)

www.state.gov (State Department)

www.whitehouse.gov (White House)

Other

Three former White House social secretaries (Ann Stock, Capricia Marshall, and Catherine Fenton) were interviewed for this book, and other former White House employees were contacted to substantiate certain recollections and details. Menu items and other culinary details were primarily culled from Walter Scheib's personal records.

Acknowledgments

I'd like to publicly thank the following people for their help making this book, and the story it tells, a reality.

First of all, my deepest personal thanks to:

My wife, Jean Scheib, who shares every part of this story with me, from making me apply for the White House job, to helping me remember all the details from those eleven years, to testing the recipes by my side. Thanks also for putting up with my schedule and ever-changing demeanor over the years;

Andrew Friedman, my collaborator, a remarkable wordsmith who gave the story its voice and shape, and in the process became a friend;

My sons, Walter and Jim, for their typing services on the recipes, and more important, for making their old man proud;

Senator Hillary Rodham Clinton, for taking a chance on me—you literally changed my life, and I'll be in your debt forever—and President William Jefferson Clinton, for your good humor and social grace. I actually believe it when you say you're happy to see me;

President George W. Bush and First Lady Laura Bush. It was my pleasure to serve you;

Ann Stock and Capricia Marshall, the social secretaries with whom I worked during the Clinton years. What great fun we had. I continue to marvel at your dedication and smarts. Thanks also for being interviewed for this book, and to Capricia for your help putting in me in touch with the William J. Clinton Presidential Library and Museum;

Cathy Fenton, former White House social secretary under Laura Bush, for sharing your time and memories with us; and

Gary Walters, White House Chief Usher, for your complete devotion to your work, your reverence for the "people's house," and for managing the monumental changes that took place in the 1990s. We didn't always see things exactly the same way, but my respect for you couldn't be greater.

For their help on the book, my heartfelt appreciation to:

Linda Ingroia, our editor at Wiley, for her belief in the project, her passion for getting it right, and her creative ideas and inspirations;

Lisa Queen, my agent, for her help getting this book together and getting it sold;

David Black, for his early advice and proposal wisdom;

Nealon DeVore, of the William J. Clinton Presidential Library and Museum, for his patience and cooperation in assembling the photos from the Clinton years; and

Amy Tucker, for her invaluable research assistance and recipe-editing skills.

And from my years at the White House, thanks to:

The journalists who quoted me correctly and treated me fairly—you know who you are, and aren't;

The White House butlers, and especially to Buddy Carter, for your help keeping everything in perspective;

Denzil Benjamin, Brian Williams, and Mary Beth Williams, for introducing me to those mobile kitchen trailers, and for being my friends;

The White House Ushers, especially Dennis Freemyer, for helping me re-imagine the kitchen, and for giving me invaluable insights into the Usher's Office in general and Gary in particular, and Daniel Shanks, White House Assistant Usher, for all the great wine pairings and camaraderie over the years we worked together;

My White House Assistant Chefs, Cristeta Comerford, John Moeller, and Keith Luce, and to Staff Kitchen Cooks Paula Moutsos and Rachel Walker, who helped us out upstairs all the time. Nobody will ever know what it took to do what we did. Thank you!

My White House Service By Agreement Cooks, especially Leland, Patrice, Gordon, Francis, David, Vincent, Jason, Nathan, Alex, Heiko, and Lance—you were the cavalry, an army of helpers coming to our rescue whenever we needed you.

The members of the United States Secret Service, for keeping us safe at all times. What unsung heroes you are every day; and

Everyone who dined at the White House during the eleven years I worked there; it was an honor to serve you.

Index

Page numbers in *italics* indicate illustrations; pages with * indicate recipes.

G

and Bush transition team, 206

and chain of command, 55–56, 173, 213

and firing of Scheib, 291–292

and hiring of Scheib, 12, 13, 14–15, 17, 19, 25, 27

instructions from President Bush, 232, 253

on job security, 209, 270

on media relations, 28, 29

in meeting with Lea Berman, 280

and outdoor events, 103, 104, 117

preference for Bush White House style, 212

purchasing decisions by, 47

during September 11, 2001, 255, 260–261, 262

at weekly meeting, 44–45, 278

wine selection by, 125, 146

Wang, Vera, 143

Washington Hilton, 260

Washington Post, 29, 30, 126, 145

Weather conditions, outdoor events and, 120

Weekly meeting, 44–45

Weinstein, Harvey, 143

Western-themed menu, 181–182, 187

* Whiskey-Tortilla Sauce, 189

White, Marco Pierre, 281

White House Historical Association, 138, 257

Will, George, 241

Williams, Brian, 5, 117–119, 157, 260, 261

Williams, Maggie, 4, 19, 25, 27

Williams, Mary Beth, 257, 260, 261

Wine selection

American wines, 146

for state dinners, 125, 126, 146, 224

Winfrey, Oprah, 126

Wonder, Stevie, 109

Working lunches, 267–272

Y

Yeltsin, Boris

at G8 Summit, Denver, 183

Hyde Park, N.Y. lunch for, 166–169

state dinner for, 140–144

Z

* Zucchini, in Vegetable Slaw, Summer, 111

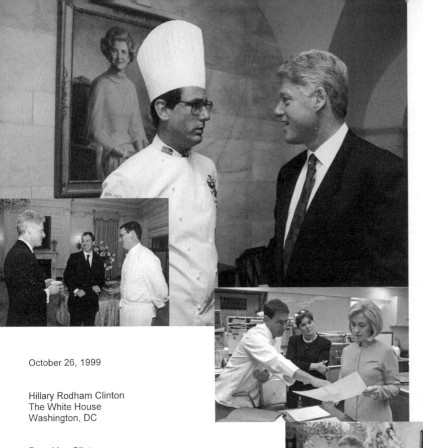

MENU

POZOLE DE CANGREJO DE MARYLAND Y CHORIZO
VERDURAS FRESCAS VERANIEGAS
Mi Sueño Chardonnay "Carneros" 1999

BISÓN CON EMPANIZADO DE PEPITAS
PURÉ DE PAPAS CON CHILE POBLANO
RAGÚ DE HABAS Y SETAS CHANTERELLE
SALSA DE MANZANA Y CHILE CHIPOTLE
*Shafer Cabernet Sauvignon
"Hillside Select" 1994*

ENSALADA DE TOMATES ROJOS Y AMARILLOS
VERDURAS DE HOJITAS VERDES
ADEREZO DE JEREZ

HELADO DE MANGO Y COCO
MELOCOTONES
SALSA DE CHILE ROJO   TEQUILA SABAYÓN
Schramsberg "Cremant" 1997

October 26, 1999

Hillary Rodham Clinton
The White House
Washington, DC

Dear Mrs. Clinton:

How very kind of you to host a luncheon for all of us the other day in your beautiful White House. I have been there several times, starting with the LBJ administration, where everything was beautifully handled.

During subsequent visits, I was not as impressed. But, when I returned for the Sara Lee Frontrunner awards luncheon, I was delighted to find the White House sparkling, and the service beautiful and attentive, and the food delicious. It was a very heartwarming experience.

Thank you so much. With all good wishes

Julia Child

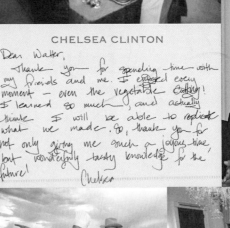

CHELSEA CLINTON

Dear Walter,

Thank you for spending time with my friends and me. I enjoyed every moment — even the vegetable eating! I learned so much, and actually think I will be able to replicate what we made. So, thank you for not only giving me such a joyous time but wonderfully tasty knowledge for the future!

Chelsea